*Paths to Middle-Class Mobility among Second-Generation Moroccan Immigrant Women in Israel*

# *Paths to Middle-Class Mobility among Second Generation Moroccan Immigrant Women in Israel*

**Beverly Mizrachi**

WAYNE STATE UNIVERSITY PRESS DETROIT

17 16 15 14 13 5 4 3 2 1

Library of Congress Cataloging-in-Publication Data

Mizrachi, Beverly.
Paths to middle-class mobility among second-generation Moroccan immigrant women in Israel / Beverly Mizrachi.
pages cm. — (Raphael Patai series in Jewish folklore and anthropology)
Includes bibliographical references and index.
ISBN 978-0-8143-3881-0 (cloth. : alk. paper) — ISBN 978-0-8143-3858-2 (ebook)
1. Women immigrants—Israel—Social conditions. 2. Moroccans—Israel—History. 3. Immigrants—Israel—History. 4. Social mobility—Israel. I. Title.
HQ1728.5.M597 2013
305.5'13095694--dc23
2012029605

*Typeset by Alpha Design & Composition of Pittsfield NH*
*Composed in Adobe Garamond Pro and Walbaum*

This book is dedicated to my dear friend, Like Roos (1933–2004)
who made so many things possible

and

To those women who struggle daily, in myriad ways,
to create a life of their own choosing

# *Contents*

*Acknowledgments* *ix*

1. Introduction 1
2. Moroccan Women in Morocco and in Israel 13
3. Becoming a Semiprofessional 35
4. Transforming One's Self and One's Body 51
5. Acquiring Educational Credentials 67
6. A Divorcée Does It on Her Own 81
7. Comfortable in Her Own Skin 95
8. Privilege and Its Discontent 107
9. Discussion: Paths to Middle-Class Mobility 121

Methodology Appendix: Classifying the Women 151

*Notes* *155*
*Bibliography* *179*
*Index* *195*

# *Acknowledgments*

I am delighted to have this opportunity to thank several people who have helped me in various ways in the writing of this book and to express my appreciation to the institutions that have funded the research and the publication of this work.

I offer my most profound thanks to my friend Christopher Phillips who was willing to immerse himself in the topic of this book and to devote enormous amounts of time to going over the manuscript word by word to make it meet his demanding standards. His friendship knows no bounds nor does my gratitude for it. I would also like to express my appreciation to Dick and Judy Wurtman, friends who offered support and encouragement during the writing of *Paths* . . . and always made me feel that I was capable of producing good, scholarly work. I am particularly indebted to Judy, who read several chapters of the book and made insightful comments. My thanks to Professor Judith Lorber for her willingness to take time from her own research to read and comment upon some of the early chapters of this book.

Several people from my academic world have shared their knowledge with me and offered their significant support. First of all, I would like to thank Professor Moshe Lissak of the Hebrew University, Jerusalem. Professor Lissak was my PhD adviser and during that time and throughout the writing of this book was always willing to share his vast sociological knowledge with me and to listen patiently and with good humor to my endless dilemmas and questions. Professor Harvey Goldberg of the Hebrew University, Jerusalem, was very helpful by graciously devoting time to reading several chapters of this book, commenting on them and contributing his extensive anthropological knowledge about ethnicity in Israel. I would also like to thank Professor Amia Lieblich of the Hebrew University, Jerusalem, my other PhD adviser, for making me aware of the power of life history narratives. I feel indebted to Professor Reuven Kahane, also of the Hebrew University, Jerusalem, who, unfortunately, is no longer with us, for being my mentor during my student days and during my early academic career.

Helene Hogri's considerable experience in working with sociological and anthropological texts was evident in her editing of this book and added greatly to its readability. Her input often went beyond her responsibility as editor, and her patience was always appreciated, even when I resisted her wise advice. The professional expertise of the librarians at Ashkelon Academic College and the Bloomfield Library of the Hebrew University, Jerusalem, was very useful in helping me find important, relevant sources. The Israel Social Sciences Data Center (ISDC) at the Hebrew University, Jerusalem, made the statistical data used in this book available to me.

The following institutions generously offered financial support for the research and publication of this book, and I offer them my sincere gratitude. First and foremost I would like to thank Ashkelon Academic College that funded both the research and various stages in the publication process. I also gratefully acknowledge the grants awarded me by the Hebrew University, Jerusalem; the Israeli Ministry for Education, Culture, and Sports; the Memorial Foundation for Jewish Culture; and Yad Tabenkin, all of which enabled me to conduct the early stages of the research that informs this work.

# Chapter 1

# *Introduction*

> It is, I suspect, an experience every field anthropologist has . . . to come upon individuals in the course of research who seem to have been waiting there . . . for someone like you, bright eyed, ignorant, obliging, credulous to happen along, so as to have the chance not just to answer your questions but to instruct you as to which ones to ask: people with a story to tell, a view to unfold, an image to impart, a theory to argue, concerning what it is that they . . . "really," "genuinely," "truly"—in fact—are.[1]

These words, written by the anthropologist Clifford Geertz, expressed exactly what I felt while I was collecting data on the mobility into and within the middle class of a group of second-generation Jewish Moroccan immigrant women in Israel. Although these women belong to a large ethnic group, albeit a subordinate one, in Israeli society little information about them exists. What we know about first-generation Moroccan immigrant women is based on scant statistical facts and on stereotypes that I sensed were founded on partial truths and assumptions, if not inaccuracies. We know even less about second-generation women from this ethnic group, particularly about their middle-class mobility. Therefore, I began this research with many questions. Why did these women want to enter the middle class or to be mobile within it? What issues did their mobility raise? How did they achieve their middle-class goals? I came away from each meeting with the women in my study with more complete and more accurate answers to these questions. I also came away with genuine humility, awe, and respect for the obstacles they had overcome as daughters of immigrants and for the human agency they exhibited in achieving their middle-class mobility for themselves, and, ultimately, for their children.

The subject of second-generation immigrant women's mobility into and within the middle class has received little research attention not only in Israel, a Western-oriented society, but also in Western societies, such as the United States and Western Europe, which have many immigrants in their midst. By studying this topic, this book aims at achieving a dual goal; it analyzes a subject that has not received in-depth academic analysis in studies on Israeli society, and by using the specific case of Israel it addresses a subject that has global relevance. In this way this book is intended to be a corrective to this overlooked topic.

In starting this research I knew that studying the field of women, immigration, and mobility is important for several reasons. First, women account for a significant number of immigrants worldwide, so that the sheer size of the group justifies research about them. The number of women who leave one country in order to live in another is such that for some time now researchers have referred to the feminization of immigration.[2] Statistics reveal that women immigrants outnumber men in countries as varied as the United States; Western European countries such as Austria, Belgium, France, Italy, the Netherlands, and the United Kingdom; Eastern European countries such as Albania, Bulgaria, Czech Republic, and Hungary; Mediterranean countries such as Cyprus, Gibraltar, Greece, and Israel; and Australia and New Zealand.[3]

Women who come to settle in their new societies—the first generation—arrive with great differences in their human capital. Some resemble the traditional immigrants of the past and have little formal qualifications with which to accomplish upward mobility. Others are highly educated professionals who, because their adopted societies do not always recognize their occupational credentials or because they encounter discrimination or negative ethnic stereotyping, experience downward mobility.[4] It is not surprising, then, that studies on both these groups of immigrant women in Israel, the United States, and Western Europe show that they generally begin their new lives in the working class and lower socioeconomic strata of their new societies and experience little upward mobility.[5] But what are the prospects of the second generation—of the daughters of this large and diverse group of women—for reaching the middle class or rising within it?

Second, the upward mobility of women who were either immigrants themselves or who were born to immigrant women is important on both the individual and societal levels. On the individual level, mobility gives these immigrants a vision of their "life chances,"[6] which includes their opportunities for attaining economic security, access to things, experiences and practices they value, their hierarchical position vis-à-vis others, and their sense of self-worth.[7] On the societal level, this mobility is important because it affects social cohesion. Immigrants who feel they have opportunities for upward mobility have positive feelings toward their society[8] and want to be part of it. Conversely, social cohesion is weakened if they sense that their upward mobility is blocked. Under such circumstances, feelings of discrimination, injustice, and alienation can arise that undermine the social fabric. Substantial research exists on the connection between such feelings among first-generation immigrants and social cohesion in the countries in which they have come to reside,[9] and, perhaps intuitively, we expect immigrant integration and social cohesion to be only a first-generation issue. However, the recent riots and violent protests of second-generation immigrants against obstacles, real or imagined, to their upward mobility in France, Denmark, and Spain and the potential for such eruptions in other Western European countries, such as Italy, Belgium, and Germany, offer ample evidence of the powerful negative emotions and deleterious social consequences of the lack of mobility among this later generation of immigrants. By studying the middle-class mobility of the second-generation Moroccan immigrant women in this research we can understand the issues involved in this process among others like them and we can then use this knowledge to contribute to the lessening of the types of social schisms that thwarted mobility can produce.

Third, immigrant women's mobility, particularly their middle-class mobility, is important because a combination of cultural norms and economic and social benefits have made the middle class the desired class location for working-class women in Western societies.[10] From the cultural perspective, entering the middle class has become a dominant norm to which working-class women are expected to conform. Elaborating on this line of thought, Steph Lawler pointed out, "Middle-classness becomes the norm against which others are measured: it is also the norm to which working-class people are supposed to aspire."[11] Wondering why anyone would not strive to enter the middle class, Lawler asked how a person could fail to want what society determines to be "*inherently* desirable, and *inherently* normal."[12] From an economic perspective, the neoliberal economy that characterizes Western societies in late modernity has created a demand for female labor and, along with it, opportunities for working-class women to enter the middle class through education and employment that have become the "site[s]" where their upward mobility occurs.[13] If, as noted previously, first-generation immigrant women tend to remain in the working class, those of the second generation may feel more integrated into the cultural milieu of their society and into its educational and occupational frameworks than did the previous generation, and therefore they, like other women from working-class origins, may desire middle-class mobility and may use the same sites to achieve their goal.

As we shall see, mobility into the middle class is a dominant norm in Israeli society as well. Therefore it is not surprising that second-generation Moroccan immigrant women share this cultural and economic/social goal and want to enjoy the benefits of this class position. Sharon, the high-ranking secretary who we shall meet in chapter 6, and who recently entered the middle class, stressed that she had striven to acquire her education, "good" income, and occupational position because it would make her feel part of Israeli society.

Research has shown that working-class women who have a desire to be upwardly mobile initiate a process that changes their class identity.[14] This change involves not only a shift in class identity but also a change in female gender identity, particularly in *feminine* gender identity.[15] Femininity is part of gender, but it is not the same. While both are cultural and social constructions, femininity is more specific than gender. It relates to appearance, deportment, achievements, and activities that are respected, valued, and admired by the group to which women belong and to the presentation of these traits in public. Furthermore, femininity can change according to time and place and between groups of women. For instance, it can be constructed differently during various periods in a society's history, can vary between religious and secular women, between women of different classes, ethnicities, and different age groups. In this study we shall see how these upwardly mobile second-generation Moroccan immigrant women constructed a middle-class-oriented femininity. For instance, Ruth, the kindergarten teacher's assistant in chapter 4, distinguished between Moroccan working-class women and Moroccan feminine middle-class women and was careful to construct a middle-class persona that would present her as a feminine middle-class woman.

The link between middle-class femininity and mobility led me to think about the connection between *ethnic* femininity and mobility, for if middle classness requires a particular kind of femininity, so does ethnicity, which also defines what is appropriate or inappropriate for feminine women in an ethnic group.[16] This connection is particularly relevant in light of Herbert Gans's research that claims that by the third and fourth generations ethnicity wanes as the immigrants' descendants become mobile; ethnicity once practiced on a daily basis turns into something symbolic that is expressed in various types of "ethnic behavior" that is determined by the individual.[17] Gans's theory, and that of others who support his view,[18] raises several questions. For example, what is the association between ethnic feminine identity and mobility among second-generation immigrant women for whom ethnic identity may still be more important and more immediate than it is for later generations? Do expressions of ethnic feminine identity wane with the second generation's mobility into the middle class? If so, does symbolic ethnicity replace ethnicity lived on a daily basis among this generation, or is this primarily a third- and fourth-generation phenomenon?

Second-generation immigrant women may feel that they want to make changes in their ethnic feminine identity or some of its components—their "ethnic behavior"—in order to be mobile. After all, ethnic femininity may include a variety of ethnic-based norms and behaviors, such as constructions of wifehood and motherhood, gender relations, preserving customs and ceremonies, forms of dress, and preparing ethnic food. Indeed, these may be components of ethnic femininity within an ethnic group,[19] but other components, such as education and employment, may not be part of this femininity; they may not be part of the ethnic feminine "tool kit"[20] of a particular ethnic group or of a portion of women within a particular ethnic group. Therefore, if study and work are the sites where the mobility of working-class women into the middle class occurs in contemporary societies, then those second-generation immigrant women who want to leave the working class and enter the middle class will initiate changes in their ethnic femininity to include education and employment in order to achieve their goal. Miriam, the kindergarten teacher's assistant in chapter 3, raised this point when she talked about how both education and work have become part of her life and the lives of mobile second-generation Moroccan immigrant women, a fact that distinguishes them from those second-generation women from her ethnic group who do not study and do not work outside their home and therefore are not mobile.

To be sure, not all second-generation immigrant women see a need to transform their ethnic feminine identity to include education and employment in order to be mobile. For instance, Georgina Tsolidis found that the second-generation Greek high school girls in Australia she studied did not see the need for such a change because Greek ethnic feminine norms legitimized education and employment.[21] Similarly, researchers who studied second-generation Moroccan-Muslim and Turkish-Muslim women in the Netherlands noted that individualistic ethnic norms in the Moroccan communities allowed women the freedom to choose whether to pursue an education and occupation, and this freedom resulted in some women achieving high levels of education and employment. In contrast, the more collectivistic ethnic norms in the Turkish communities were less supportive of women acquiring an education and being employed, and, indeed, these women achieved less in these spheres than the Moroccan-Muslim women did.[22] Furthermore, some women within an ethnic group may want to study and be employed to achieve mobility while others may not. Consequently, there may be in-group differences in mobility and ethnic feminine identities; multiple and simultaneous ethnic feminine identities may coexist composed of those who are mobile and those who are not. Naomi, the high school teacher in chapter 7, exemplified this point when she told me that she had always known she would have a complete education that included university studies and a profession, which meant she would be mobile, while most of the other women I interviewed for this research did not assume that such studies were in their future and, in fact, were less mobile.

If second-generation immigrant women from different ethnic groups are found in the same society, then their presence raises the issue of a hierarchal relationship between those in the hegemonic group and those in the subordinate one[23] or between those ethnic feminine identities that are considered superior or inferior. A woman's position in this hierarchical order may become another source of her identity in addition to those of feminine gender, class, and ethnicity. These hegemonic and subordinate relationships, along with the probability that socioeconomic disparities accompany these different locations in the hierarchy, place the two groups of women in different structural positions in which those from the hegemonic group, in all likelihood, have preferential access to mobility resources. Under such circumstances, ethnicity matters, perhaps more to the women in the subordinate group than to those in the dominant one who, because of their privileged position, may have the luxury of being oblivious to this aspect of the social order. This idea parallels Beverley Skeggs's claim that "class is not a problem for those who have the privilege to ignore it."[24] Carolyn Kay Steedman supported this line of thought when she urged that it is important to examine the stories of women whose lives are not "central to the dominant culture."[25] In the context of my study, this suggests that the paths to mobility into and within the middle class of second-generation Moroccan immigrant women will undoubtedly be different from those of women in the hegemonic group, women of European/American origin. For example, in chapter 8 we meet Colette, a high school teacher who felt that her path to upward mobility has been blocked despite her two academic degrees (a BA and an MA) because she is Moroccan, while European women do not incur such obstacles.

I decided to study the middle-class mobility of second-generation Moroccan immigrant women at midlife (forty to fifty years old) because this stage of their lives probably shows their ultimate class attainments. In this my research differs from many of the existing studies on both the United

States and Western Europe that concentrated on the educational and occupational attainments of second-generation immigrants as adolescents or young adults[26] and their mobility accomplishments in their later years. More specific research on second-generation girls and adolescents stressed a connection between parental and/or ethnic group socialization toward academic achievement and mobility in adulthood.[27] However, I contend that all of this research that focuses on young people is not as deterministic as it would lead us to believe. It is particularly problematic in regard to girls and women in subordinate racial, ethnic, and class categories who, perhaps to help support parents and siblings, may have interrupted their studies in their youth but have returned to continue their education later in life.[28] In addition, the need or desire to work in order to contribute to their own family's income and to improve the life chances of their children may also motivate these women to pursue an education and work in adulthood, and therefore to be mobile. Likewise, changing opportunity structures—more varied educational frameworks or the restructuring of the labor market—may induce women to study and to be employed. Cultural factors, such as exposure to class and ethnic feminine identities in the wider society, which may be different from those to which young girls were socialized by their immigrant mothers, may also alter life plans. Sara, the high-ranking secretary in chapter 5, demonstrated my contention. She dropped out of high school to help support her parents, then married early and had children in quick succession in order to conform with Moroccan feminine gender norms, a decision that further interrupted her education. It was only in her mature years, after she had been exposed to the norm of upward mobility that existed outside her ethnic group, that she completed the education that enabled her to enter the position that placed her in the middle class. Finally, adult life experiences, such as changes in marital status, whether through death or divorce, may cause women to adopt different goals than those they espoused in their earlier years.[29] Sharon, the divorcée, and the high-ranking secretary in chapter 6, brought up this point when she told me that her mobility and class awareness had become important to her after she separated from her husband in her mid-thirties and had to provide for herself and her children. Had I interviewed these women in their earlier years, I would have reached different conclusions about their mobility attainments.

In concluding my discussion of my reasons for studying the mobility of second-generation Moroccan immigrant women into and within the middle class in Israel and the issues it has raised, it is important to add that carrying out this study in this society presented the advantage of adding a comparative perspective to research on the topic. Since the few studies that do address this subject have concentrated on Western Europe or the United States, they have a decidedly Euro-American slant. Thus focusing on Israel expands our knowledge on the topic and provides a wider perspective. While no social contexts are entirely similar, and therefore it is difficult to present grand theories that would include and be accurate for all second-generation immigrant women in subordinate groups in all societies, a comparative approach that includes Israel can add a new dimension to a topic that has global importance.

ꕥ

When I began the study, I did not know any second-generation Moroccan immigrant women who were in the middle class. So in order to meet some who could participate in this research, I put up a notice in neighborhood centers in Jerusalem asking Moroccan women, who were born in Israel to two Moroccan parents and who were between forty and fifty years old, to contact me. I chose to focus on Jerusalem because it is the city with the largest concentration of urban Moroccans among the three major cities in Israel.[30] Controlling for residence was important because statistics on Moroccan immigrant women in the first and second generation show significant differences between those living in major metropolitan areas and those living in the more peripheral areas in regard to critical factors, such as education and employment.[31] I decided to include only women who had two parents who were born in Morocco in order to increase the likelihood that they came from a similar cultural background. As I mentioned, I concentrated on the forty- to fifty-year-old age group because I wanted to study women who had probably reached their maximum occupational/class achievements.

Only one woman answered my notice. She was happy to give me the name of a woman she knew who suited my criteria for inclusion in the study, and that woman gave me the name of another. Thus I found myself using the "snowball technique"; letting one woman lead me to another who matched my criteria. I sifted this group to find the women who were in middle-class occupations. (Readers interested in a discussion of my considerations for allocating the women into class categories may consult the methodology appendix.) Some of these were academic professionals, such as high school teachers with BA and MA degrees, while most were clerical workers—high-ranking secretaries who had administrative responsibilities—or kindergarten teachers' assistants. I divided these women into the high, middle, and low segments of the middle class. The division of the women in my study into the three segments of the middle class according to their occupations is as follows:

**Table 1.1.** Middle-class positions and the occupations of the women in this study

| Segment of Middle Class | Occupation |
|---|---|
| High | Academic professionals (high school teachers with academic degrees) |
| Middle | High-ranking secretaries in national and municipal services |
| Low | Semiprofessionals (kindergarten teacher assistants) |

While no class division will satisfy all scholars and be appropriate for all societies, the divisions into the segments of the middle class that I made seemed to me to be in keeping with the theoretical and empirical work conducted on women, class, and mobility[32] and had internal logic and consistency for this study.

It turned out that all these women were married, with the exception of one, who was divorced, and all had children. All were daughters of Moroccan parents who had immigrated to Israel between 1948 and 1956, which meant that their parents were part of the same wave of immigration. I have changed the names of the women and the names of the neighborhoods they lived in (except Rechavia—a unique neighborhood known throughout Israel) to protect their anonymity.

In choosing these Israeli-born, second-generation women for my research, I was aware that I was studying not only a group who had certain demographic characteristics in common but also a group who constituted a generation. According to Karl Mannheim, a generation is not only a biological cohort but is also a group that shares a social location—a temporal-historical period and a social-cultural context—which predisposes its members to particular thoughts, discourse, experiences, and actions.[33] This means that second-generation Moroccan immigrant women who accomplished mobility into and within the middle class did so in a different social context and cultural milieu than the one that characterized the immigrant generation and that these, in turn, will be different from those in which third-generation Moroccan women will accomplish their upward mobility.

I used the qualitative methodology of life history narratives to study the mobility of these women. Over the years this methodology has been lauded for several reasons. First, because it "allows access to the agents themselves."[34] It offers firsthand, direct information about interviewees that has not been filtered or interpreted by researchers. A review of studies on Middle Eastern immigrants in Israel reveals that many researchers have focused on what Israeli society "has done" to these immigrants,[35] rather than enabled us to read what the immigrants and their children themselves relate about their feelings and experiences. Therefore, using the methodology of life histories gave me access to precisely the kind of information that has been lacking.

Second, life histories expose the unique, the diverse, and the individual, rather than the homogeneous and the similar within groups that quantitative methodology provides.[36] Since I was interested in mobility as an individual-level process, I wanted to understand each woman's motivations and ambitions, as well as her dilemmas and the choices she made in order to enter or to rise within the middle class, alongside her interpretation of the societal barriers and opportunities she perceived to achieving this goal. In this way the narratives linked the individual woman with the social structure, or the micro with the macro, and fit in well with postmodern theories that connect the individual with constraints and opportunities in the social structure.[37]

Third, life histories offer an approach that reveals an ongoing process rather than a static state of being. Because mobility is a process that occurs over a lifetime, I wanted to use a methodology that follows individual lives over a long period, as life histories do.

Finally, life histories have the ability to generate grounded theories that derive from empirical data on a topic about which little is known.[38] Since so few studies have been carried out on second-generation immigrant women, mobility and the classed and ethnicized femininities they construct, I did not begin this research with theories or hypotheses I wanted to test, prove, or disprove. Instead, I looked to the narratives, the data "from the ground," to lead me to theoretical insights on the topic. Indeed, the narratives supplied the theoretical framework that informs this book.

The full study included twenty-five women. When I called the women to invite them to participate in the research, I told them I was interested in studying Israeli-born Moroccan women. I was pleasantly surprised to discover how eager the women were to take part in this study. In my previous work I had never encountered such willingness among interviewees to participate in a research project. In fact, the women were so enthusiastic about the research that at midpoint they suggested that when the project would be completed all twenty-five women and I should celebrate its conclusion by taking a trip together to Morocco. The trip did not take place for a variety of technical reasons, but their enthusiasm led me to ask myself why these women were so eager to be part of this research. I came to the conclusion that perhaps my original intuition was correct—these second-generation Moroccan women wanted to tell their life stories because they felt that people did not really, truly, know them. So my desire to learn was matched by their desire to tell.

All the narratives had some common themes that ran through them. However, they also had themes that were unique to mobility into the particular segment of the middle class to which each woman belonged. In order not to be repetitive but still to present the common and the unique, I included six of the total of twenty-five narratives in this book. I chose two narratives from two women in the same occupation who represented each of the three segments of the middle class. I selected the two that seemed to me to be the most compelling, strongest, and most articulate from that segment. Together they provided a nuanced and rounded-out representation of the women in each segment. Throughout this book I have used the narratives to generalize from them to other second-generation Moroccan immigrant women in the same segment of the middle class.

The interviews with each woman consisted of three meetings of two hours each for a total of six hours of in-depth interviewing. The first interview began with my asking, "Would you please tell me about yourself?" I deliberately asked a general question so that each woman would feel free to construct her life story as she chose to. Because of the good rapport that evolved between the interviewees and myself, I felt comfortable asking the women to clarify points they raised that sometimes were not clear to me. I recorded each interview and transcribed it later.

The meetings for the interviews took place at locations chosen by the women. The main consideration of all the women was a place that offered quiet and privacy. Miriam, the kindergarten teacher's assistant in the low segment of the middle class, chose her son's bedroom, removed from the noise her children were making in the living room; Ruth, the other kindergarten teacher's assistant, chose a quiet neighborhood café; Sara, the high-ranking secretary in the middle segment of the middle class, wanted her interviews to take place in the after hours of her busy office; Sharon, another high-ranking secretary, preferred her apartment when her teenage children were out and going about their after-school activities; Naomi, the high school teacher in the high segment of the middle class, preferred a quiet time at home; while Colette, another high school teacher, chose to have her interviews take place in a sunny corner in the garden of her home.

This book consists of nine chapters. After this introductory chapter, the second chapter examines Moroccan immigration to Israel against the backdrop of Jewish immigration into the country. In that chapter I also describe aspects of life in Jewish communities in Morocco that had implications for Moroccan women's class position in their new society. The chapter includes group statistics about the class mobility of immigrant and second-generation Moroccan women in Israel and compares these with those of the women in the hegemonic group, the women of European/American origin. Next come the six narrative chapters themselves, starting with two from the low segment of the middle class and proceeding to the middle and high segments. In these chapters I show these women's presentations of their motivations for mobility, their interpretations of the obstacles and opportunities they encountered, and their paths to mobility in their own words as well as my analysis of their narratives. This format enables me to allow for both the perspective of the interviewees and my own more formal analysis of their stories. In my analysis I summarize, explain, and, in some cases, compare my findings with those in the literature, but I do not "go against the grain"; I accept what the women told me in the construction of their paths to mobility because the point of using their interpretation of their life histories is to give voice and validity to their accounts of their lived experience and to avoid intrusive interpretations that amount to conjectures and second-guessing. In the last chapter I compare the paths to mobility of the women in the three segments of the middle class and analyze the theoretical issues raised by studying the mobility of these women and, by implication, the mobility of other second-generation immigrant women from subordinate groups in Western and Western-oriented societies. This chapter also discusses the significance of my findings for a comparative approach to studying second-generation immigrant women's mobility.

## Chapter 2

# *Moroccan Women in Morocco and in Israel*

The mobility of second-generation Moroccan immigrant women as a group into and within the middle class is best understood within the context of the mass immigration of Jews to Israel between 1948 and 1956 that followed the establishment of the State in 1948;[1] by examining their historical background and the "cultural roots"[2] they brought with them from their country of origin; the mobility resources of the first, immigrant generation of women in their new society and those accrued by the second generation; and the significance of these attainments for these Moroccan women as they compared them with those of second-generation women in the hegemonic group. Family formation patterns and the representations, stereotypes, and perceptions that exist about Moroccan women in Israeli society are also relevant for understanding their mobility.

## Immigrants in Israel

Two large Jewish groups entered Israel upon the establishment of the State. One was composed of 372,400 newcomers from Asia and North Africa and included Moroccan immigrants.[3] The other was composed of 344,600 Europeans and Americans (primarily Europeans).[4] Both the Asians/North Africans and the Europeans/Americans joined the 649,700 Jews[5] who already lived in the country, the majority of whom were pre-State, European immigrants associated with the various socialist pioneer movements of the founding fathers plus a smaller group who formed an emerging middle class.[6] By 1952 the North Africans became the largest immigrant group in the country.[7] In that year they constituted 42 percent of the immigrant population and they remained the largest group until 1957.[8] Shortly after their immigration, the Asians/North Africans and the Europeans/Americans became divided into the Mizraḥi (plural: Mizraḥim) or the Ashkenazi (plural: Ashkenazim) bloc (respectively) both in academic research and in Israeli discourse and came to be referred to as ethnic groups.[9] The clustering of the immigrants into these categories has been based on similarities in education, occupation, income, and cultural characteristics among the members in each category, even though there were significant differences among the groups that composed these two blocs. For example, while the German, Polish, and Romanian immigrants were all considered Ashkenazim, the Germans were usually better educated and had higher occupational achievements than the newcomers in the Polish and Romanian groups.[10] Likewise, while the Iraqi and Moroccan immigrants were considered Mizraḥim, the Iraqis usually had higher educations and higher occupational attainments than the majority in the Moroccan group.[11]

The trend in studies on immigrants in Israel has been to compare the status achievements, that is, differences in prestige and honor, between the Mizraḥi and Ashkenazi immigrants who arrived in the country during approximately the same period, rather than with veterans or the native born. This comparison has included a wide range of measures. Among these are: education,[12] occupation,[13] income,[14] intergenerational transmission of wealth,[15] residence,[16] political affiliation,[17] the power of the Ashkenazim as elites,[18] and Israeli society's greater appreciation of Western culture than Middle Eastern culture. This cultural preference has often been explained by Edward Said's theory of Orientalism that argues that Western societies place greater value on their culture than on Eastern/Middle Eastern cultures.[19] This body of research has shown that as a group the first generation of Mizraḥi immigrants had lower status attainments and less power than the Ashkenazim.

In analyzing the status attainments of second-generation immigrants, scholars agree that there has been a general improvement in education, occupation, and income among Israeli-born, second-generation immigrants.[20] However, differences of opinion exist regarding the significance of these improvements. There are those who maintain that the inequalities between Mizraḥim and Ashkenazim have persisted and even widened in the second generation and, thus, the ethnic stratification that existed in the immigration generation has been "institutionalized"[21] and reproduced in the second generation.[22] The few studies that have focused on first- and second-generation immigrant women found lower educational attainments among Mizraḥi immigrant women than among Ashkenazi women and lower levels of participation in the labor market among the former than the latter.[23] Yet while there have been improvements in the levels of education and an increase in participation in the labor market among both Mizraḥi and Ashkenazi women, the gaps that existed between these women in these two areas in the first generation have been reproduced and even increased in the second generation.[24] In contrast, other scholars presented statistics that showed that while educational, occupational, and income disparities between the second generation in the two ethnic groups have continued, Mizraḥim are less homogeneous in their socioeconomic positions than in the past.[25] According to analyses of mobility among second-generation Mizraḥim, about one-third of the Mizraḥim have moved from the working class into the middle class.[26] Generally supporting these conclusions, Meir Yaish found that the Israeli stratification structure is very open, and that a large number of Israeli men have been mobile. He concluded that it is doubtful whether stratification in Israeli society since the early 1970s is primarily based on ethnicity.[27]

The overlapping between position in the stratification hierarchy and ethnicity that was rooted among the first generation of immigrants and continued into the second—to a lesser or greater degree, depending on the interpretation of data by different researchers—created a subordinate and hegemonic relationship between the members of these two groups. The Mizraḥim became the subordinate group and the Ashkenazim became the hegemonic group.[28] This designation of subordination and hegemony indicates a social relationship of inferiority and superiority that can be as meaningful, if not more so, than the educational, occupational, or income disparities between Mizraḥim and Ashkenazim that statistics reveal. Under such circumstances, ethnicity matters and survives, even if it is not always salient. Sammy Smooha referred to this latent aspect of ethnicity as a "submerged issue" in Israeli society that resurfaces from time to time because the Ashkenazim have maintained their hegemonic position,[29] while Dan Horowitz and Moshe Lissak argued that ethnic divisions have the potential to cause social schisms in Israeli society.[30]

The subordinate position of the Mizraḥim was exacerbated by negative stereotypes of the group that created feelings of discrimination against them by Ashkenazim and led to a series of riots and protests. The first prominent riot occurred in 1959, in Wadi Salib, a slum neighborhood in Haifa, and was led by David Ben-Harush, an immigrant from Morocco.[31] The second, actually a series of protests, began in 1971 and was led by the militant Israeli Black Panthers whose leaders were also Moroccans living in a slum neighborhood in Jerusalem.[32] Mizraḥim formed ethnic political parties to counter discrimination and to create greater equality between them and Ashkenazim. The most recent of these parties is named Shas and is led by Moroccans, though the spiritual head is an Iraqi rabbi.[33] Mizraḥi protests were also expressed through their support of Likud, the opposition party in government, and against the ruling Mapai Party, which was in power during their immigration and early settlement in Israel and which they blamed for their low socioeconomic positions and for ethnic discrimination against them. In fact, the Mizraḥim were a decisive force in ousting the Mapai Party from power in the 1977 elections and installing the Likud Party as the ruling party.[34] However, the perception of ongoing inequalities between Mizraḥim and Ashkenazim continues and explains recent research findings that showed that Mizraḥim feel that ethnic discrimination against them exists even if they have not experienced it personally.[35] These feelings persist alongside the long-standing ideological opposition, if not taboo, in Israeli society against acknowledging or dwelling upon divisions along ethnic and class lines.[36] This taboo is based upon the belief that Israel was created in order to bring about an ingathering of Jews from the Diaspora who, once they returned to Israel, would all be considered equal. This ideological stance dictated a pro-immigration policy for Jews that offers them incentives for immigration and various types of special services and support for first-generation newcomers. A corollary of this belief was the assumption that immigrants would shed their original cultural traits and, through the process of a melting pot, would then produce a new Israeli culture. However, the persistence of ethnicity among immigrant groups led to a general feeling that the goal of bringing about a melting pot had failed. This aim was replaced in the late 1950s and in the 1960s by a belief in cultural pluralism that created greater legitimacy and tolerance of ethnic differences in the society.[37]

The trends described above in studying first- and second-generation Mizraḥi and Ashkenazi immigrants' stratification attainments reveal certain limitations. One has been the practice of analyzing differences in these attainments according to the broad ethnic categories of Mizraḥim and Ashkenazim rather than according to differences among the specific ethnic groups that compose these two entities. Consequently, we have been deprived of a more nuanced understanding of the factors associated with second-generation status accomplishments.

Another limitation has been the tendency to conceptualize stratification differences between Mizraḥim and Ashkenazim in terms of status rather than class, which refers to objective attainments in the marketplace, such as income or occupation. I argue that focusing on class is important because much research has indicated a consistent trend toward the crystallization of classes in Israeli society, particularly of the burgeoning of the middle class.[38] Continuing this line of thought, Uri Cohen and Nissim Leon argued that a distinct Mizraḥi (including Moroccan) middle class has emerged that is based on common characteristics such as occupation, level of education, consumption patterns, and residential areas.[39]

In discussing the particular importance of the middle class in Israeli society, Smooha observed that this is the desired class location of the average Israeli: "By definition, these people of the middle [class] constitute the average Israeli, who labors daily to maintain Western living standards, owns an apartment in a decent neighborhood, raises a family of two or three children, and is very much concerned with the education and support of his children, material well-being."[40] Perhaps the most notable aspect of the formation of the middle class in Israeli society for all groups has been the entrenchment of the norm of credentialism and professionalization as a means of mobility into the middle class that has spread throughout Israeli society since the 1950s.[41]

Taking into consideration the importance of studying a specific ethnic group led me to focus on Moroccan immigrants and their mobility into the middle class. I chose to study this group for several reasons. First, the Moroccans were the single largest ethnic group to enter Israel during the mass immigration that followed the establishment of the State in 1948.[42] Second, with some exception, little research has been conducted on this group.[43] Third, as a group, Moroccan immigrants started at the bottom of the stratification ladder after their arrival in Israel, and, indeed, they constituted the largest ethnic group of poor and near poor. Therefore they formed a subordinate group in Israeli society.[44] Adding to their poverty was their tendency toward large families,[45] which meant that few resources had to be divided among a large number of family members.

An examination of the class position of Moroccan men in the immigrant generation, who were forty to fifty years of age, shows that about 10 percent were unemployed, 67 percent were in the working class, and 22 percent were in the middle class.[46] Among the Israeli-born second generation, the percentage of men in this age group in the working class dropped to 43 percent, the percentage of men in the middle class remained relatively stable (20 percent), and the percentage of men who were unemployed rose to 17 percent.[47] This suggests mixed trends in these men's mobility and that the upward mobility of Moroccan men into the middle class in the second generation has been an individual phenomenon more than a group one.

But what are the middle-class attainments of Moroccan immigrant women? It is important to analyze their mobility achievements separately from those of men because women occupy a different position in the gender hierarchy than men do. This location exposes them to different norms, mobility resources, opportunities, and experiences in their path to upward mobility than those of men. Pamela Abbott and Roger Sapsford emphasized this point when they wrote that studies on mobility should incorporate "women as people in their own right rather than . . . as some deviation from the male norm."[48]

To understand the mobility of second-generation Moroccan immigrant women into and within the middle class in Israel requires us to examine these women's background in Morocco, because it affected the initial placement or starting point of first-generation Moroccan women in the class hierarchy in their new society, and because it enables us to analyze both the changes and continuities in their lives that subsequently affected their paths to their middle-class attainments.

## Jewish Women in Morocco

Jews in Morocco were always a small, ethnic-religious minority within the predominant Muslim society. At the beginning of the twentieth century there were approximately 100,000 Jews in Morocco who comprised about 3 percent of the total population.[49] By 1947, prior to their immigration to Israel, their number increased to about 203,850 within the total Moroccan population of 8,581,890,[50] which constituted about 2 percent of the entire population. At the time of Moroccan independence from the French Protectorate, which began in 1912 and ended in 1956, the number of Jews in the country was between 210,000 and 240,000. During certain periods Moroccan Jewry formed one of the largest Jewish communities in the world.[51]

In premodern times, Jews lived in traditional rural communities dispersed throughout the country. Some lived in urban areas while others were scattered in isolated communities in the Berber areas of the Atlas Mountains in southern Morocco. However, recurrent droughts, plagues, and hunger in these mountainous regions resulted in internal migrations to the cities that created a concentration of Jews in major urban areas. In 1947 Moroccan Jews were spread out over forty to forty-five communities, but more than 70 percent lived in the major cities of Casablanca, Marrakech, Fez, Rabat, and Meknes.[52] There the majority, who were poor, lived in crowded, squalid *mellahs* (Jewish ghettoes) or in their outskirts, though a small number of the more prosperous resided in the new European quarters of the cities.[53]

The occupational distribution of Moroccan Jewry during the precolonial, pre-Protectorate period revealed a high concentration in specific economic sectors, such as moneylending and petty commerce in the cities and crafts and peddling in the nonurban areas. The implementation of the Protectorate led to an influx of Europeans who set up administrative frameworks and established businesses and basic industries in urban areas. These developments broadened the occupational structure of the Jews. Although about 50 percent continued to work in commerce and 38 percent in crafts, approximately 5 percent were employed in clerical positions in European businesses and in the French government.[54] Few Jews were involved in agriculture.[55]

In these traditional and religious Jewish communities a patriarchal order existed that supported a hierarchy of authority, power, and prestige through which men dominated women. These relationships derived from Jewish religious writings, their interpretation by local rabbis, and were also influenced by the surrounding Muslim community.[56]

During the nineteenth and twentieth centuries, the major components of Jewish women's femininity were their family roles as wives and mothers. In the 1800s, brides tended to be twelve to fourteen years old and grooms fourteen to sixteen years old.[57] During the colonial period, the marriage age for girls rose constantly. In 1934 the Rabbinical Court determined that the minimum age at which a girl could be married was twelve, in 1948, fifteen.[58] In precolonial times marriages were arranged by male family members.[59] Doris Donat noted that during the colonial period, this norm of mate selection changed; increasingly individuals, rather than relatives, chose their marriage partners.[60]

According to religious dictates, the purpose of marriage was to produce children and was expressed in the religious commandment to "be fruitful and multiply." This explains why motherhood was a major component of Jewish women's ethnic feminine identity. The ability to give birth to a large number of children, especially sons, was a major source of women's status in the community. Furthermore, infertility was grounds for divorce in rabbinical courts.[61] The threat of divorce led to the practice of women wearing amulets and prostrating themselves on the graves of revered rabbis as precautions against the evil eye that could prevent their becoming pregnant.[62] Donat found that the birth rate was still high by the mid-twentieth century, though women had begun to use scientific methods of birth control to plan the births of their children and thereby to influence their reproductive patterns.[63]

The social construction of motherhood, how the community and women themselves defined what constitutes a good mother, changed during the nineteenth and twentieth centuries. During the earlier period, the emphasis had been on the physical care of children. Good mothers breast-fed their babies. Mothers usually breast-fed their male infants for two years and their female infants for a year and a half. The lengthier period of breast-feeding male children reflected the greater value of males in these patriarchal communities. Scholars have pointed out that mothers were also expected to socialize their children, particularly daughters, to be wives and mothers according to religious scriptures when they married, to do housework, to serve the male members of the family, and to maintain a hospitable home.[64] By mid-twentieth century, scientific motherhood had made inroads into the concept of motherhood. One expression of this was a growing tendency for women to give birth in hospitals rather than at home, as had been common in the past. Mothers were still the primary caretakers of their children, but by this time a good mother was no longer defined only in terms of providing for the physical needs of her children, but also in terms of her ability to socialize her children toward scholastic achievement.[65]

Through the above-mentioned historical and economic changes, segments of Moroccan Jewry experienced contact with modernity and the West. This occurred primarily, though not solely, through the French Protectorate administration and the Alliance Israélite Universelle (AIU), an organization founded by French Jews in 1860.[66] The aim of the AIU was to "enlighten" Moroccan Jews, who were considered backward and uncivilized, and to turn them into "modern" citizens through exposure to French culture.[67]

Education was considered a critical instrument in modernizing Jewish communities in Morocco. Various networks of schools developed, but the most influential was that of the AIU.[68] The AIU opened its first school in Tetuan in 1862,[69] well before the establishment of the French Protectorate. The organization instituted a system of schools that initially provided five to six years of education for boys and girls and offered them a vocational education in order to relieve poverty. The schools taught a European language, usually French.[70] The AIU opened secondary schools in 1912. By the mid-1950s the organization had established seventy-six schools.[71] However, in spite of the increase in the number and variety of schools and the growing number of children who attended them, by the end of World War II, 37 percent of Jewish youth in Morocco had no formal schooling,[72] and only about 50 percent, primarily those in urban areas, had a modern education.[73]

The AIU schools put a particular emphasis on Westernizing/Europeanizing Moroccan girls. Girls were particularly important in the AIU's agenda, because in their roles as wives and mothers they cultivated homes and inculcated values in future generations and thereby could be influential forces for change.[74] The first girls' schools, which were elementary schools, were established in Tetuan in 1868, in Tangiers in 1874, and in Fez, one of the more interior, traditional cities, in 1899.[75] The AIU schools taught girls vocational skills such as needlework, sewing, and dressmaking. During the colonial period, the AIU added courses in bookkeeping, commercial correspondence, typing, and stenography to their curriculum to enable young women to be employed in the business enterprises that developed as a result of the Protectorate.[76]

Girls in the major urban areas of Morocco received an elementary education earlier than those in the less central areas did, and girls in the new, prosperous European quarters outside the *mellah* began school earlier than did those who lived in the poorer, more conservative Jewish ghettoes. In order to prolong girls' education, the AIU schools attacked the practice of child marriages and were influential in raising the marriage age for girls.[77]

The initial reaction to girls' education was mixed. While some rabbis, primarily those in the coastal, more European cities, supported education for girls, others, such as those in Sale, a strongly traditional and religious city, were strongly opposed because they feared that girls' schooling would undermine religious hegemony in defining feminine gender.[78] Girls' parents often supported rabbinical objections; mothers complained that education would cause girls to neglect their household duties and would turn them into "little Christians."[79] I found no statistics on the number of girls who received a formal education, but for those girls who did, schooling became part of their feminine gender construction.[80]

The spread of school systems in Morocco created employment opportunities for young Jewish women who had a formal education. Many from middle- and upper-class families found employment in administrative and commercial work and smaller numbers in professional work. Wealthy women took part in moneylending and taught sewing and embroidery in their homes to young girls, while poor, uneducated women worked outside their homes by selling in the public marketplace.[81] Apparently, working was part of the feminine gender construction for many women, though the type of work they did varied according to their class position.

The women who belonged to the small middle and upper classes constituted an elite. They were educated, attracted to French culture and a French bourgeois lifestyle; they adopted French names as a symbol of Europeanization, instead of Jewish-Biblical names; they spoke French; they dressed according to French fashion; they traveled abroad, and they were more secular than religious. In contrast, women from the larger working class and the poor women who lived in the *mellah* and its surroundings were less educated, worked in less prestigious employment, were more religious and traditional in their habits, and dressed more modestly.[82]

These developments resulted in increasing class differences within the Jewish communities. If during the precolonial period these communities had been divided into a small elite composed of rabbis, various notables and those of lesser ranks, during the colonial period a small, educated elite arose, as well as a new bourgeoisie and white-collar proletariat, composed of the upwardly mobile who had been exposed to Western education and culture, worked in European establishments, and lived in the new European sections of the large cities or the *mellahs*. A large proletariat of the poor, who lived in the *mellahs* or in its outskirts, constituted the lowest social strata in these communities. The members of these different classes maintained strict social segregation and avoided contact with one another.[83]

The rise of political Zionism added to the diversity within the Jewish communities. The Zionist movement developed in three main stages. The first took place in the pre-Protectorate period of 1895–1912 during which time Moroccan Jewry was first exposed to Zionist ideology and organizations. Initially it was a small movement among the educated Westernized segments of the Jewish community. The second stage took place during 1912–48. During this time the movement was declared illegal by the French, who regarded it as subversive to its aim of integrating all Moroccans within the Protectorate framework. It also encountered opposition from the AIU, who saw it as competing with its own goals; while the AIU sought assimilation of Jews in their respective countries, the Zionist movement supported separatism and the development of a Jewish/national identity. In spite of this opposition, the movement organized activities within the limitations the French imposed. Hebrew was taught, Zionist newspapers were published, and visits by Zionist emissaries who encouraged immigration to Palestine took place. There were attempts by Jews from Fez and Sefrou to immigrate to Palestine. Zionist youth movements were organized that were affiliated with Zionist parties. The youth in the *mellah* joined Dror, which aimed at being a popular movement, while those from the upper classes preferred the apolitical Scouts. The Holocaust led to an increase in membership in Zionist organizations. During this stage the Zionist movement changed from being a marginal group to being an important force in Moroccan-Jewish communities. The third stage in the development of the movement began with Moroccan independence in 1956. During this time Zionist activity was forbidden, Zionist newspapers ceased publication, representatives of Zionist organizations were expelled, and anti-Semitism and anti-Israeli feelings erupted in response to the creation of Israel. Nevertheless, clandestine Zionist activity continued that culminated in emigration from Morocco.[84] While the wealthy, more French-oriented Jews tended to immigrate to France, the poorer, more traditional inhabitants of the *mellah* and the ideologically motivated Zionists chose to go to Israel.[85]

On the eve of emigration, Moroccan Jewry was highly heterogeneous. Some members of these communities were urban, while others were rural, some were educated, while others were not, some were religious and others were secular, they belonged to different classes, were in different stages of transition from traditionalism to modernity, and some were affiliated with political Zionism, while others were not. It was from this background that those women who immigrated to Israel entered the Israeli class structure.

## Moroccan Women in Israel: The Mobility Attainments of the First and Second Generation

A comparison between the class attainments of the first generation of Moroccan women with those of the second generation reveals a consistent path of upward mobility into the middle class among the latter. Because of the association (if sometimes only partial) between education and occupation and therefore class, and because education is a major resource for mobility, I am presenting both the educational and occupational attainments of these two generations of women, though, as mentioned previously, I am determining class by occupation.

As shown in table 2.1, among the immigrant generation of Moroccan women in Israel who were forty to fifty years old at the time of the 1983 census (meaning that they were born during French rule in Morocco), an overwhelming majority had no or only little formal education (zero–eight years) and a quarter had only a partial or a complete high school education. A small percentage had only a matriculation certificate, a necessary requirement for acceptance to a university, but these women did not continue their education at an academic institution. A similar percentage had a certificate from a postsecondary, nonacademic institution. Very few had an academic degree.

The low educational attainments of these women were reflected in their occupational/class positions (based on Erikson and Goldthorpe's class schema[86])(see the methodology appendix). As can be seen in table 2.2, more than half were unemployed, and almost 30 percent were in the working class, doing manual labor or working in sales and services. Only one-tenth were in the middle class, with about 5 percent in the low segment of the middle class in semiprofessional jobs working as technicians, low-level managers or kindergarten teachers' assistants. An equal percentage of women were in the middle segment of the middle class in clerical work. Very few were in the high segment of the middle class in academic/professional work that required an academic degree, such as high school teaching.

**Table 2.1.** Educational attainments of immigrant and second-generation Moroccan and Ashkenazi women*

| ETHNIC GROUP | Moroccan Immigrant Generation | Ashkenazi Immigrant Generation | Moroccan Second Generation | Ashkenazi Second Generation |
|---|---|---|---|---|
| EDUCATION | | | | |
| 0 yrs | 25.7 | 1.8 | 1.8 | 0.3 |
| 1–8 yrs (elementary school) | 40.1 | 18.3 | 18.2 | 3.3 |
| partial high school (9–11 yrs) | 16.3 | 16.8 | 26.9 | 9.5 |
| complete high school (no matriculation certificate) | 8.6 | 14.2 | 21.4 | 15.2 |
| matriculation certificate | 3.1 | 13.7 | 11.2 | 15.2 |
| postsecondary certificate | 3.2 | 14.7 | 12.5 | 24.1 |
| BA degree | 0.3 | 6.9 | 5.2 | 22.1 |
| MA degree** | 0.2 | 8.6 | 1.6 | 7.9 |
| PhD degree | - | - | 0.6 | 1.7 |
| other degrees, unknown | 2.6 | 5.1 | 0.7 | 0.7 |
| TOTAL | 100.0 | 100.0 | 100.0 | 100.0 |

**Sources:** Immigrant generation—Government of Israel, *Census,* 1983; second generation—Government of Israel, *Census,* 1995.

* The data reflect the highest level of education attained.

** The 1983 Census (immigrant generation) did not differentiate between MA and PhD degrees.

The educational and occupational accomplishments of the Israeli-born, second-generation Moroccan immigrant women who were forty to fifty years old at the time of the 1995 census and who were born to two parents from Morocco were noteworthy in that they revealed an impressive intergenerational mobility both in educational and class categories. The percentage of women with no or little schooling dropped dramatically, while the

**Table 2.2.** Class attainments of immigrant and second-generation Moroccan and Ashkenazi women

| ETHNIC GROUP | Moroccan Immigrant Generation | Ashkenazi Immigrant Generation | Moroccan Second Generation | Ashkenazi Second Generation |
|---|---|---|---|---|
| Unemployed | 56.8 | 31.6 | 30.3 | 16.3 |
| Working class Manual labor | 6.3 | 7.6 | 7.4 | 2.9 |
| Sales and services | 23.2 | 13.1 | 14.1 | 9.3 |
| Total working class | 29.5 | 20.7 | 21.5 | 12.2 |
| Middle Class low: semiprofessional, technical, managerial | 5.0 | 19.6 | 10.9 | 21.0 |
| middle: clerical | 4.5 | 16.4 | 19.6 | 22.1 |
| high: academic-professional | 0.5 | 7.7 | 3.1 | 15.9 |
| Total middle class | 10.0 | 43.7 | 33.7 | 59.0 |
| Other, unknown | 3.9 | 4.0 | 14.5 | 12.6 |
| TOTAL | 100.0 | 100.0 | 100.0 | 100.0 |

**Sources:** Immigrant generation—Government of Israel, *Census,* 1983; second generation—Government of Israel, *Census,* 1995.

percentage who achieved a partial or complete high school education almost doubled; the largest percentage of second-generation Moroccan women were in this educational category. The percentage who earned a high school matriculation certificate almost quadrupled, which meant that about 11 percent of these women could have attended an academic institution, but did not do so. These women also made considerable strides in their post–high school education; the percentage who attained a postsecondary nonacademic certificate quadrupled, and the percentage who earned academic degrees increased from less than 1 percent in the immigrant generation to 7 percent in the second generation (see table 2.1).

A large percentage of these second-generation Moroccan women were still unemployed, though their percentage decreased considerably in comparison with the immigrant generation. Furthermore, a dramatic shift occurred in class positions. The percentage of women in the working class declined, and the percentage of women in the middle class tripled. If in the immigrant generation the largest percentage of women had been in the working class, mostly in sales and services, in the second generation the largest percentage (one-third) was in the middle class, with the largest percentage (20 percent) in clerical work. The second-largest group in the middle class was in the lowest segment, in semiprofessional work. The percentage of women in academic/professional work was small, but tripled in comparison with the immigrant generation. Thus the class mobility of these second-generation women was most pronounced in the middle class (see table 2.2).

## Comparing Class Mobility Attainments of Moroccan and Ashkenazi Women

As the narratives of the second-generation Moroccan immigrant women in this study will show, the upwardly mobile women who entered the middle class or were mobile within it did not compare their mobility attainments with those of other Mizraḥi women, with Moroccan men, or with nonmobile Moroccan women, but rather with those of Ashkenazi women, the women of the hegemonic group. Therefore, it is important to examine and compare the mobility and class differences between first- and second-generation Moroccan immigrant women with their Ashkenazi counterparts.

As can be seen from table 2.1, first-generation Ashkenazi immigrant women had higher educational attainments than first-generation Moroccan immigrant women. Among first-generation Ashkenazi immigrant women who were forty to fifty years old at the time of the 1983 census, a notable percentage had no or only an elementary education, but this percentage was much smaller than among first-generation Moroccan women. The other Ashkenazi women were more or less equally divided among the various educational categories, and these percentages were considerably higher than among the Moroccan women in the same categories. A most striking difference between the two groups of women was the high percentage of first-generation Ashkenazi women who had earned academic degrees in comparison with the percentage of first-generation Moroccan women who earned such degrees.

Table 2.2 shows that first-generation Ashkenazi immigrant women were employed more than first-generation Moroccan immigrant women, and more were employed in higher segments of the class hierarchy than Moroccan women. About 21 percent of these Ashkenazi women were in the working class, mostly in sales and services. However, a large percentage

(44 percent) was in the middle class, with similar percentages in the low and middle segments of the middle class in semiprofessional work and in clerical work, and a smaller percentage was in the high segment of the middle class in academic/professional work, but this was a significantly higher percentage than among the Moroccan immigrant women.

Second-generation Ashkenazi women who were forty to fifty years old at the time of the 1995 census and who had two Ashkenazi parents continued to have higher educational qualifications than second-generation Moroccan immigrant women. Among the former, a negligible percentage had no or only an elementary level of education, and about one-quarter had a partial or complete high school education. There was a slight increase (from the first generation) in the percentage who earned only a high school matriculation certificate, and this percentage was similar to second-generation Moroccan women. The biggest difference between the educational accomplishments of second-generation Ashkenazi women and second-generation Moroccan women was at the academic level; the percentage of second-generation Ashkenazi women who continued their academic education was considerably higher than for both immigrant-generation and second-generation Moroccan women. About one-third of second-generation Ashkenazi women attained an academic education, and this percentage was considerably higher than among first-generation Ashkenazi women and second-generation Moroccan women (7 percent) (table 2.1).

A higher percentage of second-generation Ashkenazi women were employed than were second-generation Moroccan women. A sizable percentage of these Ashkenazi women continued to be unemployed, but this was considerably less than among first-generation Ashkenazi women and second-generation Moroccan women. An even smaller percentage of these Ashkenazi women were in the working class. The most outstanding finding was that significantly more than half (59 percent) of these Israeli-born women were in the middle class, with similar percentages in the low and middle segments of the middle class and slightly less in the high segment of the middle class, but three times that of second-generation Moroccan women in the high segment.

While both groups of second-generation women improved their educational and class positions in comparison with the immigrant generation, and thereby increased their individual mobility resources, Ashkenazi women's greater attainments in these areas perpetuated their hegemonic position that had begun in the immigrant generation. However, even though a higher percentage of second-generation Ashkenazi women than second-generation Moroccan women were in the middle class, the class mobility of the Moroccan women was actually greater than that of second-generation Ashkenazi women. Statistics reveal that the percentage of second-generation Moroccan women in the middle class increased by 24 percent in comparison with the immigrant generation, while the percentage of second-generation Ashkenazi women in this class increased by only 15 percent in comparison with the previous generation (table 2.2).

Despite these differences in educational and class attainments, there were some similarities in the way second-generation women from both groups translated their educational achievements into occupational achievements and therefore into class. The data revealed that high percentages of women from both groups with low and medium levels of education did not work outside their homes (Moroccan women: zero years—90 percent; one to eight years—47 percent; nine to eleven years—29 percent; Ashkenazi women: zero years—78 percent; one to eight years—51 percent; nine to eleven years—32 percent).[87] These categories included women who had only low educational skills to offer the labor market, women who may not have had a financial need to work outside the home, or both. Since I measured class by occupation, these women who were unemployed did not have an independent class position. Women from both ethnic groups who had low levels of education and who were employed tended to be in the working class in sales and service jobs.

The clear demarcation between working and not working outside the home for both groups of second-generation women was a complete high school education (twelve years of schooling), which was expressed in a noticeable drop in unemployment at this level of education. The women from both ethnic groups with a full high school education and a matriculation certificate, but not more, were found in almost equal percentages (approximately one-third of the women in each ethnic group) in the middle segment of the middle class in clerical work. This suggests an internal differentiation in this type of work in which those with high school matriculation certificates were probably in higher clerical positions than those without them, even though both were included in the same category of employment. The large majority of second-generation women in both ethnic groups with nonacademic, postsecondary educations and academic educations were employed.[88]

Another noteworthy similarity between second-generation women from both ethnic groups was their tendency to be clustered in the female sector of the labor market. This trend was reflected in their concentration in semiprofessional and clerical work and, thus, in the low or middle segments of the middle class (see table 2.2). However, the academic professionals, women in the high segment of the middle class, were also employed in this sector of the labor market. For example, they tended to be high school teachers.[89] This tendency resembles that of employed women in other societies.[90]

The overall trend toward improvement in educational and occupational attainments among second-generation women from both ethnic groups was probably a response to several factors. One, as mentioned, was the growing importance attributed to educational credentials as a means of access to semiprofessional and professional work and the middle class. A second factor was the expanding market for women workers in occupations that stereotypically belong to the female sector of the labor market.[91] A third was the need for many married women to contribute to their family's income.[92] Together, these factors created favorable opportunities for women to be upwardly mobile.

## Family Formation Patterns and Mobility

Women's mobility cannot be separated from their marital status and family formation patterns because class and ethnic feminine identities that include marriage and motherhood can influence both their education and occupation and, therefore, class. Among the women who were born in Morocco and were forty to fifty years old at the time of the 1983 census, about half married before they were twenty years old; slightly more than one-third married between the ages of twenty and twenty-five; and slightly less than 10 percent married at the age of twenty-six or later. The age of marriage of 4.5 percent of these women is unknown.[93] These women tended to have large families; only about 10 percent had small families of one or two children, about one-third had middle-sized families of three or four children, and almost half had large families of five or more children. About 3 percent did not have children. The percentage of those whose number of children was unknown was about 8 percent.[94]

The data reveal transformations in family formation patterns among Israeli-born, second-generation Moroccan immigrant women who had two parents of Moroccan background and who were forty to fifty years old at the time of the 1995 Israeli Government Census. Statistics show a sharp increase in the age of marriage and a decrease in the number of children. Among these women, only 19 percent married before they were twenty years old, approximately half married between the ages of twenty and twenty-five, and about 7 percent married at twenty-six or later. The age of marriage of approximately 18 percent of these women was unknown. The percentage of those with small families almost doubled, while almost half the women had medium-sized families, and the percentage of those with large families dropped considerably (to 11 percent). About 5 percent had no children, and the percentage of those whose number of children was unknown was about 17 percent.[95]

Ashkenazi immigrant women exhibited different family formation patterns than Moroccan immigrant women; they married somewhat later than their Moroccan counterparts and had fewer children. Among the immigrant generation who were forty to fifty years old at the time of the 1983 census, only about one-quarter married before they were twenty years old and slightly more than half married between the ages of twenty and twenty-five. Approximately 10 percent married at twenty-six years of age or later. The age of marriage among these women that was not known was about 4 percent.[96] Moreover, almost half had small families, slightly more than one-third had middle-sized families, while few (6 percent) had large families. About 3 percent of these women did not have any children, and the percentage of these women whose number of children was unknown was about 8 percent.[97]

Among the second-generation, Israeli-born Ashkenazi women who had two Ashkenazi parents and who were forty to fifty years old at the time of the 1995 census, the percentage of those marrying before their twentieth birthday declined to 12 percent, and the percentage of those marrying between the ages of twenty and twenty-five reached almost 60 percent. About 11 percent postponed marriage to twenty-six years of age or later.[98] The age of marriage of about 14 percent of these women was unknown. Almost 30 percent of these women had small families, almost half had middle-sized families, and few (5 percent) had large families. The percentage of women who had no children was about 6 percent, and the percentage whose number of children was unknown was almost 13 percent.[99]

In comparison with the immigrant generation, there was a similar tendency between both groups of second-generation women to defer marriage until they were twenty to twenty-five, as well as a trend toward middle-sized families. Within this trend, the size of Moroccan families decreased and the size of Ashkenazi families increased. Overall, second-generation women from the two ethnic groups came to resemble each other in their family formation patterns.

How can we explain these differences in marriage and childbearing tendencies between these women, and what were their implications for mobility? As the narratives will show, and research corroborates,[100] among Moroccan first-generation immigrant women, the priority given to domestic roles that included the norm of early marriage and having large families, which was the core of their ethnic feminine identity, explains their young age of marriage and their large number of children. In addition, the low level of education of the majority of these women meant that they had few occupational skills to offer the Israeli labor market. Together, these factors probably contributed to the high percentage (57 percent) of this generation of women who remained at home, unemployed (see table 2.2), and with few mobility resources of their own with which to accomplish upward mobility. The transformation in family formation patterns among second-generation Moroccan women may be attributed to their increased education, which brought about the postponement of marriage, the decline in childbearing, and an increased participation in the labor force that provided a source of income and therefore an increase in their individual mobility resources.

Studies reveal that this change in family formation patterns is often accompanied by a process of rationalization of resources, whereby family size decreases so that upwardly mobile parents can invest more in fewer children.[101] For example, they can invest more money, time, and energy in their children's education and thereby improve their life chances. Scholars have suggested that the transition to smaller families evident among Mizraḥi immigrants was probably due to their expectations that reducing family size would result in greater socioeconomic opportunities for their children.[102] Limiting family size was particularly crucial for poor Mizraḥi families who wanted to provide their children with both an elementary and a high school education, because during the time these women were growing up a high school education was neither compulsory nor free.[103] Compulsory and free education was legislated in stages, beginning in 1948 for children in elementary school and expanding gradually until it became available to youngsters in high school.

In contrast, the data suggest that somewhat different factors may have influenced Ashkenazi women's family formation patterns. The reasons for first-generation Ashkenazi immigrant women's tendency to marry later and have smaller families than first-generation Moroccan immigrant women are not clear. Perhaps early marriage and having large families was less significant for the feminine identity of first-generation Ashkenazi women than it was for their first-generation Moroccan counterparts. Furthermore, the higher educational attainments of Ashkenazi women meant that more of these women had occupational skills to offer the labor market; indeed, the percentage of the unemployed was lower among these women than among Moroccan immigrant women (see table 2.2). This combination of factors encouraged these women's participation in the labor market, provided them with their own income, and added to their individual resources for mobility. The continuing improvements in education and in the occupational/class position of second-generation Ashkenazi women may have led to a lesser need to rationalize their resources in order to provide adequately for larger families; those who wanted middle-sized families may have felt that they could provide well for their children's future and still increase the size of their families.

## Representations, Perceptions, and Stereotypes of Moroccan and Ashkenazi Women

Added to the class differences between second-generation Moroccan and Ashkenazi women were cultural factors in the form of representations, perceptions, stereotypes, and films about the immigrant generation that contributed to Moroccan women's position at the bottom of the social ladder and to Ashkenazi women's position at the top. By and large, these different images of the two groups of women have persisted, at least in public imagination and discourse, to include second-generation women as well.

The trend in research on these women, as in research on immigrants in Israel, has been to divide them into the Mizraḥi or Ashkenazi categories rather than to focus on women from a specific ethnic group.[104] Within this trend, Mizraḥi, including Moroccan women, have been portrayed as being in a subordinate social position and possessing negative traits, while Ashkenazi women have been depicted as being in a hegemonic social position and possessing positive traits. Scholars (such as Moshe Semyonov and Tamar Lerenthal)[105] presented Mizraḥi women as traditional and Ashkenazi women as modern and more able to adapt to Western-oriented, industrialized Israeli society. Esther Goshen-Gottstein added that Mizraḥi women were self-centered, passive, and subservient to men, while Ashkenazi women were modern, showed greater concern for their children's welfare, and were equal partners in their households.[106] Shoshana Sharni, who focused specifically on Moroccan immigrant women with zero to eight years of schooling, found that these women sensed a condescending attitude toward them from representatives of the Israeli establishment, such as social workers, who presumably were Ashkenazi, and a devaluation of their traditional culture and gender roles.[107] They internalized this negative evaluation and consequently felt incompetent and inferior to veteran Israelis. In contrast to the perceptions of Moroccan women as traditional and passive, Rahel Wasserfall found that these women counterbalanced the formal patriarchal dominance of their husbands through the informal sexual power they wielded over them.[108]

In the field of literature, Sammy Michael, a noted Israeli novelist, wrote primarily about Iraqi immigrants, though Doli Benhabib, in her analysis of his work, claimed that he intended his observations to apply to other

Mizraḥi women and to Ashkenazi women.[109] He framed the differences between these two groups of women in contrasting physical characteristics and resources. In his novels the Mizraḥi woman is dark-skinned and has limited opportunities for mobility; if she finds employment, it is only in work that is demeaning, such as cleaning, while the Ashkenazi woman is light-skinned, clean, and quiet and not a newcomer to the country, but a veteran who possesses power and wealth and thus represents the Israeli social order. Michael also showed that immigration changed the gender relationship between Mizraḥi husbands and wives; if in their countries of origin these husbands had tended to be the breadwinners and the powerful spouse, in Israel many could not find work or did not want the menial jobs they were offered. Consequently, they became bitter and resentful at their lost position in the household, while their wives became the breadwinners and gained power in the family.[110] It has been suggested that these wives' work outside their homes brought them into contact with Israeli society and turned them into agents of socialization to Israeli society for their families.[111]

Recent movies made by Moroccan filmmakers have presented Moroccan women as strong and assertive, even domineering, within their homes.[112] These contradictory impressions, whether in research, literature, or movies lead us to wonder who Moroccan women truly are and how who these women really are affected their mobility into the various segments of the middle class.

The statistics presented here offer only group trends, and the representations are only impressions that provide generalities about second-generation Moroccan immigrant women. Neither tells us much about these women's class ambitions, about the investments that they, as individuals, made that propelled them to move upward within the Israeli class structure into segments of the middle class, or about the dilemmas, opportunities, and constraints they perceived and experienced in order to achieve their impressive mobility. This more complex and complete kind of information can only be acquired from the women themselves and an analysis of their individual life history narratives. Therefore, I now turn to the narratives of the upwardly mobile second-generation Moroccan immigrant women.

# Chapter 3

# *Becoming a Semiprofessional*

Miriam, forty-three years old, is a kindergarten teacher's assistant. She represents the approximately 11 percent of second-generation Moroccan immigrant women who are in the low segment of the middle class because they are semiprofessionals. She invited me to her apartment to conduct her interviews. For privacy, we sat in her son's bedroom, which exhibited the usual teenage paraphernalia—a sweatshirt and jeans were strewn on the bed, sneakers and a backpack filled with schoolbooks were on the floor, and a basketball lay in a corner. A computer stood on his desk.

When I asked Miriam to tell me about herself, she said:

> "I am an educator."
> "Are you a teacher?"
> "No," she answered.
> "Are you a school principal?"
> "No. I am a kindergarten teacher's assistant," she replied with pride.

Miriam's achievement of becoming a semiprofessional has its roots in her parents' struggle as immigrants, together with the emphasis in Israeli society on professional attainment. Miriam's parents, their six children, and all their relatives arrived in Israel in 1955. She, their seventh child, was born shortly thereafter. At the time, both parents were almost middle aged—her father was forty and her mother a few years younger. After their arrival the family settled in a small immigrant town in southern Israel populated by religious, Moroccan immigrants like themselves. In Morocco the family had lived in a *mellah,* the poor Jewish ghetto, of a city in the northern part of the country. Her father had been a cloth merchant and her mother a housewife with servants who did the housework. Neither parent had any formal schooling (though her father had some religious education), and consequently they had little educational and occupational attainments to offer the Israeli labor market. As a result, Miriam's parents suffered humiliating occupational and class displacement that relegated the family to the manual working class of Israeli society; both her parents became day laborers in agriculture to support their family.

In talking about her parents' sense of loss of their former life and about their struggle to survive in their new home, Miriam related:

> In Morocco, my parents had considered themselves well off. They had had a good life. Here, it was very difficult for them. They had to start everything from scratch. They had to learn a new language. My father knew a little Hebrew because he had studied in *heder*, but that was not enough to help him find work in what he had done before. My mother didn't know any Hebrew at all. She never went to school. Then it was customary that women only knew housework that they learned from their mothers, and men were expected to be the providers. My father and my mother, too, started working with a hoe in the farms around the town where we lived. They took every kind of work they could find. They worked very hard. When my mother was older, she worked cleaning a bank.

Like many immigrants, Miriam's parents wanted a better life for their children than they had had as newcomers and saw education and work as a means to achieve that end. Vivian Louie, in her study on the educational attainment of second-generation Chinese American children, claimed that cultural and structural perceptions characterize parental expectations regarding their children's academic success.[1] From a cultural perspective, "immigrant optimism," a belief that mobility is possible for those who invest in education, leads parents to encourage their children's scholastic achievements, while a structural perspective, which sees an open opportunity structure, perceives mobility to be a realistic goal.[2]

Miriam's parents exemplified immigrant optimism. They believed in a direct link between education and mobility and that Israeli society had an opportunity structure devoid of barriers for those who chose to study. Consequently, they socialized all their children toward acquiring an education that would qualify them for work through which they could break out of the manual-labor working class of their parents. Essentially, theirs was an instrumental type of socialization toward education, which all the children internalized. Talking about her parents' expectations of their children and of their subsequent educational and occupational attainments, Miriam recalled:

> They always said, "Do what is best for you." But they also wanted us to study and have good jobs, to have a profession. They didn't want us to be like them—physical laborers—and we aren't. One of my brothers has a matriculation certificate and works as a computer technician. Another studied in a course to be a social worker's aide. One sister is a kindergarten teacher. One of my sisters is a special education teacher; she has an elementary school teaching certificate. Another sister started studying, but "broke down"—it was too hard for her—so now she is studying to be a medical secretary, another sister is an accounting clerk.

All of Miriam's siblings fulfilled their parents' expectations to a certain degree. They did not enter the professions, but the semiprofessions, a considerable accomplishment considering their manual-labor working-class origins, and all are in the low segment of the middle class. One could speculate that had their parents set clear educational goals, such as completing high school and doing their matriculation examinations, perhaps they might have attained higher educational accomplishments and therefore greater mobility. The importance of expressing specific educational goals to encourage children's educational attainments has been endorsed by researchers who found that children whose immigrant parents presented concrete expectations of educational achievements had higher attainments than those whose parents presented only vague expectations.[3]

After attending elementary school in the town in which she lived, Miriam continued her studies in the local high school. She studied in the academic track that would have enabled her to do her matriculation examinations at the end of twelfth grade and continue on to an academic education. However, she was ambivalent about her studies. She opted to drop out of school in eleventh grade because the studies were "too hard." She took some of her high school matriculation examinations, but not all of them, because they, too, were "too hard." Thus she does not have a high school diploma or a high school matriculation certificate and therefore cannot continue studies at a university or an academic college.

Miriam did not serve in the army, which is compulsory for all Jewish eighteen-year-old women unless they are religious, married, or have health problems, because her father thought that army service was immoral for girls. Discussing her father's decision, she remarked: "That was a primitive idea, but that's the way people thought then." Instead Miriam decided to take a two-year, nonacademic course at a regional college near her home to study to become a kindergarten teacher's assistant. Thereby, she became one of the approximately 13 percent of second-generation Moroccan immigrant women who acquire a postsecondary, nonacademic type of education (see chapter 2, table 2.1). The course granted her a certificate from the college and from the Israeli Ministry of Education that confirms she has professional training in her field and is authorized to work as a kindergarten teacher's assistant.

Miriam explained her decision to take the course by referring to a dominant norm in Israeli society—education toward professionalization and mobility: "I decided to study something. Everybody said it was important to have a profession. I realized that it was important, too." She clarified her choice of occupation by saying: "I chose to take care of children because I like children. Whatever you invest in them stays with them. Children are life. It is like planting a seed. You invest in them and they will grow. All the children who pass through my hands succeed in school. I have been doing this for twenty-two years."

Miriam feels her job as a kindergarten teacher's assistant is important and is a symbolic aspect of the semiprofessional status she has achieved. It has given her a sense of empowerment, self-esteem, and pride: "I am an educator, like a teacher. I am involved in children's education—in what they study. I work with different groups of children in small study groups and I help them learn. I teach them. Sometimes I see children with problems and I help them overcome their problems. That gives me a lot of satisfaction."

Miriam thinks that over the years she has advanced professionally through courses for kindergarten teachers' assistants that she has taken throughout her working life. Taking these courses has been both a method of gaining knowledge and improving her pedagogical skills, as well as a continuous process of fortifying her professional identity and legitimizing her status as a semiprofessional. She explained: "I take a course every year from work that deals with a different topic each year. I have to go—the Education Ministry makes me—but I love taking the courses. Each time I finish a course, I get a certificate and a small increase in salary."

Miriam feels a bond with the other women who take the courses with her that derives from their common structural position as second-generation immigrant women. She described them by saying:

> The women who take the courses with me are like me. They are forty, fifty, fifty-five years old. Some of the women didn't study at

> all or studied very little. Some of them say that the first time they have held a pen in their hand is in the courses we take. Most of the families of these women had a hard time when they came to Israel. They had to earn money to help their families and they have been working since they were twelve to fourteen years old. They didn't have the chance to study the way they wanted to and they regret it to this day. Some took care of the house and their brothers and sisters while their mother went out to work. Some had parents who told them that girls don't need to study. I've heard them say, "Why did I listen to my parents and not study?" Others, like me, just didn't want to study then.

Miriam's perception of her own motivation, as well as of her fellow students, was substantiated by the director of the courses for kindergarten teachers' assistants at the nonacademic institution in which Miriam studied:[4] "The typical women who take the courses are forty to fifty years old, of Mizraḥi background, daughters of women who immigrated to Israel—women who perhaps wanted to study but didn't. They married instead, had children, and feel good working with children."

Miriam's investment and that of the other women in their continuing education and in improving their skills as educators has received social recognition through the Israeli Ministry of Education. It is expressed in continually raising the requirements to enter a course for kindergarten teacher's assistants, in the content of the work the assistants do, in the title of their role, and in their increasing social status. The Ministry led the process of transforming the role of the kindergarten teacher's assistant from a manual-labor job into a semiprofession. Originally, the kindergarten teacher's assistant was called a kindergarten teacher's "helper." She made sure that everything was in its place for the day's schedule, which the teacher determined; she helped maintain order in the class; and she cleaned up, washing the dishes after snacks, washing the floor at the end of the day, and performing other physical duties. Today she is considered a partner in the young child's education. She works with the teacher to plan the year's educational activities, she works with the children to support the educational goals of the kindergarten, and she participates in meetings between the parents and the teacher. To emphasize the new pedagogical aspect of the role, the Ministry changed its name from "kindergarten teacher's helper" to "kindergarten teacher's assistant." Miriam is aware of the upgrading of her occupation. She told me: "We used to be called kindergarten teachers' helpers. That meant that we helped the kindergarten teacher, but mostly we cleaned up. Today we are called kindergarten teachers' assistants. That is an improvement."

To stress the professional nature of her work, Miriam made a distinction between her role as a kindergarten teacher's assistant and caretaking roles, such as mothering: "I always say that children need warmth, their morning kiss. Without that, it just doesn't work. I see it every morning. They wait for me to give them their morning kiss. If you work with small children, you have to love them. But it is not the same thing as being a mother. Being a kindergarten teacher's assistant is a profession."

Miriam also distinguished between her position as a semiprofessional and other work that she considers inferior. She differentiated between herself, a kindergarten teacher's assistant, and her friends who are secretaries. She regards herself an educator, while secretaries are merely people who carry out someone else's decisions:

> I don't think that secretaries work as hard as I do, but they earn twice as much. When I tell people what I earn, they laugh at me. When I tell my friends, who are secretaries, what I earn, they laugh and tell me that that is what they get as car allowance from their office. That makes me angry. A high-ranking secretary gets 20,000 shekels a month [the equivalent of $5,000] just for doing what other people tell her to do and we, poor things, who teach thirty children, get very little. It isn't fair.

Miriam's work as a semiprofessional has been central to her life, and she claimed that work outside the home has become important to other second-generation Moroccan women as well. Her comment implied that as a result of changing gender norms related to modernity, employment has become a component of the feminine identity of these women and constitutes a new Moroccan femininity in Israel:

> Why do Moroccan women go out to work today? Today life is more modern. Women have washing machines. They have everything at home to make life easier. It's not like in the past when women had to do everything themselves. Today everything is ready-made. Besides, the mentality has changed. A Moroccan woman doesn't feel the need to stay at home all the time. She can have a home and still work. Lots of women go out to work today—lots of them. Most of the women I know work outside their homes.

But Miriam was aware that some second-generation Moroccan immigrant women did not work outside their homes. She guessed that these were women who did not acquire a formal education. Her supposition is supported by statistics that show that almost 90 percent of second-generation Moroccan immigrant women with zero years of schooling and almost 50 percent with only one to eight years of schooling were not employed.[5] She feels disdain for these women:

> There are women who choose not to work. Maybe, financially, they can afford not to work or they don't like to work. I think that the women of my generation who don't work today are those who didn't study. Sometimes it drives me crazy to see a woman sitting at home. How much can you clean? How many times can you put the house in order? Going out to work develops a person.

Miriam married when she was twenty-four, the typical age of marriage among second-generation Moroccan immigrant women.[6] She completed her education beforehand. After her marriage, she moved to Jerusalem, where her husband lived. "He is educated," she stressed. Her husband has a high school matriculation certificate and works as an accountant. He is a second-generation Israeli-born man of Kurdish ethnic origin. Thus she chose a partner outside of her specific ethnic group, but within the large Mizraḥi bloc.

Miriam's explanation regarding the ethnicity of her husband revealed her opinion of ethnic intermarriage between Moroccans and Ashkenazim:

> I don't think that it is important that couples come from the same ethnic background. I have a sister who is married to someone of Ashkenazi background and they get along very well. You hear stories about Moroccans wanting to go out with Ashkenazim, but Ashkenazim prefer to go out with other Ashkenazim. Ashkenazi parents want their children to go out only with Ashkenazim. I once dated an Ashkenazi boy and whenever I came into their house, his mother acted as though a monster had come through the door. That's why I left him.

This comment reveals an ethnic awareness as well as a perception of an ethnic hierarchy in choosing marriage partners and shows that ethnicity can serve as a barrier in mate selection in Israel. According to Miriam, this is particularly true when a woman from the subordinate group, such as a

Moroccan, wants to marry a man from the hegemonic Ashkenazi group. While there are instances in which interethnic marriages can be harmonious, such as Miriam's sister's marriage, generally, women from the subordinate group who cross the ethnic divide and desire a spouse from the hegemonic group risk rejection, exclusion, and being treated like an inferior Other.

Miriam claimed that ethnic norms influenced her decision to marry: "I married because among Moroccans it is a norm to marry—it's part of our Moroccan culture—there has to be continuity of the family." Furthermore, not marrying has significant social consequences. As Miriam explained, "If I hadn't married, people would think it sad."

The notion of a connection between women's marital status and their social status is endemic to Jewish Moroccan culture. As mentioned in chapter 2, Jewish women in Morocco established their feminine identity and fortified their status in the community through marriage. Thus ethnic definitions of Moroccan femininity required women to marry to avoid being considered deviant and incurring social costs, such as the pity of others.

Besides conforming to the ethnic norm to marry, Miriam claimed to be indifferent to other components of her ethnic identity:

> What does being a Moroccan woman mean to me? Nothing, really. If I had been born to Ashkenazi parents, I would have been an Ashkenazi woman. I am satisfied being a Moroccan—I'm not sorry about it. If you ask me to define myself, I am first of all a woman, then a mother, then a kindergarten teacher's assistant. I wouldn't mention that I am a Moroccan.

Nevertheless, she observes a symbolic Moroccan ethnicity that she expresses through the preparation of ethnic food on special occasions, though she also contributes to the preservation of her husband's ethnicity by preparing Kurdish ethnic food: "When my family meets on holidays, we eat Moroccan food. I try to cook Moroccan food. I learned to do that from my mother. But I have also learned to cook Kurdish food, food that my husband is used to. I learned from my mother-in-law. But I don't feel anything special because I am Moroccan." Apparently, in Miriam's list of the components of her identity, her Moroccan identity is the least salient.

For Miriam, marriage primarily meant motherhood. She claimed that her main reason for marrying was that it provided a framework for motherhood: "If I hadn't married, I would have missed out on motherhood. I wouldn't have children if I hadn't married. It is a pity if a woman does not have children." Thus, complete Moroccan femininity includes both wifehood and motherhood, and failure to comply with both detracts from women's ethnic femininity and has social costs in that it arouses the sympathy of others.

Like other second-generation Moroccan immigrant women (see chapter 2), Miriam wanted to have fewer children than had been common among the first-generation. She felt that her material and emotional resources were finite and that having a large number of children would limit the resources she could invest in each child. Therefore she practiced a rationalized approach to child-bearing; she had fewer children so that she could invest more resources in each child. Miriam had her son one year after she married, her daughter three years later, and her second daughter a year after that: "I always wanted three or four children. More than that is a burden. It's not easy to be a mother. It's not easy at all. All I know is that a child is something alive that you have to nourish all the time, that you have to give to all the time. A child is a person that you have to mold, educate. Raising a child takes everything out of you."

What is the overwhelming burden in rearing children that Miriam talked about? Most of all it is a transformation in the nature of childhood and the goals of parenthood that have come about as a result of changes in Israeli society. She explained: "In the past, children had a childhood and enjoyed it. Today it's not the way it used to be. Then everything was fun—not like today that all children know are computers and technology. And today children are so sophisticated. It is so difficult. This is a totally different generation. What caused this change? Society caused this change."

This depiction of a carefree past childhood contrasted sharply with Miriam's previous comments about her early youth. By her own account, her childhood and that of the other second-generation Moroccan immigrant women she spoke about was hardly enjoyable. It was governed by economic deprivation in which children often had to leave school in order to help support their large immigrant families, as well as by parental pressure to attain an occupation that would enable them to break out of the manual working class of their parents and enter the middle class. Miriam's idealization of the past is not so much an expression of a reality as an indication of an anxiety that derives from living in a mobility-driven society in which children and parents are expected to strive to enter the middle class via the specific path of academic achievement that usually includes higher education. This road requires long-term emotional and financial investments that Miriam, as a woman who has just moved out of the working class, may find difficult to make. Therefore her worry about her ability to enable her children to attain what society values is understandable and not unfounded.

After her children were born, Miriam worked out various arrangements to enable her to combine her role as a mother with her chosen work. When her son was born, she worked from 7:00 a.m. to 2:00 p.m. in a day-care center and left him with a woman who took care of children in her home. When her daughter was born, Miriam cared for other children in her own home so that she could take care of her children and use her training in child care to provide an income. But when she had her third child, she stopped working entirely and took care of her children until the youngest entered kindergarten. Then she returned to full-time work and has continued working continuously until the present. These arrangements enabled her to adhere to her construction of motherhood: "Being a good mother means being available to your children always—whenever they need you, whenever they want your advice. That kind of connection between parent and child is very important no matter what the age of the child." Yet, almost in the same breath, she added: "I never felt guilty toward my children because I work. They always got what they needed. So why should they object? My children aren't going to dictate to me what to do, how I live my life. I am my own lord and master. I do as I please." So, while Miriam endorsed a child-centered motherhood, she made it clear that her children would not intrude upon her autonomy, which included her desire to pursue her occupational goals.

The division of labor between Miriam and her husband was a partnership in which he shared the responsibility of educating their children and housekeeping chores that left her free to devote her time to her work:

> My husband is a good husband. He helps with the children's education. That's the most important thing because a mother cannot cope alone. And he helps at home. When the children were small, he helped with taking care of the children—feeding them, bathing them, he took them to the doctors, he took them to kindergarten and to school—he helped with shopping, with everything. There isn't anything he didn't do. It just worked out that way.

This partnership was a strategy that centered on ways to preserve the family's middle-class position through the parents' occupations and on ways to promote their children's mobility through their education.

Miriam thought she had an equal partnership between her husband and herself not only in the division of family labor but also in decision making. It seems that the most prevalent topic in this area of their lives revolved around their finances and in deliberations about how to make ends meet in their middle-class family living in a middle-class consumer society like Israel. Miriam elaborated:

> We discuss things when we have to make a decision. I listen to his opinion and he listens to mine, and then if I think that we can do something, we do. If I think that we can't, then we don't. I always say that I buy what I can and if I think that I can't afford it, I don't buy it. One day a child wants a pair of sneakers or jeans and it's not like it used to be that you could buy a cheap pair of jeans. Today children want name-brand jeans—Levi's. And that costs a lot of money. My son wanted a TV. I didn't want one, but you can't always say no to everything. I always tell them, "I buy what I can afford. What I can't, I don't buy."

There was a subtle contradiction in Miriam's remarks. She claimed that she and her husband had equal power in making decisions about money matters, but if we analyze her comments carefully, we see that the power in making these decisions was not equal—she had veto power. What she was really saying was that while the process of reaching a decision was a joint project, the final decision was hers.

In fact, Miriam was the dominant spouse in the couple's biggest financial decisions, which entailed moving from an apartment in the immigrant slum neighborhood in which they lived after their marriage to a better neighborhood that was populated by upwardly mobile Mizraḥim, and then moving again to an even better neighborhood also composed of upwardly mobile Mizraḥim. The purpose of these moves was to provide her children with more pleasant surroundings and better schools than those in the family's previous neighborhoods. Her belief in the positive effects of good neighborhoods on children's academic achievement has been validated by research that shows a connection between good neighborhoods and scholastic achievement.[7] Her dominance in this process is evident from her recurrent use of the word *I*, rather than *we*:

> When I had my son, we were living in a bad neighborhood, so I bought a small apartment in Bilu, a better neighborhood. Five years later I moved again to Gordon, an even better neighborhood. We left the first apartment because it was small—but mostly because it wasn't a good neighborhood. It wasn't a neighborhood in which I wanted to raise my children—the schools were bad. But then I wanted to move to a better neighborhood that had better schools, so we took a mortgage and I bought this apartment. It has four bedrooms.

Miriam's dominance in financial decisions seems to derive not from her financial power as a dual earner but rather from a strong sense of self. Miriam told me:

> I don't think that a woman's working outside the home should make a difference in how couples decide things or spend their money. It's not right that if a husband earns more than the wife he should decide what they do with the money. I suppose that there are couples that the husband says, "I work, I earn the money and I'll decide how we spend it." But that only happens when the wife is weak. But that kind of situation can happen in any family, not only in Moroccan families. But if the wife is strong . . .

Miriam was the dominant partner in financial matters even though she was not the primary breadwinner. She earned slightly more than a minimum wage, but her husband earned an average wage, which placed the family in a higher income category than they would be based on Miriam's semiprofessional position alone. As she pointed out:

> The salary I earn is low. I couldn't manage on that. But my husband earns more, so, together, with both our salaries, I think that we are in the middle class. It's enough, but it isn't easy. We don't go away on weekends; we don't take vacations. There are always expenses—for the children's education, books, clothes, the mortgage. What I can do, I do. What I can't, I can't.

Miriam used her own occupational attainments in determining her individual class position, but she used both her and her husband's income in determining her family's class position, though she was aware that objectively hers was the less significant contribution.

Looking back at her attainments, Miriam compared herself with her mother, who belonged to the immigrant generation. She emphasized differences in the constraints in the opportunity structure available to her mother, particularly with regard to education, and those available to her, as a second-generation immigrant woman. Her remarks revealed her awareness of the statistics that show that an increasing percentage of women, including Moroccan second-generation women (approximately 7 percent) (see chapter 2, table 2.1), study at universities. For these women, higher education offers a road to mobility, increasingly through occupations that enable them to break out of the female sector of the labor market by becoming doctors and lawyers:

> The women in my mother's generation worked all the time, and they had lots of children. And they had so much physical work to do at home. My mother had seven children and she didn't have a washing machine. She cooked on a small kerosene stove. Then, women didn't have the opportunities they have today. They couldn't study. Today there are a lot of women students. My neighbors have daughters who study in the university. I have friends whose children study. Today a lot of women study. They study to be doctors and lawyers.

Comparing her children's educational and occupational mobility with those of her own, it was clear they have already surpassed her educational attainments. Her son studied in a technical track in a vocational high school, did his high school matriculation examinations, and is serving in the army. Both her daughters are studying graphic computer design in a vocational high school and will do their matriculation examinations. In a matter-of-fact tone, Miriam told me, "All my children will have matriculation certificates."

Although her children were still too young to know what their ultimate educational attainments will be, these certificates will give them the option of continuing their studies in a university and enjoying the class benefits that such an education confers. In spite of her anxiety about her ability to do so, she has reared her children to comply with the norm of mobility through education and professionalization that will enable them to exceed her class achievements.

Measuring her mobility attainments against those of other Moroccans, Miriam identified herself and those in her immediate circle as upwardly mobile. Her children were on their way "up" through their educational qualifications. Her siblings had all accomplished upward educational and occupational mobility in comparison with their parents; one has a matriculation certificate and all are in semiprofessional occupations similar to her own. The women who took courses for kindergarten teachers' assistants with her, other second-generation Moroccan immigrant women, also acquired semiprofessional credentials. Thus those around her served as a reference group and validated her perception of the possibility of upward mobility. This use of a reference group in evaluating individual mobility prospects supports research that found that members of subordinate groups who aspire to upward mobility identify with those in their group who have achieved such mobility.[8]

As Miriam spoke about her mobility attainments and of those she knew, she also mentioned other Moroccans' lack of upward mobility:

> Maybe some Moroccans feel that "their backs are up against a wall." That they can't do what they want, that they can't send their children to the schools they want. That's why some of them feel discriminated against by Ashkenazim. But I don't feel that way. I work in a kindergarten in which many of the parents of the children are Ashkenazim—they are the elite—but I don't feel any discrimination from them even though I am Moroccan. Actually, they respect and love me.

In these comments, Miriam implied that those Moroccans who were not mobile were those who sensed discrimination against them, who felt their ethnic identity was a constraint on their mobility, while she, who considers herself mobile, did not sense such limitations. In other words, her class accomplishments countervailed discrimination. Nevertheless, she was aware of a class structure in which Ashkenazim, through their greater occupational achievements, were a class above her and constituted the elite in Israeli society.

In spite of Miriam's pride in her occupation as an educator, she thought she could have accomplished more, that she was, after all, only on the margins of the educational profession. She had a sense of "unfulfilled potential," what Carolyn Britton and Arthur Baxter have defined as "'missing out' in some way at an earlier stage."[9] In Miriam's opinion, her unfulfilled potential derived from her parents' refusal to let her serve in the army, or from what might be interpreted as constraints placed upon her by ethnic feminine gender norms and by being the daughter of first-generation immigrant parents. Pondering whether serving in the army might have changed her life course—an idea that perhaps gives inordinate weight to army service—she asked herself whether her educational and occupational attainments would have been higher had she continued her education. Miriam reflected: "Maybe I should have gone to the army. Maybe it would have broadened my horizons. Maybe I would have done my matriculation exams and studied more and achieved more. Maybe I would have been in a different profession."

These remarks acknowledge the existence of alternative choices that could have been made, of options that were available but not utilized. Her comment, "Maybe I would have studied more and achieved more," suggests her perception of her failure to take advantage of educational opportunities that existed in a stratification structure she sees as open to those individuals who make certain critical choices and thereby affect their own mobility. In the construction of her life story, Miriam's sense of "unfulfilled potential" seems more like "opportunity refused" than "opportunity denied."[10]

ꕥ

In spite of the gratification that Miriam felt from being a semiprofessional, she was aware that the economic consequences or rewards of her work were limited. Her low income is particularly frustrating to a family who is in a precarious position in the middle class. The pressure to "keep up" a middle-class life suggests Zygmunt Bauman's characterization of the newly arrived parvenu who is insecure and anxious in the new class position he has recently entered.[11]

But while Miriam and others like her may feel they could have achieved "more," they also feel that their semiprofessional occupation provides two important rewards, both more symbolic than material; it enables them to break out of the working class and to have the satisfaction of being a semiprofessional. From a theoretical perspective, this narrative highlights the different dimensions of upward mobility. While many studies focus on the material or economic rewards of upward mobility, this life history is an example of a type of mobility in which the emotional rewards, such as personal empowerment, pride, and increased self-esteem, compensate for limited economic rewards. As Richard Sennett and Jonathan Cobb observed,[12] these kinds of rewards may be particularly important to individuals who belong to a subordinate group, such as second-generation Moroccan immigrant women.

While Miriam stressed the feeling of achievement at becoming a semiprofessional and entering the middle class, another woman focused on issues Miriam did not, which she felt were significant in her upward mobility. This is the substance of the next narrative.

# Chapter 4

## *Transforming One's Self and One's Body*

Like Miriam, forty-two-year-old Ruth represents women in the low segment of the middle class. She, too, is a semiprofessional, a kindergarten teacher's assistant. However, in the construction of her narrative in which she told of her path into the low middle class she stressed her transformation of herself and her body in order to enter this class.

Ruth and I met in a booth at a quiet café for her interviews. As she sat opposite me at the table, I could not help noticing her erect posture and her habit of looking directly into my eyes as she spoke. She began telling me about herself by recalling her background.

Ruth told me that after their immigration to Israel, her parents and their nine children were sent to a transit camp for newcomers. The couple had married when her mother was fourteen and her father was twenty or twenty-two. The family was religious. Ruth, their tenth child, was born in Israel. In Morocco her parents had lived in the *mellah* (the Jewish ghetto) of Casablanca, where her father had been a peddler who traveled with his horse and cart to sell his wares, and her mother had been a housewife. Her father had some elementary education, but her mother had none. In Israel her father became a manual laborer and found work building roads, while her mother continued to be a housewife. A few months after their arrival in the country, the family moved out of the transit camp and into a slum neighborhood in Jerusalem that was populated by Moroccan immigrants like themselves.

Ruth's parents socialized her and her siblings to believe that work, rather than studies, would be their path to upward mobility. As she explained:

> Both of my parents, but especially my father, would say, "If you don't work, you will never have anything," and I felt that if I didn't

> work, I really wouldn't have anything. They didn't care what work I did, as long as I worked. And I have worked every day of my life. Of all the twenty years that I have been working, I have only been unemployed a month and a half.

In her opinion, the priority that her parents attributed to work explains the fact that none of her brothers and sisters completed high school. She is the only one in her family who has a full high school education, twelve years of schooling: "My parents never supported my studying. There was never anyone who sat with me and helped me and encouraged me. That always bothered me."

In high school, Ruth's teachers placed her in the vocational track to study sewing, a stereotypical female topic of studies. According to some researchers,[1] the Israeli educational system encouraged children of Mizraḥi origin, including Moroccan origin, to enter the vocational track, which resulted in their concentration in the low income, low status, working-class sector of society and excluded them from high status, high income sectors populated primarily by Ashkenazim. These scholars argued that through this process the school system reproduced class and ethnicity. However, by placing girls from Mizraḥi origin into stereotypically female fields, the school system reproduced gender as well. This explanation draws on Jane Gaskell's study on the Canadian school system that showed a tendency to place girls from working-class and subordinate racial-ethnic backgrounds in stereotypical fields in the vocational track and girls from higher classes in the academic track.[2] Ruth was acutely aware that the choice to study sewing was not hers: "I didn't choose the vocational track; the school chose it for me. I wasn't good in mathematics, so the school decided that I should learn something useful."

Upon completion of high school, Ruth did some of her matriculation examinations, but not all of them, which means that she only has a partial matriculation certificate. She was aware of the importance of a complete certificate if she wanted to continue her education: "It always bothered me that I didn't have one. You need a complete matriculation certificate if you want to study." Therefore, she cannot study in a university and will not profit from the mobility resources that an academic education bestows.

Despite the lack of parental encouragement, Ruth wanted to continue her studies beyond high school, but had to stop. As the daughter of immigrants from a large family, she was expected to sacrifice her desire to study in order to help support her family. She regretted having to end her studies because learning enriched her soul. For Ruth, as for the mature students interviewed by Britton and Baxter and by Diane Reay,[3] studying was a passion.

She loved the mastery over knowledge for its intrinsic value more than for its instrumental use. As she explained:

> I wanted to continue studying, but I had to work to support myself and help my family, so I couldn't. I love to study, I am obsessive about studying. Studying makes me feel good about myself. But I never really stopped studying. I have taught myself seven languages. I learned English from people I work with. I learned the other languages from TV, newspapers. It was very difficult, but I wanted to know languages.

Ruth entered the army but did not complete her two-year term of duty because, again, she had to help support her family: "I didn't finish the army, either, because the family needed me to work to make money. I think that if I had completed the army, I might have gotten more out of it."

At that stage of her life, Ruth decided to continue her education by taking a two-year course at a postsecondary nonacademic college to become a kindergarten teacher's assistant. Upon completion of the course, she received a certificate that attested to her professional expertise. She explained her choice of career by telling me: "I like children. You can invest in children. Each time I teach a child, I feel as though it's the very first time. I follow up on my children after they leave me, so I know that they are doing well."

Throughout the years she has continued to improve her pedagogical knowledge and her professional skills through additional courses she has taken and for which she has received certificates. She has also taken courses to advance in her work:

> I started out by studying to be a kindergarten teacher's assistant. Now I am studying to be a senior kindergarten teacher's assistant. When I finish this course, if I have money, I want to continue studying. Eventually, I want to be a teacher. That's my dream.

For Ruth, the intrinsic satisfaction she has received from her work is more important than the material reward:

> I love everything about my work. I love the beginning of the day and the end. Work has given me advancement and that adds a little to my salary. But another 100 to 200 shekels (roughly, the equivalent of $25–$50) doesn't matter. The money I earn doesn't interest me. I am interested in the results, in watching children open up, gain self-confidence.

Then, giving voice to her longing to compensate for the educational deprivations she had suffered, that she apparently felt cannot be compensated for, she added: "I want to give other children what I didn't have. It's harder later in life."

If, for Ruth, her semiprofessional attainment has been her path to upward mobility into the low middle class, her wholehearted rejection of Moroccan feminine gender norms accompanied this process. As we saw in chapter 2, these norms require women to marry young, but she married later than expected, when she was twenty-eight. As she told me: "Moroccan women are expected to marry. I was taught that marrying was like a holy commandment—it was supposed to be my main goal in life, and I guess that I believed that, too, so I wanted to marry. I married relatively late, though. All my sisters married young—maximum at nineteen."

However, Ruth did not seek a Moroccan husband, as her sisters had done, or a Mizraḥi marriage partner, but an Ashkenazi man:

> I think that one of the reasons I married late was because I was looking for someone different from the men my sisters married. Almost all of them married Moroccan men. I didn't want to marry a Moroccan man. I don't think that it is important that a couple come from the same ethnic group. I think that people ought to be open to people from other ethnic groups. People need to be open and meet all kinds of people.

Ruth had preferred an Ashkenazi husband because she expected that he would be more egalitarian in a spousal relationship than she thought a Moroccan husband would be. This perception of Ashkenazi men as more egalitarian than Mizraḥi men (including Moroccan men) is a stereotypical image rather than a proven empirical fact, but it reflects a prevalent notion about a difference between these two groups of men. Nevertheless, in spite of her reservations, Ruth married a Moroccan man: "In the end, I also married a Moroccan man. He was born in Israel, but he is of Moroccan background. He went to school for eleven years and works as an electrician."

Ruth was determined to establish the egalitarian spousal relationship in her marriage she thought typified Ashkenazi marriages. But the relationship between her and her husband was not a partnership that evolved from a voluntary agreement between equals but rather a type of sharing of domestic obligations that she dictated:

> I told my husband from the very beginning, I told him, "If you are coming to live with me, these are the conditions. Whoever does

> not share the work, can't tell me what to do and when." My husband does dishes, helps with the laundry, washes floors, throws out the garbage, bathes the children. I got him used to that from the beginning.
>
> Why should husbands and wives both do housework? So that the woman does not become a slave, a housemaid, a creature who is supposed to do everything—who is supposed to provide a clean house, take care of children, educate them, and even work outside the home.

Listening to Ruth's opinions regarding the division of household labor between spouses, it was hard to avoid the impression that her expectations regarding acceptable gender relations between husbands and wives were influenced not only by her desire to emulate Ashkenazi spousal relationships but also by popular feminism, which entered Israeli public discourse in the 1970s during the years she was growing into adulthood. This ideology may have been particularly attractive to her because it was functional for her goals of upward mobility. Dividing household obligations freed her to pursue her work and studies.

Her determination to create a stereotypically Ashkenazi egalitarian spousal relationship placed her in direct conflict with her immediate family and put her in the contradictory position of being a Moroccan woman who advocated the spousal relationship of the quintessential Other, the Ashkenazim:

> Both my mother and my in-laws think that I am Ashkenazi because of my ideas. My family calls me an Ashkenazi. My mother says, "You are not one of us. You are Ashkenazi." She means that I am different. That I think differently. But nobody is going to tell me what to think or what to do. With all my modern ideas I rebelled against what they thought. I guess that I have always been rebellious about things Moroccan women are supposed to do.

Ruth equated being Moroccan with being traditional and being Ashkenazi with being modern and, by implication, preferable. In fact, she has sometimes felt so alienated from Moroccan feminine gender norms that she doubts her own ethnic identity: "Sometimes even I don't know whether I am a real Moroccan, or maybe they switched me at the hospital. With me it is just different."

Ruth dared to contest the conventional Moroccan definitions of wifehood because she saw them as inhibiting her independence. She explained:

"A good wife is independent. She knows how to divide her time between her home, children, work, and husband. The first priority is the children, then husband, home, work, her independence. Actually, independence will always be first." Her insistence on independence was not an abstract ideology, but was functional for her upward mobility; it empowered her agency to act to achieve her goals.

Ruth balked at the ethnic norm that dictated that a married woman's household duties should be her first priority and widened the definition of wifehood to include work outside the home:

> A good wife also works outside the home. A wife who doesn't work outside the home is "heavy." She doesn't divide up her time correctly. She devotes all her time to cleaning the house, and that is something that is never done. It is all a question of priorities. It is a question of what you want to invest in. Do you want to invest all your time so that your husband can see that the house is orderly, like a museum? A home isn't a museum. A home should serve its inhabitants, not the opposite.

Ruth claimed that some Moroccan women share her definition of wifehood, though others do not. Thus there is a plurality of constructions of Moroccan wifehood:

> Some Moroccan women think like I do, some don't. They think that being a housewife is the purpose of their existence. I think that a wife should be at home, but that she should also divide her time with other things. She should go out into the world, not close herself up from the world. Most of the Moroccan women I know think that it is important to go out and work. I know very few Moroccan women who don't work.

According to Ruth, one of the consequences of wives' work outside the home is that it changes gender relations between spouses by giving women more power:

> Women go out and work, make financial decisions at home. When a woman works outside the home, she has more power in the home. When a woman stays home, her husband is like the foreign minister—he makes the decisions, he buys. I see a real difference between women who work outside the home and those who don't.

> I see it in my case. If I say we don't buy something, we don't. I decide what goes on in the house. If Moroccan women have self-confidence, they will decide things.

In her case, her work not only gave her financial power but also made her the dominant spouse in money matters.

Ruth's dominance in the marriage brought about her family's residential mobility. When she and her husband married, they moved in with her mother in an apartment in Bilu, a slum neighborhood in Jerusalem populated mostly by Mizraḥi immigrants. After her first daughter was born, she insisted that she, her husband, and infant move to a better neighborhood. She chose an apartment in one of the new, higher-status neighborhoods, Gordon, being built on the outskirts of the city. Gordon was being populated by other couples, mostly of Mizraḥi origin and, like her, recent arrivals to the middle class. Ruth was well aware of the status of the various neighborhoods in Jerusalem:

> Moving from Bilu to Gordon was my idea. I didn't like the Bilu neighborhood. It wasn't a good neighborhood. I found a job as a kindergarten teacher's assistant in Gordon that had an apartment that went along with the job. After a while I decided to buy the apartment. I took out a mortgage on it and I have paid the mortgage—I paid the mortgage, not my husband. I did it all.

According to Ruth, not only work but also exposure to feminine gender constructions in the wider Israeli society influence whether women will be dominant or meek. In her opinion not only social roles but also psychological traits, such as docility, were part of the Moroccan feminine gender construction, but were amenable to change:

> Maybe what determines whether a woman will be dominant is what she saw, learned, picked up from her surroundings. Surroundings influence us, and Moroccan women are changing. Women who go out learn from their neighbors, from their friends, from work, from those around them. They go to school and they meet other people, they learn other things. When women go out they gain self-confidence, they know what they want, they know what they want from their partner. They become dominant and more independent than they were in the past. They develop. Women who remain at home will always be dominated by men because Moroccan culture teaches women to be closed off, to be modest.

Ruth became a mother shortly after she married. She gave birth to her first daughter one year after she married, to her son ten months later, and to her second daughter six years later. When the mandatory three-month maternity leave after the birth of each child ended, she placed him or her in a nursery school for toddlers and returned to full-time work.

Discussing the number of children she wanted, she said: "I wanted a small family so that I could give my children everything they need. I want to give them the maximum. If I had had more children, I would have had an abortion." Clearly, Ruth had a rational assessment of her parental resources and those that were required to rear her children as she would like. She felt that these resources were limited, so she was determined to limit the number of children she would have, even if the price was having an abortion.

For Ruth, motherhood was a role she chose that involved clear obligations and goals, what Sara Ruddick has referred to as mothering as work, in contrast to mothering as an identity:[4] "I was prepared to be a mother. I knew what I would do at each stage and at each age. It was a continuation of things for me. It was clear to me that I was taking on a responsibility. If you bring a child into the world, you have to know that you are responsible for it. If you can't do that, don't have children."

To Ruth, parenting meant motherhood, parenting dominated by the mother, and not a partnership between spouses. Therefore, she spoke about parenting as a singular activity for which she accepted sole responsibility and not as a shared project between mothers and fathers: "A woman who gives birth has to know that she has to raise the child, take responsibility for it, help it with every problem that arises—give it the maximum. I want to give my children everything they need. I want to give them the maximum. If you can't do that, you are a failure as a mother."

She was aware that other Moroccan women define motherhood differently than she does and that, therefore, multiple definitions of motherhood exist within her ethnic group:

> Some define motherhood as I do, some don't. Some Moroccan mothers think that it is enough to feed a child, that education isn't important. That what is important is that he doesn't turn out to be a criminal. That is probably what they saw at home and they haven't developed their own opinion about motherhood. They haven't moved forward. They haven't left the homes they grew up in. But I see things differently.

Thus Ruth maintained a distinction between Moroccan women who adhered to traditional ethnic constructions of motherhood and were, therefore, backward, and those who have been exposed to definitions of motherhood outside their ethnic group in Israeli society and were, consequently, enlightened. According to her, different constructions of motherhood are not equal in value, and there is a hierarchy of types of motherhood in which some types are superior to others. The best mother is the one who enables her children's scholastic achievement. This interpretation explains Ruth's earlier remark, "I want to give my children everything they need. I want to give them the maximum." During the period in which Ruth is living in Israeli society, in which education for mobility is valued, it is not surprising that she defines her children's needs as acquiring an education and defines the good mother as someone who can provide this education. She elaborated: "I'll do anything to help my children succeed in school. One of the reasons I want to study is because I want to know that I have something to give my children, to help them as much as I can. And if I can't help them, there are private tutors. I'll pay and they will learn."

Producing academically successful children is Ruth's major mothering project, and it is the ultimate criteria by which she judges her success as a mother. Failing to produce such children is failing at motherhood: "When I hear that my children are not doing well in school, that is the worst thing for me. If I hear that, I feel as though I failed at motherhood. I can't accept their failure at school. I overcame my failures at school over the years, but I can't accept theirs." Ruth's view of motherhood coincides with Lawler's observation that mothers who are the dominant parent have the power to "produce" children who possess socially valued traits,[5] in this instance, traits that will position them for mobility into the middle class.

Ashkenazi mothers are at the top of Ruth's hierarchy of mothering because they, more than Moroccan mothers, understand the importance of an education that includes cultivating children's bodies and enriching their minds:

> Ashkenazi mothers invest more in studying and they invest less in food. They'll invest in after-school programs for their children. Things that feed the soul, more than the body. Among Moroccans it is just the opposite. That is true of my generation, too. Very few will make studying the most important thing. They don't understand that today, if you don't study, you don't eat. If you don't study, you don't earn money, you don't have food. And food isn't only what

> you put into your mouth. It means you can't go on vacation, go to the gym, do hobbies that interest you.

According to Ruth, being like an Ashkenazi mother requires not only giving priority to children's education, but since Ashkenazi mothers are mostly middle-class mothers, being like an Ashkenazi mother means educating one's children to enter the middle class. Ruth's admiration for Ashkenazi mothering was another expression of her identification with the dominant norm of education for upward mobility prevalent in Israeli society.

Ruth thinks that Moroccan and Ashkenazi mothers also have different consumption patterns, and these, too, have consequences for their children's class position. In her opinion, Moroccan mothers indulge in conspicuous consumption that reflects an erroneous order of priorities:

> Most of the Moroccans I know go overboard. They have large weddings, lots of glitter, singers—they even compete with each other over who will have the most extravagant affair. They even go into debt for years to show that they had the most extravagant affair of anyone. Personally, I went against that, too. I made a very modest bar mitzvah for my son—respectable, but modest.

In contrast, she thinks that the consumption practices of Ashkenazi mothers are more prudent:

> Ashkenazi women know how to take care of themselves moneywise better than Moroccan women. Ashkenazi women have the right idea about using money and buying things. They invest less in cosmetics and clothes and owning things and a house that is full of expensive furniture. They invest more wisely. Their first priority is their children and their children's education and then what will be in the apartment. When an Ashkenazi marries off his children, he doesn't make a fancy wedding, not something outrageously expensive. They'll make a respectable wedding and have everything, but they won't have a too extravagant wedding—so that they will have something left to give the children for their apartment. Ashkenazim worry about what the children will need afterward, long term. They'd rather have a modest wedding, and most of the Ashkenazim I know—their children have an apartment without a mortgage. It's nice to be able to start life like that. Moroccans aren't like that.

Thus the investment of Moroccan mothers in conspicuous consumption has only short-term satisfaction, whereas the spending habits of Ashkenazi mothers have significant long-term rewards and therefore are wiser. Basing her opinion on personal experience, Ruth concluded that the investment strategy of Ashkenazim gives their children, the third generation, advantageous access to the middle class that Moroccan third-generation children may not have. By adopting the spending habits of Ashkenazi mothers and giving her son a "modest" but "respectable" bar mitzvah ceremony she, too, hoped to position her son in a more advantageous position to enter the middle class.

Ruth's image of most Ashkenazim as being wealthy enough to afford long-term major investments, such as helping their children buy an apartment, revealed her awareness of a class structure in Israeli society in which Ashkenazim occupy higher class positions than Mizraḥim, including Moroccans. Actually, her impression of differences between these groups in extending help to their children was well founded. Daphna Birenbaum-Carmeli, Nili Mark, myself, and Moshe Semyonov and Noah Lewin-Epstein have shown that Ashkenazi parents give their married children substantial financial aid,[6] particularly for the large, major expense of buying an apartment, which is part of the "local culture of property"[7] and is symbolic of belonging to the middle class. Moroccan parents, who usually have less economic resources than Ashkenazi parents, may find it more difficult to provide such aid. Thus the ability of Ashkenazi parents to help their children with significant financial resources serves as a means by which that group reproduces its middle- and upper-class position in Israeli society and contributes to the perpetuation of class differences between it and non-middle-class Moroccans.

Ruth's perception of differences between Ashkenazi and Moroccan women included not only differences in wifehood and motherhood but also extended to differences in their bodies. Thus for Ruth a woman's body is a site where feminine, ethnic, and class identities are constructed and displayed. The different ways in which Moroccan and Ashkenazi women present their bodies through makeup and clothes, their posture, even the way they use their voice—all create femininities that reflect their different ethnic origin and their different positions in the Israeli class hierarchy. Her opinion is very much in keeping with several scholars who have analyzed how management of the body displays gender, ethnicity, and class.[8]

Ruth claimed that Moroccan women possess an ethnic-specific bodily trait: beauty. She explained:

> I usually recognize a Moroccan woman when I see her. Moroccan women are very beautiful. It's something in their eyes, something bright. Most are a bit round—they are not thin women—they have very feminine bodies, like a guitar, small at the waist and wider at the bosom and hips. Where does their beauty come from? I guess God gave it to us. Moroccan women have a natural beauty. They don't have to use a million creams to be beautiful, they are naturally beautiful.
>
> There are beautiful Ashkenazi women, but it's not my taste in beauty. It's not a beauty that I enjoy looking at. But I admire them for being smart. Ashkenazi women are smart. They know what is important.

But while Ruth thinks that Moroccan women have a superior bodily trait, it depreciates in value when it is compared with Ashkenazi women's favorable characteristic: being smart.

In her narrative, Ruth equated a certain type of appearance with ethnicity, ethnicity with respectability, and respectability with being middle class. And for her, looking like a middle-class woman meant looking like an Ashkenazi woman. She explained: "Some Moroccan women are very well groomed, very careful about how they look before they go out. Their hairdo must be just right, their makeup just right. But the older women always wear bright red lipstick—that never changes." According to Ruth, some Moroccan women care very much about their public presentation of themselves, how they appear to others. They invest a great deal of time, effort, and money (good hairdos and makeup are expensive) into producing an appearance that will be accepted as respectable ("just right") and, therefore, middle class and, by implication, Ashkenazi. In contrast, other Moroccan women, those of the previous generation, are vulgar. Ruth is critical of these women because they do not know how to be refined. By their garish lipstick, they contradict the respectable appearance she considers middle class and characteristic of Ashkenazi women.

Elaborating on the differences in deportment between the two groups of women, Ruth added: "Moroccan women have a special walk. They walk differently from Ashkenazi women. Ashkenazi women have straight posture. They have more confidence. Moroccan women have less confidence. Ashkenazi women will always have more confidence than Moroccan women." In Ruth's opinion, Moroccan women, through their posture, reveal their inner selves. Their nonerect bodies show that they do not possess the confidence that comes with knowing that they are who they want to be—as respectable as middle-class Ashkenazi women.

Even younger Moroccan women who, presumably, have had more opportunities to adopt the appearance and behavior that Ruth claimed characterize middle-class Ashkenazi women, lack the self-assurance that typifies these women. These younger Moroccan women belie their lack of confidence through their shrewish voices. As Ruth explained: "The younger ones will either have less confidence or they will be overconfident and they will ruin themselves with their big mouths. Ashkenazi women are more calm and quiet than Moroccan women, more introverted." Thus through their deportment, some Moroccan women both proclaim their ethnicity and their lower-class positions and create obstacles to their mobility into higher-class positions.

Ruth thought it was possible to avoid what she considered Moroccan women's typical appearance and behavior by monitoring her body. She invested great effort in methodically transforming her body and appearance to rid herself of the markers of her subordinate ethnic and class position, being a Moroccan woman of working-class origin, in order to create her image of the body and appearance of the hegemonic, middle-class Ashkenazi women. To do this she embarked upon a project of self-improvement through "a disciplined constructing of herself"[9] to "produce the look"[10] she associated with middle-class Ashkenazi women: "I bought a book about body language. I wanted to know how to present myself to other people. Important people, like lawyers." Self-conscious about her appearance, she added:

> I learned what clothes to wear—what colors to wear—or not to wear. It's best to wear white and black or white and blue. Here, look [she said proudly, as she ran her hand over the well-ironed, white blouse she was wearing with black pants], I am wearing a white blouse that I bought for only three shekels [the equivalent of less than one dollar]. The book also taught me to look people straight in the eye when I speak to them and when to look to my left and when to look to my right. It works—I try it all the time.

Ruth believed this would make her more effective in interacting with people she felt were above her in class and ethnic status, important people, like lawyers, who are generally middle class and Ashkenazi. While she used what she learned from her book daily, her control of her body was especially helpful in presenting herself to such people.

Ruth's manipulation of her appearance and body was a process of constant self-monitoring that relieved her of regulation and judgment by others. At the same time it enabled her to "(dis)identify"[11] herself from those Moroccan women whose demeanor she criticized as being non–middle class.

Her transformation of her body became "corporeal capital"[12] that she used to declare her belonging to the middle class.

Ruth thought she and her family belong to the middle class on the basis of her occupation as a kindergarten teacher's assistant, even though she earns slightly more than a minimum wage. Her husband earns an above-average wage. Thus it is probably only through both their incomes that she and her family maintain the consumption level of the middle class.

Ruth supplements her income with other work that she does on her day off from the kindergarten. In her extra job she works for an Ashkenazi couple. Ruth described the wife as lazy and therefore, as morally inferior to her, though she implied that the couple belongs to a class above her because the husband is a lawyer and both are Ashkenazi. "One day a week, on my day off from the kindergarten, I cook and do some cleaning at the home of a lawyer. He and his wife are Ashkenazi. She is too lazy to do anything, but it is not hard for me and I make good extra money."

It is interesting to remember that previously Ruth described Ashkenazi women as less feminine than Moroccan women and here she described them as morally inferior. Constructing the women in the hegemonic group as less moral serves a purpose. As Yen Le Espiritu pointed out in her study on Filipinas in the United States, constructing the hegemonic group as morally inferior enables the subordinate group to present itself as superior in at least one trait and therefore to "reaffirm to itself its self worth in the face of . . . subordination."[13]

Ruth's life is a work in progress in which she sees an open mobility structure, largely free of obstacles. In visualizing her future, she did not dwell upon the structural-material constraints in her past that limited her and other second-generation Moroccan immigrant women in their upward mobility, such as those that compelled her to stop studying in order to help support her family, the difficulty of making up for early disadvantages, or cultural obstacles in the form of ethnic feminine gender norms. Instead, she focused on opportunities that await her: "I know how to take advantage of every opportunity and of resources I have—every relationship with lawyers I know, with people in education. I'm never embarrassed to ask questions—that's how I learn things. I never give up."

The one constraint Ruth was aware of was the discrimination against Moroccans that ascribes to her a subordinate and degrading ethnic feminine identity she feels does not apply to her and one that she resists aggressively:

> Sometimes I am ashamed to be a Moroccan woman. People have all kinds of ideas about Moroccan women. If I tell people that I am

> Moroccan, they look at me as though I am backward, as a woman who should be in the kitchen, washing floors. People think that Moroccan women are only good for doing cleaning at home.
>
> When someone says something derogatory about Moroccans, I put them in their place. I say, "I am Moroccan. Where are you from? Tell me, I want to know where you are from that makes you better than I am?" It is insulting to make derogatory comments about Moroccans.

However, Ruth thinks the upward mobility of some Moroccans has mitigated discrimination against the ethnic group. This belief has led her to conclude that prejudice against Moroccans will not be an obstacle to her future plans and, presumably, to those of her children: "But now things have changed. Now people see that there are Moroccans in high positions with important jobs. And that has made a difference in how people think about Moroccans."

Perhaps this lessening of discrimination and the accompanying acceptance of Moroccans is the reason that despite her criticism of her ethnic group, particularly of its ethnic feminine gender norms, Ruth maintains an attachment to Moroccan culture, if only to its symbolic, ceremonial aspects. This is evidenced by her comment about the *Henna* ceremony, the traditional Moroccan engagement party that by custom is a gender-specific activity organized by the mother of the bride: "I think that many Moroccans are not interested in preserving their culture, but I had a *Henna* when I married and I hope that my children will have a *Henna* too." This remark suggests that Ruth does not reject the totality of her Moroccan ethnic identity in favor of an Ashkenazi ethnic identity, but only those aspects of that identity that she perceives are obstacles to her upward mobility. For her, being a traditional Moroccan woman means being nonmobile. Therefore her aspiration is not so much to break away from her ethnic group as to break out of it in ways that will enable her and her children to continue their mobility within the middle class.

☙

Ruth, and women like her, undertook a process of self-transformation of their identity in order to enter the middle class. For them, this process involved a reconstruction and reintegration of mind, body, ethnic, and classed feminine identities and the occupation of being a semiprofessional. The totality of this recreation is an example, par excellence, of the power of agency to create a coherent new identity to achieve a goal, in this instance mobility into the middle class.

Britton and Baxter described narratives of self-transformation as those in which "changes in the self and identity are the prime and explicit focus."[14] Furthermore, they claimed that narratives of self-transformation are masculine gendered because they describe an "active self seeking individual fulfillment which is the essence of the reflexive self,"[15] whereas feminine-gendered narratives tend to focus more on the "self-in-relation" to others.[16] Basing their contention on Jo Van Every's work, they maintained that "for women to prioritise their own needs is to challenge both the cultural assumptions about women's place and the patriarchal domestic division of labour."[17] I argue that regarding the narrative of self-transformation as masculine perpetuates a stereotypical perception of the ways in which women construct their lives, particularly in the context of upward mobility. If Ruth's account of her life history teaches us anything, it is that women *do* challenge cultural assumptions about their feminine gender roles and *do* prioritize their own needs in order to accomplish mobility.

The following two narratives represent women who have achieved greater mobility than those in the low segment of the middle class. These are women who are in the middle segment of the middle class through their positions as high-ranking secretaries in the Municipal and National civil services.

## Chapter 5

# *Acquiring Educational Credentials*

Sara, who is forty-seven years old, belongs to the largest group (20 percent) of second-generation Moroccan women in the middle class: those who are clerical workers. She represents high-ranking secretaries in the middle segment of the middle class. She works in the Municipal civil service in Jerusalem and invited me to her office at the Municipality for our meetings. At her initial interview, she greeted me with a warm smile and offered me coffee and Moroccan cookies she had baked especially for our meeting. She began telling me about herself by talking about the importance of her ethnic feminine identity:

> I am proud to be a Moroccan woman, I am happy about it. My being a woman and my being a Moroccan are inseparable. I don't feel discriminated against. I think that discrimination depends very much upon the person—what she projects to her surroundings. From the first day that I can remember myself, I never went anywhere and felt that I was being discriminated against, or that I didn't get what I deserve because I am Moroccan. On the contrary, I think that because I am a Moroccan woman, people treat me well.
>
> When I hear people talking about discrimination today, people say that there is less discrimination than there used to be. But people still live the past because in the past there was so much of it. Moroccans are proud people, but when they came to Israel they found themselves inferior, and the feeling of inferiority stayed with them. Perhaps that explains their bitterness. But today you find some Moroccans in high places. Moroccans see that and slowly they will feel that there is less discrimination.

Furthermore, Sara thinks that a positive stereotype exists about Moroccan women: "When people ask me where I come from, I always say, "I am Moroccan." And when I say that, what runs through my mind are all the good things about being a Moroccan woman. When people know that I am Moroccan, they know that I know how to cook, to bake, how to run my home well. A Moroccan woman will never neglect her home."

Sara attributed her attachment to her ethnic culture to her socialization through which her mother transmitted Moroccan culture to her daughter:

> I am the daughter of traditional Moroccan parents and everything that characterizes Moroccans. I come from a closed Moroccan home—a home that was closed to outside influences. In my childhood I learned a great deal about what it means to be a Moroccan woman and about Moroccan culture. My mother kept what is called an "open house"—like all Moroccan women she prided herself on her hospitality. She celebrated all the religious holidays by inviting people and serving all the special Moroccan food that is customary on holidays. My mother placed a lot of emphasis on celebrating holidays according to Moroccan tradition, and I live the tradition all the time. I like preparing Moroccan food, especially for the holidays and for guests. And it is very important to me to cook all the Moroccan food my mother cooked. That includes the cooking, making jams, the special cakes. I also bake Moroccan cookies for other people and give them at special occasions, like a *Henna,* the Moroccan engagement party.
>
> I was always excited by Moroccan tradition. I know that I am different that way—that lots of Moroccan women my age today don't care about preserving Moroccan culture as much as I do. But it is important to me because when I look around I see that the special Moroccan culture is disappearing and I want to continue it. I don't want to see it disappear. I learned it all from my mother and I have taught my daughters so I hope that they will continue what I have passed on to them.

However, Sara thought that being the daughter of Moroccan immigrants has been an obstacle to her acquiring the formal educational credentials necessary for her to continue her upward mobility within the civil service, and hence her class mobility. As the daughter of immigrants, she was expected to help support her family. This required her to drop out of high school:

> After my parents immigrated to Israel, my father worked in construction and my mother was a housewife. In Morocco she had been a midwife, but midwives were not so much in demand in Israel, so she didn't work outside her home. Neither of them had gone to school and they immigrated when they were in middle age. After their arrival in Israel, they were sent to an immigrant transit camp, and about two years later they moved out of the camp and into Jerusalem. We didn't have much money. I was an only child, so I had to help. I dropped out of high school. First, I worked as a telephone operator at a bank. In the evenings I went to night school to finish high school, but I didn't do my high school matriculation exams then.
>
> After a while I left the bank and went to work in the National civil service as a secretary in the Ministry of Education. I worked there for ten years, took severance pay, and then left. I applied for a job in the Jerusalem Municipality and I have been working here since then. I began working as a secretary and for the last twenty years I have worked as a secretary in various departments in the Municipality—mostly in community relations and interreligious relations. I have always been the secretary in charge of the departments. That means that I had to coordinate meetings between people and write up the protocols of the meetings. I was the only secretary and everything passed through my hands, so I got to know lots of people and they got to know me. Everyone in the Municipality knows me. I am involved in important things. I have one of the highest ranks among the secretaries in the Municipality. I earn a good salary. My work gives me lots of pride.

As several researchers have noted, since the early twentieth century, clerical work has attracted primarily three groups of women in Western societies, such as the United States and Canada, and has reflected an interaction between feminine gender and class. One group was made up of educated, married middle-class women who chose not to work in female occupations such as teaching, social work, or nursing. A second group was composed of white working-class women with only a partial high school education who had sufficient language skills to do filing, correspondence, and other simple office work. A third group consisted of second-generation immigrant women, like Sara, who attained a partial or complete high school education. For these women, clerical work constituted upward mobility from the manual-labor working class or the blue-collar occupations of their immigrant parents into the white-collar middle class.[1]

The expansion of administrative and large bureaucratic frameworks, especially of the government and Municipal civil services, that occurred since the mid-twentieth century in the United States, Canada, and in Israel as well, attracted these women as clerical workers because these services offered security through tenure, welfare benefits, and social status.[2] In writing about the benefits of municipal employment, particularly for minority-status women, Joshua Behr claimed that: "Public sector jobs offer pay and prestige that provide social and occupational mobility. . . . The draw of public sector employment for a particular group must be understood within the context of all available routes for occupational mobility, both within the public and private sectors."[3]

In contradiction to scholars who have maintained that clerical work is a type of proletarization,[4] others have argued that the growing specialization and differentiation in clerical work within large bureaucratic structures has created a hierarchy of women office workers that begins with typists and ends with the highest rank of secretary, like Sara, who manage the office and thus enjoy control, power, and autonomy.[5] And as Sara pointed out, high-ranking secretaries also have the opportunity to acquire a wide network of personal relationships.

However, each rise in rank in the Municipal civil service requires additional educational credentials, formal proof of educational accomplishments. Sara was able to enter the civil service because she had a high school diploma. She did her high school matriculation examinations through a special program the Municipality offers its employees for free at the workplace. She then began her university studies, but did not complete them. She told me:

> Today you can't get anywhere without a matriculation certificate, so I did my matriculation examinations through the Municipality. Then I began studying at the Open University, but I didn't finish. I didn't finish because I married and then had a baby. I started studying after the first baby was born and after a few years I found myself with three small children. I couldn't leave home twice a week to go to classes or keep up with the homework—the university demands a lot of studying at home. I just didn't have the time, so I stopped. I am very sorry that I stopped. Every day I think, "I'll go back tomorrow." It all depends on the aspirations of the woman—what she wants to achieve. If she wants to get ahead, there is no alternative;

> she needs degrees—a high school degree, a matriculation certificate, and a university degree. If I had continued studying, I think that I would have gotten to something four times higher than what I have achieved.

Sara feels that now she has reached an impasse. Her lack of a university degree is a barrier to her continuing progression within the Municipal civil service hierarchy: "I always advanced in each job I had, but I always felt that I didn't have enough education. Today if you want to get ahead, you have to have an education and credentials—what they call "education on paper." When I apply for a promotion, I'm always asked to present my credentials, and then it bothers me a lot that I don't have enough."

Sara has taken an impressive number of courses through various informal, nonacademic frameworks to compensate for her lack of a university credential. As she explained: "I always took courses—all kinds of courses, some because they advanced me at work and others because they interested me and added to my personal development. I took some of the courses on work time, but mostly on my own time if it was a course that interested me. I have taken about fifty courses and I have about fifty certificates." However, while most of the courses contributed somewhat to her promotion at work and others to her self-enrichment, they were not equivalent to a university degree, and therefore she could not convert them into educational assets for her occupational/class advancement.

In retrospect, Sara thinks that Moroccan feminine gender norms hindered her acquiring the university credentials she needed for continuing her upward mobility. The initial area of conflict was between the priority that Moroccan culture gives to marriage for women, particularly to early marriage, as opposed to other goals (see chapter 2):

> Most Moroccan parents want their daughters to marry early, and they don't think about anything else. My parents were like that. They expected me to marry early. That was their primary concern. They wanted me to marry someone who would take care of me, who would respect me, spoil me, treat me like a queen. They didn't think that he had to be educated. They didn't think about other areas of life. That's all they ever talked about. My mother couldn't have any more children, so I was an only child and they put all their energy into marrying me off. I married at eighteen—not as young as my mother who married in Morocco when she was twelve—but I married young. Not marrying was not an option.

Apparently, at the time Sara internalized the ethnic feminine gender norm of early marriage. She also thought it was appropriate to marry young, if only for the respect accorded married women: "But I also wanted to be married, to have a home of my own. I can't imagine never being married. When a woman never marries, people look at her as though she is "loose," immoral. But when they know that she has a husband and a family behind her, they treat her with more respect."

Sara married a man of Moroccan origin, three years her senior. He is a son of immigrants, and after completing elementary school his parents apprenticed him to learn a trade and become a carpenter. Since then he has taken several courses to upgrade his skills, and Sara thinks he is well regarded in his field.

According to Sara, a second impediment to her completing her academic education was her wish to give birth as soon as possible after her marriage. This desire harkened back to the importance of women's fertility, which secured their status as feminine women in Jewish communities in Morocco (see chapter 2). She gave birth to her three children at close intervals; one daughter was born one year after her marriage, a second daughter one year later, and another daughter was born one year after that:

> I would have been very unhappy if I hadn't had children. I think that I would have felt less of a woman if I hadn't had children. Society sees women who don't have children as less feminine than women who do and as less important. So I wanted to prove that everything was OK with me—I wanted children right away. God forbid I would have had problems.

The constraint that ethnic feminine gender norms imposed on Sara's education, and therefore on her mobility, was exacerbated by what Sara considered ethnically derived gender relations, particularly the division of labor between spouses in which the husband was the provider and the wife the housekeeper and dominant parent. Sara and her husband had shared this definition of spousal roles when they married, but she began to question the fairness of this arrangement after she had children and her desire to acquire an academic education for her continued mobility became important to her. It was then that she began to advocate a more egalitarian relationship that would be a partnership for her mobility:

> My husband never participated in child care. Moroccan men just don't think that it is their job. After a while I began asking myself

> about it. I never understood why he didn't get up at night when the children needed someone. He had to get up in the morning to go to work, but so did I. Actually, I wanted more children, but I didn't have them because I saw that he wasn't helping me with them.

However, Sara acknowledged that the inequality in the division of domestic labor between two working spouses is offset somewhat by women's increasing power in decision making regarding family expenditures:

> I think that when both spouses work, they cooperate more in decision making than when one works. The power relationship between the couple is different when the wife works outside the home. She feels more of a partner. The husband can't come and say, "I earn the money, I get to make all the decisions." When the woman works, everything is more equal.

Furthermore, Moroccan women who work outside their home not only have greater power in financial decision making in the family, but also, as Sara explained, their income makes a financial contribution to their families:

> Most Moroccan women work. Maintaining a household requires it. Today you can't fulfill your husband's and your children's needs just by having food on the stove, a clean house, and a wife who receives her husband with open arms when he returns home from work the way it used to be in Morocco. Today the demands are great—a mortgage, educating children. Women can't allow themselves not to work.

Sara and her husband earn equal middle-class salaries, and she regards them as equal breadwinners. Actually, she thinks she has greater financial power than he does because her work in the Municipal civil service and the extensive contacts she has made through her work have enabled her to get loans and a mortgage on good terms. She used this advantage to initiate her family's residential mobility so that her children would grow up in a neighborhood with a good school. As a result of her initiative, the family moved from a small apartment in a slum neighborhood in Jerusalem populated mostly by Mizraḥi immigrants to their present home, a larger apartment in the Gordon neighborhood populated by more mobile Mizraḥim:

> My mother was very much against my leaving the Ministry of Education. She always told me that as long as I work for the government, I will have people's respect. Everybody thought that I was crazy to take severance pay from the Ministry of Education to buy an apartment, but I knew I could buy a better apartment in a better neighborhood with it. I wanted to get my children out of the slum neighborhood and into a neighborhood with a better school. This isn't the best neighborhood in Jerusalem, but it was the best I could do.

Sara's experience of lacking the university degree she needs to continue her upward mobility through her advancement at work has led her to change her ethnic-based construction of motherhood and its order of priorities from one that emphasized satisfying the physical needs of children to one that stressed academic achievement, a value associated with middle-class motherhood. This transition began through her exposure to parenting outside her ethnic group. Consequently, she began to groom her children early for their educational mobility:

> I sent my children to nursery school so that they could begin developing early. But the biggest change came when my children started going to school—in first grade. I volunteered to be on the PTA and I found myself meeting people who spoke a different level of Hebrew than I did, who I sensed were on a different level—they all had university educations. I began thinking that being a mother is more than just buying shoes and cooking food. I realized that when a child comes and asks for help with homework, you have to know how to answer him, you have to become his private tutor.

She added:

> Moroccans come from a situation in which books weren't important, what is on bookshelves isn't important, that it is not important to invest in extracurricular activities for children. They thought that it was important that the child looks well, that he not go barefoot, that he be dressed well. They put the emphasis on the basic things—food and clothing—but as time goes on we see that that is not enough.
>
> Today there is awareness that studies are important. Today we know that books and extracurricular activities are important. Today

> we know that a child can wear cheap shoes so that the rest of the money can be spent on books and extra studies. One has to save for high school and if he wants to go on to university, one has to provide books at home, encyclopedias, dictionaries. From the time my children were very young, a month didn't go by that I didn't buy a book or some kind of encyclopedia. I could pay for them in installments because I worked in the Municipality.

According to Sara, other second-generation Moroccan women who work with her in the Municipality share her definition of middle-class mothering: "All my friends—they are also Moroccans and they also work in the Municipality—did the same thing. None of us have a high education, but we realized that providing our children with a good education was important for their future."

However, Sara thinks that not all second-generation Moroccan immigrant women support this type of mothering, which means that there are multiple constructions of motherhood within her ethnic group. According to her, the distinguishing trait between the types of motherhood is the emphasis that each places on educational credentials. Sara considers that those who invest in their children's education, and thereby in their mobility to be advanced while those who do not are backward and limit their children's mobility: "Today there are changes in the importance attached to studying—at least among the most advanced Moroccans. But you can still find things that were customary among my parents' and grandparents' generation."

To Sara, Ashkenazi motherhood exemplifies middle-class motherhood because it values educational attainment above housekeeping, traditionally Moroccan women's area of accomplishment. Thus different motherhoods have different consequences for mobility: "An Ashkenazi mother won't keep after her daughter to make sure that her closet is neat. For her, it is more important that her daughter read a book, but a Moroccan mother will not let her daughter get away with not keeping her closet orderly and with the floor dirty."

But while Ashkenazi mothers are "advanced" mothers because they foster their children's education, they lack a trait that characterizes Moroccan women and makes them more feminine than Ashkenazi women. According to Sara, an outstanding attribute of Moroccan women is their beauty, with its emphasis on sexual allure:

> Moroccan women are beautiful and they are warm. They care about how they look—they are very well groomed, they like to

> use perfume. Moroccan mothers teach their daughters to use their beauty with their husbands. They tell them, "When you know your husband is coming home, you have to take a shower, put on makeup and perfume, smile and be beautiful—more beautiful than any woman he sees outside. When he opens the door and sees you, he won't need any woman he sees outside."

Sara implied that the beauty of Moroccan women is the source of their power over men. They use their "corporeal capital"[6] to dominate their husbands in their homes: "Moroccan women are very domineering, very strong, and they are very proud of being domineering. What I have seen is that Moroccan men without Moroccan women advising them—nothing gets done at home. Perhaps even more, nothing is done without her control and men don't have much to say about it."

Sara claimed that Moroccan women's beauty is empowering not only vis-à-vis men, but also vis-à-vis Ashkenazi women:

> Moroccan women may not be the most educated, have the most university degrees, but they know that when they stand next to a woman who has everything, they know that they are beautiful, they get attention. Their beauty gives them self-confidence—it's something that they are born with. Ashkenazi women are beautiful and they also have degrees, but they don't have the warm nature of Moroccan women—they are cold. They don't dye their hair and they don't use a lot of makeup and they don't pay a lot of attention to dressing up and always being in style.

In these remarks, Sara constructed opposing femininities between Moroccan and Ashkenazi women in which Moroccan femininity is superior to Ashkenazi femininity because it is "true" femininity. But even though Moroccan women have the advantage of corporeal capital in comparison with Ashkenazi women, Sara concluded that it is the Ashkenazi woman who has "everything" because she is the woman who has educational credentials. Perhaps it is not surprising that Sara regards educational credentials as "everything"; they are what she lacks in order to continue her upward mobility.

In spite of Sara's admiration of Ashkenazi ethnic femininity, she is not willing to give up the last bastion of her Moroccan femininity, her domination of her household that is symbolized through her control of her kitchen. Traditionally, Moroccan women have prided themselves not only on their cooking on a daily basis, but especially on their preparation of special dishes for traditional ceremonies such as the *Mimuna,* the spring festival, and the *Henna,* the Moroccan engagement party,[7] which can be seen as their gender-specific contribution to these ceremonies. It is not surprising then that Miriam protects the domain of her kitchen by refusing to let her husband share it, for sharing it would diminish her femininity and therefore her status in the family. She told me:

> I don't let my husband cook. I don't see him cooking for me, even though he knows how to cook. The kitchen is mine. The whole experience is that he waits for me, he waits to eat what I prepare. I don't let him do the dishes. I also don't see him doing housework. That is just the way Moroccan women are raised. That is what I am used to. Even during hard times—when I broke my leg and couldn't stand, I didn't let him cook for me—my sister-in-law helped me. He is the one who has to be the provider, she is the one who raises the children.

Sara added:

> This week I was at a meeting and I heard some women say that they are antikitchen, that they don't cook—that they won't go into the kitchen—and that their husbands do all the cooking. Some said that they told their husbands when they married that they don't cook and they stuck to it and the husbands accepted it. Personally, I don't see how a woman can be antikitchen. There are things that are my space—the kitchen is my space.

It is worth noting that, perhaps not by coincidence, Sara's preservation of her domination of her home through her control of her kitchen is also the component of Moroccan ethnic femininity that does not conflict with her goal of pursuing educational credentials and mobility.

While Sara's comments revealed her determination to hold on to her supremacy within her household, they also exposed certain contradictions. In these latter comments she maintained that a husband should be the provider for the family and the wife should care for the children. Yet previously she expressed resentment at her husband's refusal to participate in child care because it was a barrier to her acquiring the university credential that would enable her to continue her mobility. Furthermore, while she claimed here that the husband should be the provider, she noted earlier that not only was she an equal provider for her family, but also that she had more financial power than he did because her work in the Municipal civil service gave her financial advantages beyond her salary. How do we explain these contradictions? They seem to be an expression of a clash between her desire to hold on to a central component of her traditional ethnic femininity and, at the same time, to be mobile, to be a substantial contributor to her family's income and thereby to construct a new ethnic femininity and a different ethnic spousal relationship. These inconsistencies seem understandable in situations in which ethnic-based gender relations are undergoing a process of change.

Sara's feeling that her ethnic feminine gender norms prevented her from acquiring the university credential she needed to continue her mobility within the middle class has led her to socialize her daughters to different feminine gender norms than the ones she lived by. She referred primarily to giving the acquisition of educational credentials, including academic credentials, and acquiring a profession priority over early marriage:

> When I married, I didn't have any goal for myself then, something that I could say, "OK, first I'll finish studying, I'll get a profession. I'll first make something of myself and then I'll marry." At the time everything was geared to my marrying. Maybe, today, looking back, I would have married later. Today, when I think about these things, I think differently. I don't think that I was right in the past. I am sorry that I gave them legitimacy. It shouldn't happen.
>
> When my daughters finished the army, the first thing I did was tell them, "Finish your studies. First get your high school diploma. Go to the university. Get degrees. Study as much as you can." These things didn't interest my parents. All they cared about was "have a home and children." Then it wasn't like today that parents want their children to study first—get a degree in something and then get married.

Her opposition today to the unequal division of household labor between husbands and wives has led her to socialize her daughters toward greater egalitarianism in their marriages. She expected that this kind of relationship would make it easier for them to combine their domestic roles with a work role and, presumably, would lead to their further mobility. Apparently, in rearing her daughters to equality in marriage, she has resolved the contradictions in an area that has plagued her in her own life. Furthermore, it seems that her daughters have internalized their mother's socialization:

> I tell my daughters that you have to establish these things from the beginning—taking care of the house together, taking care of the children together. Both parents have to take care of the children and of the home. It is not just the mother's responsibility. There is no reason why the woman should shoulder all the responsibility. It has to change. And my daughters agree. They say that when they have children, their husbands will also take part in taking care of the home and of the children.

For Sara, even beauty, the unique trait of Moroccan women, has lost its priority:

> Beauty is not enough. I always tell my daughters that. I tell them that today you are beautiful, but beauty fades, so it is important to have educational credentials and not rely on your looks. I see it in myself. When I was young I was beautiful, and when people told me that I was beautiful, it used to make me happy. But today I am much more pleased when people compliment me on my work, my experience, or on my wisdom. Today I trade beauty for wisdom.

Sara's investment in her daughters' socialization has brought about the results she hoped for. Her daughters have high school matriculation certificates that enable them to continue their higher education. While they have not attended universities, they have chosen to study graphic arts, fashion design, and textile design in colleges that specialize in the arts and that will award them academic degrees. Her oldest daughter is married, has a baby, and maintains an egalitarian division of household labor with her husband. "She and her husband are equal partners," Sara told me with pride.

By advocating these feminine gender norms for her daughters, Sara has been an active agent in constructing a new ethnic feminine identity for the third generation of Moroccan women. Over the years, she reached the conclusion that while the ethnic feminine gender norms she inherited from her mother may have been functional for the immigrant generation, they have become less functional for her and her goal of mobility through educational credentials. Therefore, she has transmitted different ethnic feminine gender norms to her daughters so that their path toward mobility will be easier than it has been for her. Sara exemplifies the dynamic aspect of constructing an ethnic feminine identity that changes with time and place and illustrates Nancy Foner's comment that the family is not just a site where cooperation for mobility occurs, but also a site where cultural change occurs in a process of "gender and generation."[8]

The changes Sara initiated were not without contradictions and pain. They have required her to let go of and reformulate an ethnic feminine identity she valued and loved in order to enter the middle class and to enable her daughters to do so. Ultimately, in this balance or trade-off between losses and gains, Sara feels that while she has given up something of value, she has received something she values more—occupational advancement that places her in the middle class. Thus the costs of this mobility should not lead us to overlook the overwhelming sense of gain she feels. In spite of her frustration at not having the university credential that would enable her to continue her mobility within the Municipal civil service hierarchy, she is proud of her achievements. She is particularly proud that she has attained her occupational/class achievements on her own, without the advantageous access an Ashkenazi name provides. As Sara remarked when we concluded her interviews: "Because other than my education, I feel very good about myself—that I have achieved things on my own that not everyone achieves. I am no one's princess. I didn't have an Ashkenazi name." When I asked, "Who is 'everyone'?", she replied, "Other Moroccan women."

∽

For Sara, and women like her, education and its accompanying credentials have primarily an instrumental value; they are formal evidence that they possess the human capital necessary to move up from one segment of the middle class to the next. If acquiring a partial high school education, a partial matriculation certificate, and accreditation from a postsecondary nonacademic institution were adequate credentials for Miriam's and Ruth's entry into semiprofessional positions and the low segment of the middle class, Sara needed higher educational credentials to enter the middle segment of the middle class and advance further. In addition to a complete high school diploma, a complete matriculation certificate, and a partial university education that Sara acquired during various periods in her life, she now needs a complete academic education to advance beyond the high-ranking secretarial position she occupies at present. Without the credential that such an education bestows, her additional mobility is blocked.

While this narrative represents married mothers who are in the middle segment of the middle class, divorced mothers face unique challenges in their mobility into this position in the class hierarchy. They are represented in the following narrative.

## Chapter 6

# *A Divorcée Does It on Her Own*

Sharon is forty-seven years old. She also represents women who belong to the middle segment of the middle class through their position as high-ranking clerical workers. However, in contrast to Sara, she works in the National civil service as a high-ranking secretary in the Israeli government's Ministry of Social Welfare. She is a divorced mother and typifies women who have entered the middle segment of the middle class without a marital partner.

Sharon invited me to her home for our meetings. As I looked around the living room where we sat, I could not help thinking how much it resembled the conventional middle-class living rooms that are pictured in women's magazines. A sofa upholstered in deep burgundy stood against a wall, with an end table and lamp on each side. Facing the sofa, across a mahogany coffee table, were two armchairs covered in the same deep color. Velvet draperies, also in burgundy, bordered the windows. A beige carpet with flowers set the living room off from the dining nook on the right side of the room.

Sharon began her narrative by telling me about her parents' background. They came to Israel from Casablanca in their late thirties with their nine children. Sharon, their tenth child, was born in their new country. In Morocco her father had been a merchant and her mother a housewife. Neither of them had any formal schooling. In Israel both parents became manual laborers, members of the working class. As Sharon explained:

> After my parents came to Israel, they learned very quickly that you need a permanent job, security, with social welfare benefits, and they tried to pass that on to their children. My father got a job as a maintenance man in a university and my mother got a job cleaning offices in government buildings.

> My mother always told me, "You have to work in a government office. Working for the government gives you a permanent job and gives you security and stability. It lets you plan ahead for the future. The money isn't important. The important thing is not to make a lot of money today, but to know what is going to happen tomorrow. What is important is security and stability so that you can sleep at night." That was my mother's greatest gift to me, her biggest legacy to me. And I have made it my life's work—making long-term plans. It is important not to look only at today but also at tomorrow and to plan ahead.

Sharon followed her mother's advice. Although she dropped out of high school in the eleventh grade, she served in the army (the only one of her sisters to do so), and then entered the Israeli National civil service. She has been employed there for the last twenty-four years. During this time she completed her high school studies and then did her matriculation examinations in a special program for government employees that the Ministry offers. She attended a university but did not complete her studies. Therefore she does not have a university degree and cannot advance further in the civil service hierarchy and in her class position. Throughout her period of employment, she has taken many nonacademic courses and workshops to improve her managerial skills. She attends such a course or workshop as often as once a week. She explained her present job:

> I am a high-ranking secretary in the human relations department in the Ministry for Social Welfare, and I am responsible for 1,400 to 1,500 social workers. It is a job that requires a lot of sensitivity in dealing with people and managerial skills. I have a big responsibility. I am successful at my job. I get a lot of feedback that says so.

The security of working in the National civil service proved to be particularly important when Sharon divorced and became a single parent with two children:

> I married when I was twenty-three and a half. I wasn't a child. I wanted to marry and have children. That is how Moroccan girls are raised. But after twelve years of marriage, I wanted to get divorced. Among Moroccans it is important to marry, and it is a stigma to be divorced. Moroccans used to say that it is better to be a widow

> than to be divorced. But I didn't see marriage as a holy institution anymore, the way I had in the past.

Perhaps it was Sharon's dis-identification with her ethnic group that made it easier for her to defy ethnic-based feminine gender norms and to divorce:

> Being a Moroccan woman means nothing to me. My mother didn't keep Moroccan culture and it doesn't matter to me that I am Moroccan. I'm an Israeli woman. If someone presses me—then I am both Moroccan and Israeli. I don't deny my Moroccanness. I'm not ashamed of it the way some Moroccans are. It just isn't important. I don't understand people who say that it is important. If you live like an Israeli, raise your children like an Israeli, why should being a Moroccan be important? Are you raising them in Morocco? And my children are like other Israeli children—they eat French fries. I don't cook Moroccan food. And I don't particularly want to go to visit Morocco. I'd rather go to America.

But even if Sharon disassociated herself from her ethnic identity, others imposed it upon her:

> There is a stigma to being a Moroccan. People think that you are not intelligent, that you are primitive, disturbed, loud. People always tell me that I don't look Moroccan, and they think that is a compliment. In the past, people used to be ashamed of being Moroccan, used to hide being Moroccan. They used to change their names to Hebrew names so that people wouldn't know that they were Moroccans. But today, some Moroccans have achieved high positions, so Moroccans feel that they have something to be proud of. That draws them closer to their Moroccan culture.

However, in spite of her avowed disassociation with Moroccan culture, Sharon observes some Moroccan customs. For example, she intended to organize a *Henna*, the traditional Moroccan engagement party, for her daughter and added, "I hope she agrees to have one," a comment that suggests that Sharon wants to keep some symbolic attachment to her ethnic culture.

Sharon divorced her husband because he tried to impose what she claimed was a traditional ethnic division of gender roles upon her and to dominate her, a trait she considers characteristic of Moroccan men. In essence, he wanted to restrict her autonomy. He particularly opposed the fact that work outside the home had become an integral part of Sharon's feminine identity:

> I didn't want to marry a Moroccan man, but I did. He didn't suit me. He acted as though he owned me. It was as though I didn't exist. He didn't let me decide things. My opinion didn't matter. He didn't want me to study. He didn't want me to work. Moroccan men who object to their wives working are afraid that their wives will open their eyes and see the world and demand things. He wanted me to stay home and take care of the apartment and the children. When my first maternity leave ended, I told him, "If you want to, stay home and you raise the children. I'm going back to work." And that is what I did. We had different ideas about what marriage was about.
>
> A woman who is just a housewife feels that she is nothing special. What kind of thing is this, just sitting at home! Go out and work—not for the money, but to be among people! To have something to talk about with your husband when you come home. There are some Moroccan women who are housewives—the ones who have financial security and think that because they have money they should serve their husbands. The women who stay at home are the ones who don't study, who have no profession and no training to do anything. But I feel that even rich women are jealous of me—not because I have money and I am rich, but because I have a rich life. How many times can you travel abroad? How many times can you make the rounds of the boutiques?

Sharon continued:

> If, in the past, Moroccan women were supposed to stay home and raise their children, women today don't agree with that. But that is true not just about Moroccan women, that is also true about all Israeli women. Work is part of life and a way of life. It is about learning about other cultures, about being conscious of the world around you, about meeting people. It enriches one's life—one's soul.

In contrast to the relationship she had with her husband, Sharon believed that marriage should be a partnership that should offer each spouse equal opportunities for self-fulfillment and that there should be an equal division of labor between husbands and wives. She attributed her image of the ideal marital relationship to the socializing influence of her parents:

> I was raised in a home in which my father helped at home and also worked outside the home. When he came home, he rolled up his sleeves. So I saw the way things should be with my own eyes, not from books. When we were children, he used to bathe us, he would take down the laundry. If he was home he would sweep, make the beds. And my mother was never afraid to speak her mind. I can explain it by the fact that my mother worked outside the home. Both my mother and my father worked outside the home and both had to work at home and both shared the authority at home.

Sharon's perception of an egalitarian relationship between spouses that is a result of the wife's employment supports research that claims that immigrant women who work outside their home after their immigration are able to translate their new economic power into greater equality within the household.[1] However, Sharon, a second-generation immigrant woman, was unable to convert this power into an egalitarian partnership between her and her husband, and therefore she divorced.

With the end of her marriage, Sharon joined the growing number of divorced mothers in Israel. While this number has increased in recent years, the incidence of divorce is lower in Israel than in Western societies.[2] This low percentage is generally explained by the fact that Israel is a familistic society, which means that marrying, having children, and maintaining family stability is central to the society's values.[3] In the early 2000s, about 55 percent of the heads of single-parent families were divorcées.[4] At the time these statistics were compiled, approximately 41 percent of single-parent families in Israel lived below the poverty line.[5] Only slightly more than half of the divorced Jewish mothers could afford to buy their own homes, because in Israel home ownership requires two steady incomes that pay at least a minimum wage or one high income, usually provided by a male head of family.[6] Divorced mothers also owned less basic appliances, such as a television, a telephone, and a washing machine, than married mothers did.[7] Because single-parent families in Israel, like those in Western societies, have fewer financial resources than two-parent families,[8] the Israeli government's National Insurance Institute offers allowances and special assistance to them.[9] However, divorced women who are employed and earn above an allotted income and whose former spouse pays child support are not entitled to these benefits.[10] Because Sharon earned above the allotted income, and because her former husband usually paid child support, she did not receive supplemental financial support from the government.

When Sharon divorced, she was aware of the existing negative stereotype that portrays all divorced mothers as "welfare mothers."[11] She told me: "When people think about a divorced woman, they think about a poor woman who lives in a rented apartment with her children and is miserable." Sharon was determined to prove that the stereotype would not apply to her. Therefore, her first project after her divorce was to buy an apartment. In Israel the "local culture of property"[12] attaches great importance to owning one's dwelling. As Noah Lewin-Epstein, Yuval Elmelech, and Moshe Semyonov pointed out, more than three-quarters of all Jewish heads of households in their sample owned their own homes,[13] though this percentage was higher among Ashkenazim (80 percent) than Mizraḥim (59 percent).[14] However, studies have shown that researchers have differences of opinion about the class significance of home ownership for men and women. Some scholars argue that men more than women consider owning their home to be a symbol of their class position.[15] Other researchers contend that the class significance of home ownership among the middle class is gender neutral because both men and women regard home ownership as equally important in contributing to their position within the class structure.[16] Sharon's comments, which placed home ownership at the top of her list of priorities, clearly support the theory that for middle-class women like her residential ownership is as important to women as it is to men. For her it constitutes a considerable contribution to her middle-class identity.

In explaining how she was able to afford the purchase of her home, Sharon told me:

> I bought this apartment five years after I divorced. It was my first project after I divorced. We lived in a rented apartment until then. My permanent salary at the Ministry helped me buy it because I knew that I had a salary I could depend on. Financial security gives you courage. And courage helps you to succeed in life. I looked at how long I needed loans and what loans I could get through work. I got interest-free loans as a government civil servant from the employees' fund. That gave me some room for maneuvering. I also took "revolving loans"—I borrowed from one place and borrowed from someplace else to pay them off.
>
> This apartment is quite an accomplishment. It's my life's work. It's small, not anything special, it's not in the best neighborhood, but for me it's a lot. I sat and calculated how I could afford it. How I could repay loans per month, how many years it would take me to return the loans, the mortgage. I actually drew it all out. I figured

> out that by the time my daughter would be eighteen, I will have paid off everything I owe on the apartment.

Sharon's next project was buying a car, a possession associated with the Israeli middle class:

> Two years after I bought the apartment, I figured out that I could buy a car, so I bought a car. I worked weekends for three years to buy the car. Physically, it was hard, but I had the will power. If there's a will there's a way. It was all a project. I succeeded in my financial planning because I encouraged my children to participate and I included them in the financial planning. I put it positively. I didn't say, "We can't have things," because I didn't want them to feel insecure. I said, "Let's see how we can save so that everyone will be better off." It's the way that it is done that's important, not just the goal.

Recently, Sharon decided to refurnish her apartment. Some scholars have claimed that women, more than men, are concerned with the internal contents of the home, or its material culture, as a symbol of class position.[17] Providing a social-historical perspective, Bonnie Smith traced the evolution of this idea in her book about bourgeois women in nineteenth-century France:

> During the nineteenth century the domestic world of women overflowed with artifacts and produced patterns of behavior, the sum of which has been labeled "domesticity." . . . Domesticity flowered from this period until the present day. . . . As a result, by the twentieth century women found themselves almost exclusively concerned with interior decorating, fashion, cuisine, etiquette, needlework and childrearing; and by extension, these occupations came to be considered intrinsic to the female personality.[18]

In her plans to redecorate her apartment, Sharon concentrated on the living room, which, as Grier pointed out, is the public face of the middle-class home because it immediately displays class to anyone who enters.[19] Sharon continued:

> My next project is renovating the apartment instead of buying a better one. During the past year, I have been thinking about how I could finance it. I calculated whether it was worth it for me to sell

> and buy and what would be the difference—if I could afford the difference. I calculated that to move to a bigger apartment would be very expensive. I sat down and calculated how much renovations would cost—how much the building materials would cost, how much the labor would cost. I got appraisals.

Buying a piano, a symbol, par excellence, of middle-class display,[20] was a prominent item in Sharon's plans to refurbish her apartment:

> I also want to buy a piano. I think that I'll enjoy learning to play the piano. One day I'll have it. It's in my plans. I have already gone to the Academy of Music to see whether they have old pianos that they want to replace with new ones. They sell their old pianos cheaply. They have five pianos that they want to sell. I'm interested in one of them.

Sharon also plans to hire domestic help, a practice that is common among middle-class employed women in Israel and in other Western societies:[21]

> Now I am going to hire someone to clean the apartment. I'm going to put it into the family budget. Now that my daughter is living away from home, my telephone bill is less and I'm going to use the money I save on the telephone and put it toward paying someone to clean the apartment. I keep a strict family budget. I am very responsible about that. If I wasn't careful about the family budget, I wouldn't manage at all.

Explaining the courage that these expensive undertakings demand, Sharon told me:

> I'm not afraid because I have always had a list of priorities. And if I sometimes wanted something, I took an extra job and then I knew that the job was for a specific purpose and not for the rest of my life. I took work over the telephone on weekends and selling jewelry or dolls. I took extra jobs all the time. I bought these tables and lamps with the money I got selling towels.

Sharon interrupted her narrative to point proudly to the end tables and lamps that stood on each side of the sofa, and then continued:

> This became a part of my lifestyle since getting divorced. If after the divorce everything I had in the apartment was secondhand, my goal was to replace it all with new things.
>
> I did the same thing with clothes. Instead of buying new clothes, I changed the clothes I had. I took off a collar, did something with the sleeves. But there were times when I couldn't allow myself anything. I would say to myself, "Maybe next year will be better." But I have will power—when I set a goal, I have the will power, the strength, the motivation.

While Sharon did it on her own, she, like the single mothers depicted in Ruth Sidel's book *Unsung Heroines*,[22] also had a familial support network composed of her mother and other family members who helped her succeed in her aspirations. This support included financial aid and child care:

> Yes, my family lent me money—they weren't gifts. I had to repay them all. And when I had to work in the evenings, I used to take the children to my mother and she would take care of them. We also used to eat at her house to save money. When she used to shop for herself, she would shop for me. When she cooked for herself, she cooked for us, too. She did that for many years. She gave the children pocket money.

Sharon was aware of the negative stereotype not only about single mothers, but also about their children. These reinforce a stigma that such children, especially those from subordinate status groups, are at greater risk of dropping out of school, developing emotional and behavioral problems, using drugs, and becoming delinquent.[23] She was determined that this stereotype would not apply to her children:

> When I divorced, my son was eight years old and my daughter was seven. And I knew the statistics. The statistics say that children of single-parent families fail. I wanted to prove them wrong. I never told anyone at their school that I was divorced. I didn't want them to suffer from the stigma, but I also wanted to prove that my children could be as successful as children who come from a two-parent family. I wanted them to have what other children have and to do what other children do.

When Sharon elaborated, she made it clear that "what other children have" and "what other children do" were getting a good education and having contacts with Ashkenazi children, both of which would be instrumental in improving her children's life chances: "For my children to succeed they have to do well in school and they have to have the right friends and live in a good neighborhood."

Sharon began her educational project for her children by giving them a head start:

> I sent my children to day care very early—when they were two years old. I wanted them to develop themselves and to develop early. When the time came for them to go to school, I went to study. I studied at the Hebrew University for three years. I studied psychology and education so that I would understand my children. I wanted to raise them well. But then I got divorced, it became difficult to study, so I stopped.

However, a crisis in her son's schooling threatened to put her children's educational project at risk:

> My son caused me a lot of worry at the end of tenth grade. He was always a very good student, a gifted student. But at the end of tenth grade, his school marks went down drastically and he didn't want to study. It was a crisis. It frightened me. I thought that perhaps he had a psychological problem. I immediately took things into my own hands and got to the bottom of things. His father, the teachers, and I all met and talked things out. My son said there was no problem, he just said he didn't feel like studying for a while, but that he intended to catch up on his school work. But I was in a terrible state—I was afraid that I was going to fail as a divorced mother. I went to counseling to get help so that I wouldn't feel that I had failed.
>
> I insisted that both my children have a matriculation certificate—that's the ticket—and both of my children did their matriculation examinations. My daughter finished her high school studies with honors. I have taught them that life is about studying and then studying some more—at the university. In fact, both are studying in the university now. Today a matriculation certificate isn't enough. Today you need a university education. Thirty years ago a matriculation certificate was worth a university degree, but not today. In

another ten years, maybe you'll need a doctorate—that's what I tell my children. When I didn't want to study, my mother didn't insist. She had many other children to worry about. But I have only two children. I earn a good salary and there is no reason in the world why my children shouldn't study.

But Sharon did not believe a university education was enough to ensure her children's future mobility, which she defined as success. An additional requirement was having a network of the "right friends," middle-class friends who would provide an "association with high achievers"[24] and thus would function as another resource for her children's mobility. In Sharon's opinion these friends would be Ashkenazi children who, she believed, were more prevalent in an established middle-class neighborhood than in the predominantly low middle-class, Mizraḥi neighborhood in which she lived. Because of the interaction among ethnicity, class, and residence in Israeli society, Sharon's children would, in fact, have more opportunities to meet middle-class children in an Ashkenazi neighborhood than in a Mizraḥi neighborhood.[25]

For Sharon, this consideration meant embarking upon residential mobility, not by gradually moving up the residential ladder, but by making a big leap that would be an indisputable, visible indicator of her children's middle-class position. Therefore she considered moving to Rechavia, the upper-middle-class elite Jerusalem neighborhood composed primarily of Ashkenazim. Sharon explained:

Five years ago I thought of moving to Rechavia. It was important to me how society would judge my children, and since then I have been turning myself inside out to try to move to a better neighborhood than the one I live in—to move to an Ashkenazi neighborhood. It is important to me to "market" my children well. I know that the neighborhood they come from makes a difference, it makes a difference for their future. People evaluate people according to the neighborhood they live in.

Aware of the "hidden injuries of class"[26] and ethnicity that Moroccans suffered in the past, Sharon was determined to spare her children such indignities:

I won't repeat the mistakes of the 1950s and '60s and '70s, when children who lived in a certain neighborhood were automatically thought of as belonging to a certain group and being inferior. Then

> if a Moroccan said he lived in an elite neighborhood, people would ask what his father did. If you said you lived in a bad neighborhood, they didn't ask what your father did. In other words, if a Moroccan lived in a good neighborhood, he had to explain why, but if he lived in a bad neighborhood, he didn't have to explain why—it was taken for granted. And people inherited where they lived from their parents. It was not something they could attain on their own.

She believed that the present class structure in Israel is more open to Moroccans than it was in the past: "Today money changes everything. If you and I can live in the same neighborhood and in the same building and I am a secretary and you are a professor, it's socially acceptable. If people work and earn money, they can live in the same neighborhood. Money opens the door to everywhere."

Apparently, Sharon has transmitted her class and ethnic awareness to her children:

> My children came to me and asked if we could move to Rechavia. I told them that I couldn't afford to buy an apartment there, but that I could add another $200 a month to rent an apartment in Rechavia. They said that they would be willing to share a room if we moved. In the end, we gave up on the idea. But they don't have any friends here in this neighborhood. All their friends are in Rechavia. They have always known how to choose friends. All their friends are Ashkenazi.

Listening to Sharon's narrative, I could hear not only a drive to see her children positioned within the middle class but also a sense of obligation to push them toward further mobility. Now, having accomplished this goal for her children, her mothering project is done:

> I gave all my life to my children and left nothing for myself. I invested 100 percent in them and left no percentage for myself. My children have everything that they need. They have been my biggest investment—like in a stock exchange. Everybody who knows me, knows that. That is why I never remarried. I didn't want to remarry. If I would have remarried, my investment would have been divided.

However, Sharon's financial and emotional investment in her children's mobility has exacted a price. She feels burned out from all the years of working, worrying, scrimping, and saving:

> Now that my children are grown and are studying at the university, I say to myself, "Take 20 percent for yourself. You deserve it." So now I don't run home as soon as I finish work at four o'clock. Sometimes I go out for coffee with friends or I go shopping and even stay out late to go to a party. I am taking some free time for myself. I am tired of working and worrying. There are financial resources and there are spiritual resources. Sometimes the spiritual resources become depleted.

But alongside her weariness, Sharon is proud of her accomplishments because she achieved what she set out to do and she has done it on her own: "All in all, I am proud of myself—I'm not a divorcee with two children who lives in a rented apartment and lives from hand to mouth. The apartment is mine. The car is mine. I have a job. If you have financial security, you have peace of mind."

In her study on single mothers, Sidel noted that the interviews of her subjects were pervaded by a sense of loss:

> loss of a partner or a spouse; loss of emotional support, social support, financial support; loss of self-esteem; and loss of status within their immediate community, within the larger society, and, perhaps, most important, in their own eyes.[27]
>
> . . . Yet, despite significant personal and structural barriers, many of them have managed to empower themselves to move toward greater control of their own and their children's lives.[28]

Sharon definitely belongs to the latter group.

ᔓ

Sharon's narrative is important to this study because it focuses on the mobility of second-generation Moroccan immigrant women who are divorced mothers, a topic that has received little research attention even though divorce is a growing phenomenon in Israeli society. In significant ways, Sharon's narrative was similar to those of the married second-generation Moroccan immigrant women who participated in this study; she aspired to the same middle-class mobility for herself and her children as they did, she noted the same constraints, and she applied the same means to overcome them. The structural impediment of being a daughter of working-class Moroccan immigrants that the married mothers spoke about, particularly the childhood deprivations, such as a sporadic education and her efforts to overcome this disadvantage through increasing her education later in life and through her employment, was present in Sharon's life story. The desire to reconstruct her ethnic feminine identity in ways that would foster her mobility was also present. So was the determination to position her children to surpass their mother's mobility. While all the mothers in the previous narratives stressed the advantages of upward residential mobility for their children's education in order to move up within the middle class, Sharon gave considerably more weight to residential mobility as an opportunity for her children not only to improve their education but also to acquire the social networks that would enable them to penetrate the hegemonic group and thereby to improve their life chances. She also saw residence as an expression of middle-class material culture more than the other women in the middle segment of the middle class did.

But for Sharon, and divorced mothers like her, the most compelling structural constraint to her mobility into the middle class derived from having the financial resources of a single breadwinner while having mobility aspirations that equaled those of married women who have a co-breadwinner. Added to this structural obstacle was the cultural bias in the form of stereotypes that regard divorced women and their children as those who do not belong in the middle class. In spite of these barriers, Sharon's single-minded resolve to achieve her mobility goals for herself and her children—and to do it on her own—explains the feelings of pride, self-esteem, and self-empowerment that her success has generated and reveals a unique feminine ethnic identity that she and those she typifies have created: the second-generation Moroccan divorced mother who is in the middle segment of the middle class.

The following narrative will present a woman who was born into the middle class, has moved upward beyond the middle sector of the middle class, and is satisfied with her class attainments.

## Chapter 7

# *Comfortable in Her Own Skin*

Naomi, who is forty-five years old, represents the small percentage (3 percent) of second-generation Moroccan immigrant women in the high segment of the middle class. She was born into the middle class and for her upward mobility meant becoming an academic professional. She earned BA and MA degrees as well as a teaching certificate, which enabled her to be a high school teacher. Naomi invited me to her house for her interviews. During our meetings we sat around the dining room table to talk. At our first session a cocker spaniel, the family's pet (what Katherine Grier has described as part of the "domestic ethos" of middle-class life[1]), lay curled up at her feet.

From Naomi's narrative I learned that both of her parents had belonged to the segment of Moroccan Jewry who had joined a Zionist youth movement (see chapter 2) and had immigrated to Israel because of their membership in the movement. They came as young people in their late teens with what were, at the time, educational and occupational middle-class resources. Therefore they entered the Israeli middle class directly after their arrival in the country. Prior to their immigration, both parents had lived in Casablanca, in the new European quarters that developed since the establishment of the French Protectorate in 1912. Each was more educated than the majority of Moroccan immigrants who arrived in Israel at the time.[2] Her father had completed high school at the French Alliance Israélite Universelle school in Casablanca, and her mother had completed her elementary education in another Alliance school. As part of their education in these schools, the parents had learned French.[3] As Aziza Khazzoom pointed out, knowing a foreign language was an advantage in Israeli society, which was composed of immigrants who came from European countries and from French-speaking countries in North Africa.[4] Khazzoom also observed that Moroccan men who arrived in Israel unmarried and without children "did better" than those who came with children.[5] This claim was supported in this study by the fact that the fathers who immigrated as educated young men, who spoke French and were bachelors free from family responsibilities did, in fact, enter the middle class directly after their immigration. Naomi's parents met and married in their new country and gave birth to three children.

According to Alejandro Portes and Rubén Rumbaut, immigrant parents who have high levels of human capital offer their second-generation children certain advantages.[6] Among these is their better ability to help their children in two ways. "First, they have greater information about opportunities and pitfalls in the surrounding environment; second, they can earn higher incomes giving them access to strategic goods,"[7] such as education. Naomi's parents offered their children these dual advantages: their membership in a Zionist movement gave them knowledge about Israel before their immigration that served as a head start in their new country, and their education enabled them to earn middle-class incomes that they invested in their children's studies.

Naomi told me that her father had had high aspirations for his children and himself in his new home:

> My father was very ambitious and he had a lot of will power. After he immigrated, he decided he wanted to work in accounting because he thought that he could use his knowledge of languages—he knew French—and the accounting he had learned in school to advance in business. So he started working as an accountant at a regional branch of a national department store chain in the country. He began as a low-grade accountant and worked his way up to be the head of the national accounting department. He always took courses in accounting and he has certificates from the courses he took. He earned a good living.

Naomi's parents' ambition for their children revolved around providing them with a good education, and they had the material and cultural advantages to do so. Because of his high income, her father was able to provide his three children with a complete, continuous education that included high school and university. From the cultural perspective, both parents appreciated education for its intrinsic value and with the help of their own educations had the ability to support their children's schooling on a daily basis through the supervision of homework and additional studies during summer vacations. It was Naomi's mother who undertook these daily duties:

> My mother wanted to be a housewife and to raise us—that was her goal in life. That was good for us. We always had peace of mind. There was always someone to talk to, to turn to. Our mother always prodded us to succeed at school. At the beginning of summer vacation she would buy workbooks for us to work on during the vacation and she made sure we did them. She would always check our work.

Naomi's mother's devotion to her children's studies coincides with findings in other research that also noted the intense involvement of middle-class immigrant parents in their children's education and thus suggests that this may be a norm among these parents.[8]

In talking about her later studies, Naomi told me:

> I went to Cremieux Gymnasium high school. It was associated with the Alliance. We learned French and I did my matriculation examinations there. After high school I went directly to the university. I did my BA in history and geography. I decided that I wanted to be a teacher, so when I finished my BA, I studied for a teaching degree. While I was studying, I started substitute teaching at elementary schools, and then when I had my degree I taught history in high school and was a homeroom teacher. A few years later, I went back to do an MA in history and geography, and I have been teaching those subjects all these years. I also do remedial teaching. I love teaching because I love children.

In Israel, as in other countries, teachers in elementary, junior, and high schools are mostly women.[9] According to recent Israeli government statistics, out of a total of 38,710 secondary school teachers, 33.57 percent are men and 66.43 percent are women. These female teachers are more academically qualified than the male teachers; 48.98 percent of the women have academic and teaching degrees as compared with 19.42 percent of the men.[10] Naomi is among the minority of Mizraḥi teachers who have an academic degree at the MA level.[11]

Research has shown that teaching is attractive to women primarily for two reasons. Firstly, it serves as a path to mobility into the middle class for women from lower social class origins, women from subordinate status ethnic groups, nonwhites, and women from rural backgrounds who have attained the educational credentials required to enter the profession.[12] Secondly, teaching, as a stereotypical feminine profession, attracts women who want to work in an occupation with professional status that offers a flexible work schedule, enabling them to give priority to their domestic duties, which they, and society, see as the appropriate order of priorities for women.[13] In their study of secondary-school teachers in Israel, Dahlia Moore and Abraham Gobi also found that the women in their sample attributed higher priority to their domestic roles than to their work roles.[14] Nevertheless, their teaching was important to them. Lya Kremer-Hayon and Zahava Goldstein found that secondary-school teachers in Israel attributed great significance to their success as teachers; this was expressed in their preoccupation with teaching issues in their after-school hours.[15]

Naomi belongs to that group of women referred to in the above-mentioned research who entered teaching not because it was an avenue for mobility into the middle class (she was born into the middle class), but because it enabled her to work in an academic profession that offers self-fulfillment and fits in well with her construction of her domestic roles:

> I work, first of all, to fulfill myself, but also to add to the family's income. My children don't object to my working. If they did, I would explain to them that everyone has his own needs, that I have my needs, and that it is very important to me to satisfy them. If my husband objected, I would listen to him and try to convince him of my opinion. He would have to raise some very strong arguments to convince me to leave teaching. And if he would convince me to leave teaching, I would go work in something else. I wouldn't stay at home. I would never stay at home.

Naomi was aware that working for intrinsic satisfaction was a luxury that only the minority of Moroccan women, perhaps those in the high segment of the middle class like herself, could afford. She thought that most Moroccan women worked for the additional income they provided for their families: "Today I think that most Moroccans want women to work so that they add to the family income."

Naomi wanted to marry. However, it is important to note that she framed these desires not in terms of ethnic-based expectations of women, whereby they have to prove their femininity and social respectability by marrying and having children (see chapter 2),[16] but rather in terms of her individualized concept of self-fulfillment, which freed her to exercise her agency to choose between options and lifestyles that would suit her:

> I married when I was twenty-one and my husband was twenty-seven. We met while we were both students at the university. I wanted to

> marry because marriage is a way for me to fulfill myself. I don't think that people would have treated me differently if I hadn't married, but marriage was a way of fulfilling myself.
>
> If I hadn't married, I would have found another way of fulfilling myself. I think that if a woman marries and has children, she develops a whole different side of herself than if she doesn't and perhaps is lonely. But I would have surrounded myself with other people if I wasn't married—I wouldn't have been lonely. I would have done other things with my life. Everyone is an individual and everyone can do what he wants to with his life.

It is likely that Naomi's sense of having the option of marrying or not was enhanced by her class position. Andrew Cherlin[17] noted that for some women marriage is, indeed, an expression of their individuality rather than a "marker of conformity"[18] to socially scripted roles and expectations. Although he did not attribute this "deinstitutionalization" of marriage specifically to class norms, his research suggested that the choice of whether to marry applied more to women in higher-class positions than in lower ones. Gary Becker, in his book *A Treatise on the Family*, supplied an economic explanation of why women in high-class positions may feel free not to marry. He argued that women who are economically independent can "afford" not to marry because they can support themselves and do not need a husband to provide for them.[19] Naomi's middle-class origins, her higher education and high middle-class occupation would have enabled her to support herself without the aid of a husband. But it is probable that Naomi's decision to marry was influenced not only by her desire for self-fulfillment but also by the norm of "familism," the tendency to marry and have children that is prevalent among all sectors of Israeli society.[20]

In describing her choice of husband, Naomi told me:

> My husband is also of Moroccan origin—his parents came from Morocco. I think that it is important that people come from the same ethnic background. There is less tension if both come from the same ethnic group. He is an engineer in the civil service—he works for the government. He has a BA and an MA.

Naomi's husband was born to parents who were in the manual-labor working class, but through his education and subsequent occupation he entered the high segment of the middle class. Thus among the husbands of the women in this study, he was the only one with an academic degree, one whose education equaled that of his wife's and who, like his wife, belonged to the high segment of the middle class.

Naomi and her husband adopted a rational approach to childbearing that enabled them to maintain the middle-class position she was born into and the high middle-class position they had created for themselves and their children: "We each earn a good middle-class income and we have two daughters. We didn't want any more children. That is the number of children we can raise well—give them a good education and a good home in a good neighborhood—so we were careful not to have any more children. I used birth control for a very long time."

If marriage was a source of self-fulfillment for Naomi rather than an ethnic/cultural imperative, so was motherhood:

> I wanted children very much. I love children. Children are a way for me to fulfill myself. I wanted to raise them. I never sent my children to day care. When they were young, my mother used to take care of them while I was at work. That gave me a lot of peace of mind. I always knew that they were in good hands. I wasn't like my friends who sent their children to day care or hired someone to care for them and were always worried when they were at work about their children, whether their children were being well cared for. I always tried to work hours that would enable me to be with my children. My mother stayed with them in the morning and I arranged my work schedule so that I would finish teaching at 12:00. When they went to kindergarten, I also finished teaching at 12:00, so I was home when they came home at 1:00. That way I was with them most of the day. And I never worked on Fridays. Fridays were always devoted to doing things at home and cooking Moroccan food.

However, Naomi's image of the ideal gendered division of family labor did seem to reflect the traditional ethnic spousal division of labor in which the Moroccan woman is the homemaker and the dominant spouse in the home:

> I think that women have more presence in the home than men do. If you look at women in politics—those who are members of Knesset [Israeli Parliament]—they sound as if they are satisfied with having a career and having the husband take care of the home and children. But that doesn't sound right to me. It sounds unnatural—like going against nature—for a woman to be a public figure—to

> be outside the home so much. These women hardly spend any time with their children; they are hardly a presence in their children's lives. And I think that children feel that. I'm not against women holding a public office; they are contributing to society, but they are doing it at their children's expense. Their children are paying the price of their mother's career. I think that children have a very basic need to come to their mother first and tell her things. A father's job is more outside the home.

Naomi's husband was not a partner in the division of household duties or in child care. Moreover, she justified his lack of participation in domestic duties:

> My husband is very ambitious and is always working. He always worked several jobs when he was a student. He was one of the few people who had his own car when he was a student. That was unusual at the time. He also had bought his own apartment before we married.
>
> My husband participates at home only on rare occasions, such as when we have a lot of guests and there is pressure. I think that he could improve a great deal in that department, but he is very busy.
>
> When the children were babies he would sometimes help with them when he came home from work—he would change their diapers and sit with them. But I didn't mind his not helping with child care because I like to take care of them. I always thought that it was my job to take care of them. I always felt that it was my duty to dress them, feed them, wash them, and be there when they went to school and when they came home from school.

Why did Naomi not resent her husband's lack of partnership in household duties or regard it as an obstacle to her mobility, as did the women in the middle segment of the middle class? Several possible reasons may explain her attitude. One may be that she admired and respected her husband's middle-class ambition of mobility through education and work. It had enabled him to enter the high segment of the middle class and to rise above most other Moroccan men in his generation,[21] and she did not want to divert him from this path. Second, she perceived this division of labor as her choice and as a means of self-fulfillment rather than an arrangement that he imposed upon her. Therefore she did not feel that she was his "slave" or "servant":

> Women's position has changed. There used to be a stigma to being women—that they are weaker than men and less equal to men. I think that there has been a lot of progress regarding women's equality. There are some groups of Moroccan women who are more equal to men than others. It depends on their education. The less educated women have a lower place in the hierarchy than men. These are women who cannot fulfill themselves and they are, basically, slaves at home. I am talking about homes in which the husband demands something and she runs to do it immediately. She is a servant. There is a stereotype that Moroccan women are subordinate to men. But that is not true of all Moroccan women. That stereotype exists because there has not been anyone to contradict it. There are many women who feel equal to men, but we don't hear about those women. People talk only about the stereotypical woman. But I don't think that that is something unique to Moroccans. I think it applies to Ashkenazim, too.

A third reason that Naomi did not resent her husband's lack of sharing home responsibilities was because his refusal supported her construction of her ethnic feminine identity that defined her as the spouse in charge of the household. Finally, she created a substitute partner, the hired cleaning woman, who helped with the drudgery of the physical labor involved in housekeeping so that Naomi did not have to rely on her husband or do it all by herself: "I do most of the housework. But I have household help. A cleaning woman comes in twice a week. She has been coming since the children were young. I work along with her—we work together." This, of course, was a solution that she, as a woman in the high segment of the middle class, was able to afford. But it was significant, as Naomi pointedly mentioned, that she worked alongside the cleaning woman; through this arrangement she had the help she wanted without it detracting from her feminine identity as homemaker. Furthermore, as Floya Anthias and I (elsewhere) have both noted, hiring domestic help is a symbol of middle-class status.[22] Thus Naomi responded to the potential tension of her husband's lack of participation in household duties by legitimizing it and turning into an opportunity to display both her ethnic feminine gender and class identities.

While Naomi and her husband were not partners in housekeeping duties, they did share major financial decisions: "I decide the small things—what to buy, what not to buy—in everyday things. But we decide the big things together—like buying a refrigerator, a car, a new apartment. If we have a difference of opinion, we try to convince each other."

The biggest expenditure in the couple's life has been housing, which for them has been a steady process of "moving up the housing ladder."[23] As Naomi mentioned previously, her husband owned a small apartment when they married so that they did not have to begin their climb up the ladder from the lowest rung, but could begin from a higher position. A few years after their marriage, they bought a larger apartment in Armon, a Jerusalem neighborhood populated by upwardly mobile Mizraḥim, but one in which their daughters shared a bedroom. After several years they moved to a spacious two-family house surrounded by a garden in Nativ, an established, ethnically mixed, middle-class neighborhood in which each daughter now has her own bedroom within which to study and the parents have a study. In contrast to the women in the low and middle segments of the middle class, Naomi and her family do not live in an apartment building, but in a house. Within the hierarchy of residential properties and neighborhoods in Jerusalem, Naomi and her husband have accomplished significant residential mobility.

Naomi enjoys middle-class pursuits such as traveling for pleasure. She is well traveled; she went abroad when she was single and has continued this leisure-time activity with her husband. Ian Munt, basing his approach on Pierre Bourdieu's theory of classificatory struggles between classes,[24] contended that tourism, particularly independent, nonmass travel, is a way by which members of the middle classes distinguish themselves from those of inferior classes.[25] Naomi's comments about her traveling exemplify Munt's contention and serve as another reminder of her position in the high segment of the middle class: "I have traveled abroad a lot. Before I was married I traveled with my girlfriends, and since I married I have traveled with my husband. We have been to Paris several times, to Scandinavia, to the Far East, and now we are planning a trip to Europe. We traveled less when the children were young, but now we travel a lot more."

Naomi's view of Moroccans in Israel is colored by her middle-class background and her position in the high segment of the middle class. She identifies with second-generation Moroccan immigrant women like herself who are in the high segment of the middle class and whose parents, like hers, came from the French-influenced sector of Jewish society in Morocco. To her, these women represent second-generation Moroccan immigrant women even though statistically they are the minority: "Moroccans like to dress well—tip, top. They also have European table manners. I think that that is part of their culture. I know that the French ruled in Morocco for a long time and Moroccans adopted their French culture."

When comparing her mobility achievements with those of her parents, Naomi knows that she has surpassed their position in the middle class, particularly her mother's:

> First of all, I am much more educated than she is. I studied at the university and work in an academic profession. From the financial perspective, I am in a much higher status than my mother and father. I have a much higher standard of living than my mother did. I think that is understandable. She stayed at home and had three children. I have only two children.

Her children also belong to the high segment of the middle class. Both daughters are university graduates and are working in academic professions.

Naomi claimed that her Moroccan identity was not important to her, apparently others did not impose it upon her and she had no complaints about ethnic discrimination:

> Being Moroccan is not important to me. I was born to Moroccan parents, but that's it. Being a Moroccan is a cultural heritage that I inherited from my parents. I think that those women who say it is important to them that they are Moroccan are reacting to prejudice and discrimination against Moroccans that they feel. It's their way of saying that they are proud of their ethnic heritage in spite of discrimination. I never felt discriminated against, even when I was a child, or in school or in the university, though my parents used to talk about it. But feelings of being discriminated against may have something to do with personality, the way people interpret things and the way they cope with things. And some people may be more sensitive than others. I'm not very sensitive and emotional. I am more rational.

In other words, discrimination, to the extent that it exists, is waning in comparison with her parents' immigrant generation. In any case, in Naomi's opinion it is not institutionalized and when it exists is experienced only on the individual level.

Naomi's comment about the lack of importance of her Moroccan identity indicated that she felt she was free to choose her ethnic identity, that she had "ethnic options,"[26] the freedom to choose whether to claim Moroccanness as her ethnic identity. Since Naomi had not experienced the ethnic discrimination that other second-generation women talked about and since she had not encountered offensive stereotypes that ascribed a subordinate ethnic identity to her, it was not surprising that she thought she had a choice about whether to identify herself as belonging to the Moroccan ethnic group.

Even though Naomi claimed that her ethnic identity was not important to her, she maintained a symbolic Moroccan ethnicity that she expressed by cooking ethnic food and performing Moroccan ceremonies such as the *Henna*, the traditional engagement party:

> Being a Moroccan woman to me means cooking Moroccan food. Those are the basic things I keep. On Fridays, when I do not work, I cook Moroccan food. I learned Moroccan cooking from my mother and grandmother and after I married I asked them for all their recipes and I have kept them to this day. For me, cooking Moroccan food is a way of keeping the tradition. On Sabbath evenings it is customary to eat certain foods and I prepare them.
>
> I also like celebrating holidays according to the Moroccan tradition and keeping Moroccan customs, like the *Henna*. Other than that, I am entirely Israeli. I accept all the Israeli norms and whatever Israeli women do. My children identify themselves as Israelis whose parents belong to Moroccan culture.

Although Naomi thinks that ethnic differences can cause tension on the interpersonal level (witness her remark that married couples should come from the same ethnic background), she perceives Israeli society to be a culturally pluralistic one in which she and members of other ethnic groups can practice their cultures: "Every ethnic group has something special about it, its special foods, forms of dress. It's become something popular and political."

Naomi's impression that cultural ethnicity has become popular in Israel has been confirmed by social scientists who claimed that the failure of the melting pot ideology and the persistence of ethnicity has made cultural pluralism a legitimate goal.[27] Consequently, members of ethnic groups feel encouraged to express their cultural differences publicly. This trend has been particularly evident among those groups, like the Moroccans, who were at the bottom of the social ladder and who now feel free to exhibit ethnic pride, especially since some members of their group have accomplished upward mobility. The trend toward cultural pluralism has also found political expression in the tendency of politicians to turn public ethnic festivals into opportunities to present themselves as supporters of various ethnic groups and thereby to curry the group's support as well as to acknowledge its electoral power.[28]

However, Naomi opposes political ethnicity, the institutionalization of ethnic differences in the form of political parties, because she thinks it fosters divisive tendencies in Israeli society: "I am very much against ethnic political parties. We are in Israel and the goal should be toward integrating everyone, uniting everyone, and not to emphasize ethnic differences. It is much nicer to accept everyone and not to create ghettos according to the different ethnic groups." Thus, while Naomi favors the preservation of cultural pluralism, she thinks that ethnic identities, including hers, should be submerged within the broader collective identity of being an Israeli.

ఌ

In writing about modern society, Bauman claimed that "modernity is the impossibility of staying put. To be modern means to be on the move."[29] It requires a "need to get out of one's skin"[30] in order to become someone else.

However, Naomi represents second-generation Moroccan immigrant women in the high segment of the middle class who are comfortable in their own skin; they are who and where they want to be. They have no further mobility ambitions. The initial advantage of being born into the middle class has afforded them classed opportunities and choices more than constraints. Among these are the luxury of making major lifestyle choices, such as marrying, having children, and working, from considerations of self-fulfillment rather than financial need. In fact, they seem to assume it is natural that their lives would offer them these possibilities. Through their own efforts, they have built upon their initial class origins to rise within the middle class, entering the high segment as academic professionals. Naomi and women like her do not feel that their class, ethnic, or feminine gender identities have been obstacles to attaining their high middle-class position. Thus they are at peace with these identities. Furthermore, they are confident that their children's position in the high segment of the middle class is secure.

However, not all second-generation Moroccan women in the high segment of the middle class are as content as Naomi with their mobility accomplishments. The following narrative represents women who have additional mobility ambitions, but who feel that these have been thwarted.

# Chapter 8

## *Privilege and Its Discontent*

Colette, a forty-six-year-old woman, also represents women in the high segment of the middle class. She, like Naomi, was born into the middle class and through her own efforts became an academic professional. She has a BA and an MA degree as well as a teaching certificate. She is a high school teacher. However, she is discontent because her additional mobility is blocked. As we sat on the patio of her house, surrounded by a blooming garden, Colette began telling me about herself by describing her parents.

Colette's parents, like Naomi's, came to Israel because they were motivated by Zionist ideology. They came to the country as young, secular, single people unencumbered by children and family obligations. Most importantly from the perspective of their mobility prospects, each one entered the country with educational and occupational qualifications that they, like other young people from cosmopolitan, middle-class Jewish-Moroccan families, had acquired in the French-oriented Alliance Israélite Universelle schools in their country of origin (see chapter 2). These accomplishments enabled them to enter directly into what was then the middle class in Israeli society. Colette told me:

> My mother lived in the European sector of Casablanca and my father in Rabat. My mother studied at the Alliance school where she got her high school and vocational education. She studied to be a seamstress, which was considered an elite occupation for women because wealthy people did not buy ready-made clothes and preferred to have them sewn for them. My father also completed his high school and vocational education at an Alliance school. He studied accounting. They met and married in Israel.

Both parents knew how to use their educational and occupational achievements to become incorporated into the more remunerative segments of the Israeli labor market. Naomi's father became a bank manager, and her mother became a seamstress in the exclusive female sector of the market—sewing for the elite. Colette told me:

> After my parents married, my father began working in a neighborhood bank and very quickly worked his way up to become the branch manager. He always wanted to expand his knowledge. He used to read encyclopedias and he memorized English and French dictionaries, even though he knew French, because he thought that at the time people in Israel spoke foreign languages more than they spoke Hebrew. My father earned a good living, and we always had everything we needed. We lacked for nothing. My mother worked as a seamstress which, at the time, was also a prestigious occupation in Israel because well-to-do people preferred to have clothes that were sewn according to the European styles that they saw in magazines rather than buy clothes they saw in local shops.

Colette's father knew how to rationalize his resources in order to maintain the middle-class existence he wanted for his family in the Israeli milieu. One way to do this was to limit the number of children he and his wife would have. Colette explained: "My father said that the financial situation in Israel was difficult and that providing for more than two children was difficult, so he only wanted two children. My parents had two daughters and I am the oldest."

Colette's parents had the educational resources to be actively involved in their daughters' schooling. Undoubtedly, their commitment to their daughters' studies laid the foundation for their subsequent educational success. Each parent contributed her and his unique capabilities and invested both time and energy in their children's scholastic activities. Her mother used her education to supervise her children's daily homework and their supplementary studies during summer vacations from elementary school. Her father, "who was good with numbers," helped with math homework. Colette continued: "We were spoiled. We were not expected to do anything at home but study. Our parents didn't expect us to help with the housework, just to study. We were always good students. I was always a perfectionist in my studies."

Colette's father was the family's sole provider because her mother became a full-time homemaker after the children were born. She recalled: "My father didn't want my mother to work. He wanted her to stay at home and devote herself to our education." The family spoke French and all the children were given French names. Her parents created a middle-class culture for their family that very much resembled French bourgeois family life emulated by middle-class Jews in Morocco (see chapter 2).

Colette's father's salary as a bank manager enabled him to provide his children with a privileged education. She and her sister attended private high schools that required the payment of tuition:

> The tuition for our high school studies was very expensive, but my father very much wanted us to succeed. And success meant going to high school and then to a university. When we had to choose which high school to attend, my father went with me to every high school in Jerusalem and interviewed the principal. Eventually, we decided that I would go to the Academy of the Arts High School. We were required to study the regular high school curriculum and to learn to play a musical instrument as well. That was a wonderful experience. The school contributed a great deal to my cultural development and exposed me to other cultures. When I finished high school, I completed all my matriculation examinations. I didn't serve in the army so I started studying at the university for a BA right after high school. I wanted to be a university graduate very much because I think that through studying one can enter society and become somebody. One can cope better in society and one is respected if he has a university education.
>
> When I started the university, I wanted to be a Renaissance woman. That's my ideal—someone who knows a lot about many topics. I studied comparative literature and art for my BA. I also wanted to continue my music studies. Those are fields I love. I never thought about the financial aspects of what I studied—whether I could make a living from it, the way some people do. I just studied what I loved for the pleasure it gave me.
>
> When I finished my BA, I studied another two years at the university to get a teacher's degree. When I finished studying for my teachers' degree, I did an MA in history. Since then I have taken university classes every year in a subject that interested me. I took several classes in anthropology because I thought that that is related to history and art in some way, and I took additional classes in literature and music and that led me to study theater. I don't think that a person has to focus on one subject only when he studies. I think that a person should study many things that enrich him. It is

> very important to me to enrich my intellectual life by widening my knowledge in many fields. I also took specific courses for teachers, such as courses on how to teach music, because I felt that I lacked the techniques for teaching music.

After completing high school, during the period of her university studies and throughout her adult life, Colette traveled abroad frequently to Europe and the United States. As mentioned in chapter 2, young women from well-to-do Jewish families in Morocco tended to enjoy this type of activity because it was popular among young, middle-class French women, and therefore it was another way by which they expressed their identification with middle-class French culture. Apparently, young middle-class second-generation immigrant Moroccan women like Colette continued this practice in Israel. Colette's frequent trips abroad also contributed to her becoming the well-educated, well-rounded Renaissance woman she wanted to be because it exposed her to the influences of the major cultural centers of the world. And, as Munt noted, in postmodern societies, middle-class travelers distinguish themselves from other tourists by having unique travel experiences,[1] for example, itineraries that offer intellectual enrichment. Separately or together these explanations suggest that Colette's frequent trips abroad were another expression of her privileged existence:

> I have traveled a lot. I went to France before I began my university studies and I have been there many times since then. I've also been to many other countries in Europe. I have visited Eastern Europe—mostly Prague and Budapest. I've been to Prague and Budapest several times. I'm going to the Unites States again soon. It will be my fifth trip there. I like to get to know places in depth, not superficially.

Toward the end of her first year of her BA studies, when she was twenty years old, Colette married. She married a man of Moroccan origin. He was twenty-five years old, a high school graduate, and today works as a regional manager of a national petroleum company:

> I didn't especially want to get married, but we had dated for two years and decided that we should marry. He is proud of being Moroccan. He speaks Moroccan. He goes to a Moroccan synagogue. He likes me to cook Moroccan food. I don't think that it is important that both spouses come from the same ethnic group. I know

> mixed couples who are successful, and I know people from the same background who are successful.

From Colette's perspective, the less attractive side of her husband's living his ethnic culture has been his attempts to impose an ethnic feminine identity upon her by perpetuating ethnic-based gender norms according to which men are the dominant spouse and women the subservient one. She resisted these attempts because they conflicted with her expectations of spousal equality, though eventually she acquiesced:

> My husband behaves like a typical Moroccan husband. He thinks that he is a sheik and that I am his servant. I don't think that a wife should be a servant at home, but I am. I don't agree with some of the things I do, but I do them anyway. My husband can be sitting with his friends, and he expects me to serve them all. I don't agree with that. Or, if he is sitting down, he expects me to serve him coffee. I don't agree with that either. There are things he wants me to wash by hand. I don't agree with that either. Why do I do them? Because I got used to doing them, and I got my husband used to my doing them. We talk about it a lot, but nothing changes.

In other words, Colette made a "bargain with patriarchy"[2]; she agreed to her husband's patriarchal demands in order to keep the peace at home.

It is interesting to note that both Naomi and Colette used the term "servant" to describe wives who fulfill their husband's expectations of Moroccan femininity. However, while Naomi did not see herself as her husband's servant, Colette did. Perhaps the difference in these women's perspective about their husband's expectations is related to the element of choice and self-ascription of roles. Naomi shared her husband's perception of the ideal Moroccan wife, while Colette did not and felt that it was imposed upon her.

Colette continued:

> He also never helps at home or with the children. I think that he should help because if both husband and wife work and contribute to the family's income, then both should share family responsibilities. When women work, they have more power in decision making. Today people in the Moroccan ethnic group think that women working outside the home is a positive thing because it helps financially. I don't know how much they think about women working for their own development. But his not helping didn't hold me back

> at work. I moved ahead even without his help and I would have advanced in any work I took on even without his help.
>
> He accepts my studying and my working, but lots of time he says, "Why are you studying so much?" Sometimes I think that he feels threatened by my studying. Knowledge is power.

Colette's analysis of her husband's demands that she comply with his wishes may be correct; they may, indeed, be his strategy for reasserting his dominant position in the traditional Moroccan gender hierarchy that is jeopardized by her superior education. Constantina Safilios-Rotschild and Marcellinus Dijkers found similar patterns of husbands' behavior among the Greek couples they studied in instances where wives were more educated than their husbands.[3]

To resolve the conflict surrounding her husband's unwillingness to be a partner in household labor, Colette resorted to a solution that her middle-class position afforded her and hired domestic help: "Several years ago, I hired a cleaning woman to come once a week, so it is easier. I decided that I couldn't be superwoman."

Toward the end of her BA studies, Colette gave birth to a son and shortly thereafter to a daughter, and later to another daughter. The births of her children were planned so that they would not disrupt her teaching schedule:

> I wanted to have children because of the continuity and because society thinks that women who can't have children are pathetic—there is a stigma to not having children. I planned the birth of my children so that I would give birth around school vacations.
>
> I am the dominant parent in everything that concerns the children's education. It is very important to me that my children succeed in their studies. I am a very achievement-oriented mother. My children have to get 100 in their exams, 99 is not acceptable. I am a perfectionist with my children, not only with myself. All of my children have finished university and are in the professions. Two of my children—my son and daughter—are lawyers and my other daughter is an economist.

By breaking out of the female sector of the labor market, her daughters have enhanced their opportunities to surpass their mother's class mobility.

Colette was also the dominant partner in the family's residential mobility. Each move from one dwelling to the next was motivated by her desire to create an environment conducive to learning for her children. Consequently, the family moved from a small apartment in a working-class neighborhood in which Colette and her husband lived when they married, to a house in Basle, an ethnically mixed, middle-class neighborhood whose residents are upwardly mobile. In this new house, each child had his own nook for studying. When the children began their university studies, she initiated a move to their present house in the same neighborhood, but one that offered each child his own spacious bedroom in which to study. She took a mortgage to buy their present home.

Having children determined Colette's choice of occupation. She chose a stereotypically female type of work, teaching, because it enabled her to combine her work and family roles and thus suited her construction of her feminine identity:

> After I gave birth to my son, I decided that I wanted to be a teacher. My work is very important to me because I think that work is part of the normal development of a person. It was very important to me to combine everything, but after I gave birth, motherhood became more central to my life than my studies and my work.
>
> I thought that teaching would coincide well with my family life. That I could be home when my children were home every day and that I would be home during their summer vacations. So when my children were young and in elementary school, I taught in elementary school so that I would finish my workday when they finished school. When they moved on to junior high and high school, I also began teaching in junior high and in high school because they then had a longer school day and so did I. Since then I have taught only in high school. I have always taught full time. I usually don't have guilt feelings toward my children about my work, though sometimes I do because when I have to choose between being with my children at home after school or being with the children at school on some project, I go to the school and live with the guilt. It is part of the reality of my life.

But Colette also had an ideological reason for choosing to teach: "I thought that I could help weak students escape poverty. I love to teach and to achieve success. When I see a child go from zero to forty, for me that is progress—great progress. It is very important to me to advance children who are average or below average. These are mostly Mizraḥi children."

Colette's sensitivity to the social distinctions between Mizraḥim and Ashkenazim is rooted in her own childhood experiences:

> My parents always talked about how they were treated by the immigrants who had come to Israel before them, the Ashkenazim. They said that there was always a sense of "them" and "us." My father always said that he could have advanced more if he wasn't a Moroccan.
>
> But that isn't something that existed only in my parents' generation. I felt it when I was in school. When I went to elementary school, there was also a feeling of "them" and "us." There was always the feeling that somehow we were inferior to the Ashkenazim. The Ashkenazi children felt that they were the veterans in the country and we, the Moroccans, were the new immigrants, even though they were immigrants, too. They felt that they were superior and that the Moroccans were inferior to them.
>
> We, Moroccans, came from a European-French culture; we had our own food and table manners that were beautiful and European in every way. It's true that the Ashkenazim had a better command of Hebrew than we did, they were quicker to adapt to things than we were, and they knew how to get things done. Even today I see that they know how to run things. They take control easily. Over the years the feeling that we were different from them had a psychological impact upon us. Their attitude of superiority created a feeling of insecurity among Moroccans that exists even today.

For a certain period in her life, Colette internalized the Ashkenazi devaluation of her Moroccan culture and of her:

> My surroundings influenced me. While I was growing up, people tried to repress their being Moroccan, and I did, too. I wanted to cut myself off from my Moroccan culture. I always tried to be like the Ashkenazim to cover up my insecurity. When I was in elementary school I wouldn't let my mother speak Moroccan with me. I used to speak with a Moroccan accent and the children in school made fun of me. So I worked on myself to get rid of the accent. When I was in high school, it was the same thing. I once dated an Ashkenazi boy. One day when we were out with his parents, I heard one of them say, "Here is another *Frenk*" [a disparaging ethnic slur for Moroccans]. I was terribly hurt. I wanted to be "in."

Colette has followed a convoluted and painful road to formulating her ethnic identity. She has gone from disidentifying with her ethnic roots, which she considered more European-French than Moroccan, to embracing a European-Ashkenazi-Israeli identity, which proved to be an "illusion in assimilation,"[4] and finally to accepting her Moroccan ethnicity as part of her ancestry. Her reconnection with her Moroccan ethnicity has been encouraged by greater appreciation of cultural pluralism in Israeli society:

> Along the way, I tried to cut myself off from my Moroccan culture, and I got a real slap in the face when I saw that that was impossible. Then I started to understand that a person who has no roots can't fly. I am the daughter of Moroccans—I was born into it and that has remained in me somewhere. It is a given. I think that if someone is proud of his roots, he is treated with respect. That's why I think that it is important to strengthen one's roots.
>
> I went through a process of becoming Israeli. I think of myself as Israeli. I grew up in Israel. All my culture is Israeli and not Moroccan. What does Morocco have to do with me? I prefer not to be considered Moroccan. Lately, though, I have returned to accepting my ethnic roots. I try to preserve them, but that's all. There are some nice things in Moroccan culture—the holidays, for instance—but there are nice things in every culture. I think that most Moroccans want to preserve their culture. I preserve it through food, cooking Moroccan food. Today people are going back to the ceremonies like the *Henna*, the traditional Moroccan engagement party. I had a *Henna* for my married daughter. She wanted it. My children are proud of being Moroccan. But wanting to preserve one's culture is also due to people's attitudes today. There is less of a condescending attitude to other people's culture. Today there is greater legitimization of people's culture.

In spite of the growing appreciation of cultural diversity in Israel, Colette claimed that discrimination against Moroccans was both informal and institutionalized in the educational system, and that it constituted a structural barrier to her occupational, and therefore her class, mobility. She made a great investment in her work that resembles the commitment one makes to a career. In her family life, she planned the birth of her children around the exigencies of her career, and on occasion when conflict arose, she chose her work responsibilities over her family obligations. Propelled forward by ambition, during her work history she advanced from being a teacher to being a homeroom teacher, then to being the head of her department at her high school. Now she wants to move on to a higher administrative post in the school hierarchy; she wants to be a vice principal and then a principal.

According to Colette, discrimination on the informal level is expressed through stereotypes about Moroccans that surface in interpersonal relations between teachers:

> I remember one day in the teachers' room when the Moroccan Shas[5] [Political] Party started. I didn't support the Party because I don't believe in ethnic parties, but when I walked into the teachers' room, one of the teachers, an Ashkenazi woman, said in a derogatory tone, "Here is one of the Shas supporters." My feelings were terribly hurt. I thought to myself, "What kind of talk is that?" I said something to her, I don't remember what exactly. I didn't hold back. I was very angry.
>
> I think that an ethnic party, like Shas, is not the answer. I think that it portrays the whole ethnic issue in an undignified manner. It presents all Moroccans as underdogs. I think that we should stress the ability and talents of the Moroccans and what they can contribute. People in the Moroccan ethnic group should take the initiative and show all the positive things in the group, what Moroccans can do, not the negative things, not what they can't do.
>
> Some Moroccans are in positions to influence the positions of other Moroccans, but they don't. Moroccans who succeed just care about their own individual success and don't care about the Moroccans who are less successful. They attribute their success to their own individual talent and don't support the group.

Colette objected to the other teacher's comment because it suggested that Ashkenazim do not make the differentiation between mobile and nonmobile Moroccans that is important to her, and they ascribe or impose a stereotype on all Moroccans, including her, that presents them as downtrodden. To some extent she also blames this stereotype on mobile Moroccans who regard their mobility as a unique, individual-level achievement and disregard those within their ethnic group who have not attained their class accomplishments. Thereby, they contribute to the image of all Moroccans as "underdogs" lacking the resources with which to accomplish mobility.

On the organizational level, Colette claimed that she has experienced discrimination firsthand. She elaborated: "The principal of my school is an Ashkenazi woman, and I see who is close to her and who isn't. I see who gets promoted and who doesn't."

Scholars who have studied the recruitment of women teachers into administrative positions in schools in the United Kingdom, the United States, and Israel found that their desire to give priority to family roles rather than career or breadwinner roles has restricted their entrance into high administrative posts, such as vice principal or principal.[6] Furthermore, their tendency to concentrate their studies in humanities and social sciences rather than in educational administration, which men favor, has limited their probability of being appointed to high administrative posts.[7] However, all the studies mentioned above have noted that gender discrimination, opposition to women as women, restricts their chances of being assigned such positions. In addition, research, such as that of Patricia Ann Banks, has shown that women teachers who belong to racial or ethnic minority groups are further discriminated against in their selection to these administrative posts and so confront double discrimination.[8]

While most of the teachers in Israeli schools are women, their percentage among school principals, particularly secondary school principals, is low, though there are differences between the Jewish state sector, the Jewish religious state sector, and the Arab sector educational frameworks.[9] According to Audrey Addi-Raccah and Hanna Ayalon, the lower percentage of women in these jobs attests to discrimination against women who vie for these positions.[10] However, Addi-Raccah, in her study on gender, ethnicity, and school principalship in Israel, found that belonging to an ethnic minority status group, such as the Mizraḥi group (which includes Moroccans), limited women's chances of being appointed to the position of principal of a school.[11] Thus statistics support Colette's feeling of ethnic discrimination against her in her ambition to become a school principal.

When the research cited here so clearly supports a claim to both gender and ethnic discrimination in appointments to the post to which Colette aspires, why does she complain about ethnic discrimination and not gender discrimination as an obstacle to achieving her goal? Stated differently, why does Colette consider her ethnic identity and not her gender identity a constraint on her advancement? Mary Waters, in her discussion of ethnic options, maintains that structural reasons, such as discrimination, sustain ethnic identities.[12] I argue that this is also true regarding gender. Colette had never encountered the structural impediment of gender discrimination, and therefore she did not see her gender identity as an obstacle. While she resented the unequal ethnic feminine gender role she had accepted as a wife, it had not been a barrier she could not overcome and in fact did overcome by hiring domestic help. Also, outside her home she had chosen a stereotypically female job that usually did not conflict with her maternal obligations, which added to her feeling that her gender was not a barrier to her attaining her aims. Furthermore, as long as Colette remained within her female stereotypical job as a teacher, she was shielded from the gender discrimination she would likely encounter once she applied for a stereotypically male post, such as a vice principal or principal. Probably an additional explanation for not seeing her gender as a barrier was the fact that her own principal was a woman, which showed her that mobility into that position was possible for women. This explanation is in keeping with Jay MacLeod's contention that personal experience and the experience of people one knows influences one's assessment of opportunities for occupational and class advancement.[13]

In contrast, Colette's own life history had taught her that ethnic discrimination could be a barrier to her mobility. The compounded effect of ethnic discrimination in her parents' immigrant generation, during her own childhood, and now in her adult life had made her feel that being Moroccan stood in the way of her achieving her goals. Looking around her at those women who were appointed to the position she wanted at her school, Ashkenazi women, validated her belief in the deleterious influence of her ethnicity. Thus MacLeod's explanation is equally valid when explaining Colette's expectations that ethnic discrimination would be a constraint on her occupational and class mobility.

Colette's narrative has been about fortifying the middle-class position into which she was born as well as moving beyond it through her own accomplishments in order to move into the high segment of the middle class. She sees herself as belonging to the middle class on the basis of her occupational position and on the basis of her and her husband's joint salaries, though he has been the main breadwinner throughout their marriage because he has always earned more: "If I compare ourselves to managers who earn large salaries, we belong to the middle class on the basis of both our salaries." However, achieving the position of vice principal would enable her to improve her class position both in the occupational/class and income hierarchies.

ᔕ

Although Colette represents women who have achieved upward mobility from the middle-class position into which they were born and are academic professionals in the high segment of the middle class, and their children are also in this segment of the middle class, they are discontent. Their discontent derives from their blocked mobility that they attribute to their ethnic identity.

To women like Colette, the most galling aspect of the barrier imposed by their Moroccan ethnic identity is that it ignores their privileged middle-class identity. These women do not compare themselves with other privileged, middle-class women, Ashkenazi women. For them, Ashkenazi women are not a reference group whose mobility achievements they strive to attain because they know that they are equal to them in their class accomplishments. Nevertheless, they are aware that an ethnic gender hierarchy exists that places Ashkenazi women in the hegemonic position and them, as second-generation Moroccan women, in a subordinate position. Thus the stratification system denies them the class position, prestige, and appreciation that are the full rewards for their class achievements. If Colette studied because "through studying one can enter society and become somebody. One can cope better in society and one is respected if he has a university education," this respect is withheld from her and others like her. Instead of the inclusion and equality these women seek, they are offered subordination and a pervading sense of inferiority and insecurity that positions them as the quintessential Other. This means that for second-generation immigrant women in the high segment of the middle class who belong to a subordinate group, mobility achievements do not bring the same rewards they offer hegemonic women. This has been shown to be true among first-generation immigrant women,[14] but according to Colette's narrative, this is equally true among second-generation immigrant women who belong to a subordinate group. Thus ethnic identity can put a glass ceiling on the mobility of these women who aspire to continued upward mobility.

## Chapter 9

# *Discussion*
## Paths to Middle-Class Mobility

The narratives show that these women used their human agency over multiple social sites and social structures simultaneously to acquire the individual mobility resources that brought them to their class goals while at the same time constructing new classed and ethnicized feminine identities. These sites were areas, arenas, or social spaces in their lives—education, employment, gendered spousal relationships, motherhood, residential mobility, the body, emotions—that they manipulated to achieve middle-class mobility for themselves and their children. The sheer range and number of sites they used and activated indicates the totality and extensiveness of the process of mobility for these women. While it is generally acknowledged that women use education and employment in order to "get ahead," this finding that women use so many sites concurrently to achieve middle-class mobility is a new contribution to studying second-generation immigrant women's mobility.

There were similarities in the sites the women used to acquire their mobility resources. However, the way they used and activated these sites varied according to the segment of the middle class to which the women belonged. The variations in the use of these sites and the resources the women acquired through them justified my placing them in three different segments of the middle class.

There was some resemblance in the way the women in the low and middle segments used the sites for mobility that was different from the way the women in the high segment used them. Thus, in the context of the debate about whether differing middle-class occupations produce intraclass differences in lifestyles, values, and behavior,[1] my data suggest that they do in many areas, but among second-generation Moroccan immigrant women in the group I studied, the more significant differences were between the women in the two lower occupational categories (segments) of the middle class and those in the high occupational category (segment).

The motivation for these women's mobility was their identification with a dominant norm that has characterized Israeli society since the 1950s—namely, mobility into the middle class through education and professionalization.[2] This was a common theme that ran through all their life stories. The centrality of this norm in the narratives demonstrates that life stories are not neutral or coincidental, but are themselves temporal constructions that reveal dominant cultural norms during a particular period.[3]

The goal of middle-class mobility was accompanied by a class awareness among these women. This awareness was based on their perception that Israeli society is composed of a hierarchy of unequal positions (classes) that presents individuals with different obstacles and opportunities and thereby determines their individual life chances.[4] These women imagined the Israeli class hierarchy to be a three-tiered structure that had an ethnic component—an upper class, the elite, who was predominantly Ashkenazi and was composed of those who had acquired the educational and occupational attainments that entitled them to their class position; a middle class that consisted mostly of Ashkenazim but also of a growing number of Moroccans who had middle-class educational and occupational attainments; and a working class made up primarily of nonmobile Moroccans who lacked these achievements. It was striking that their imagery of the class structure did not include Ashkenazim in the working class, which leads to the conclusion that they thought that all Ashkenazim were either in the upper or middle classes. They considered Ashkenazim in upper- and middle-class positions to be a group phenomenon, while they viewed Moroccans in these positions as an individual phenomenon. Nevertheless, these women believed that this ethnic/class connection was weaker in their generation than it had been in their parents' immigrant generation, and therefore that the Israeli class structure was more open to mobility than it had been in the past. This perception of the class hierarchy as permeable and the belief that they could rise within it led these women to pursue mobility ambitions for themselves and their children.

The middle class was a significant social category in these women's lives, even if they did not always speak in "class terms." Louise Archer and Carole Leathwood pointed out that "Middle-class identities and norms are . . . unspoken yet ever present, shaping and structuring the conditions and contexts within which working-class girls and women maneuver and position themselves."[5] Fiona Devine supported this opinion when she wrote that people can talk about class without "using the language of class."[6] In the present study, these women's reference to class, and especially the middle class, was evident from their discourse, the critical life choices they made, their practices, and their image of Israeli society that directed their actions. More specifically, their language showed that the women were talking about class because some used the words "class" and "middle class" explicitly; all spoke about mobility into and within the middle class as climbing up a stratification hierarchy based on differences in education, occupation, and income; and all talked about mobility as a way to improve their and their children's life chances. Thus the desire to belong to the middle class that Archer and Leathwood claimed was typical of working-class women,[7] and Smooha claimed characterized the average Israeli,[8] was also evident among these second-generation Moroccan women and presumably exists among other second-generation immigrant women as well.

In the following, I analyze both the similarities and differences in the ways the women in the three segments of the middle class used the various sites to achieve their mobility, the ways by which this mobility led to the construction of new classed and ethnicized feminine identities, and how these identities were related to the subordinate/hegemonic relationship between these Moroccan women and Ashkenazi women. I then discuss the innovative ways the women used their human agency and social structures to achieve their goal of upward mobility. The chapter concludes by discussing how the theoretical framework from the Israeli data can contribute to a comparative perspective on paths to mobility among women in subordinate groups in Western societies.

## The Semiprofessionals: The Low Segment of the Middle Class

A prominent characteristic of the women in the low segment of the middle class, the kindergarten teacher's assistants, was their working-class origins. Their immigrant fathers were physical laborers, as was the mother who was employed, while the other was a housewife and thus shared the working-class position of her husband. The importance of immigrant parents' initial position in the class hierarchy for their children's mobility attainments has been attested to by several researchers.[9] Scholars have observed that the class starting point of parents—their education, occupation, and income—is important because it determines the mobility resources they can provide for their children.[10]

### *Education*

The class origins of the parents of the women in the low segment of the middle class created an interaction between material and cultural factors that presented their daughters with specific constraints for accomplishing mobility into the middle class. The most critical material constraint was financial. In Ruth's case, she could not do her matriculation examinations because she had to work to help support her family.

Among the cultural factors that affected these women's education was parental attitudes toward schooling. Not all the parents encouraged their daughters to acquire an education as a means of mobility out of the working class. Miriam's parents socialized their daughter to regard education as a way to achieve this goal, while Ruth's parents taught their daughter that work, rather than education, would be her path to upward mobility. Another cultural factor that may have affected these parents' attitudes toward their daughter's education was their own cultural capital; they did not have the ability to help their children with schoolwork, and therefore they may not have wanted to encourage what they could not actively participate in and support.

However, while these narratives showed that the initial class position of the women's parents and their attitudes toward schooling were significant for the early educational paths of their daughters, they were not totally deterministic. After some apathy, ambivalence, and stops and starts, these women, on their own, turned education into a site for mobility by identifying opportunities for continuing their studies. They made investments in their education that enabled them to acquire a postsecondary nonacademic certificate and become semiprofessionals, thereby entering the low segment of the middle class.

Elsewhere, I have characterized the education of adult women from subordinate social groups who have a disrupted education that culminates in a postsecondary nonacademic institution of one type or another as a nonmainstream path of education.[11] I maintain that this type of education provided the women in the low segment of the middle class with an option to attain the resources necessary for their mobility into the middle class by enabling them to acquire training and credentials as they chose and as opportunities arose. However, as other research has shown and this study corroborates, the rewards of a nonmainstream path of education are limited in terms of occupational/class positions, income, and other benefits.[12]

## *Employment*

The women in the low segment of the middle class entered the world of work early in their lives, as adolescents, and their employment was initially meant to answer their most basic needs and those of their working-class families. It was not until their adult years that they defined the significance of work for themselves. It was during this stage in their lives that they chose the specific occupation they wanted and made the life-long investments and commitment necessary to advance in their chosen work, and thereby in their mobility. Thus their employment became a site for acquiring their own individual mobility resources. While some Jewish women in Morocco and some in the immigrant generation had worked outside their homes to help provide for their families,[13] these second-generation women were unique in that they legitimized wives' employment not primarily for financial reasons, but in order to accomplish mobility. Furthermore, for them, their work was not "just a job," but part of their identity, indivisible from who they were. In fact, these women saw employment, in addition to education, as the defining trait that separated mobile from nonmobile women and "modern" from nonmodern women.

These women chose occupations in the female sector of the labor market. As scholars have pointed out, this type of work characterizes women's employment both because the labor market prefers them for certain types of occupations, such as the semiprofessions and white-collar work, and because women choose these fields of work.[14] Karen Aschaffenbur argued that women opt for employment in the female sector because it coincides with societal expectations of appropriate roles for women; because it suits their construction of their feminine gender identity, especially their construction of motherhood; and because they can acquire accreditation for this work in an educational institution that has low entrance requirements.[15] This explanation is particularly applicable to the women in the low segment of the middle class, who chose to study in a nonacademic postsecondary college, which has low entrance criteria, and earned certificates as kindergarten teachers' assistants that enabled them to enter this segment of the middle class.

## *Marriage and Gendered Spousal Relationships*

The women in the low segment of the middle class had been socialized by their immigrant mothers to feminine ethnic norms that gave priority to domestic roles for women. Included in these norms was an emphasis on early marriage and motherhood. In fact, marriage was as central to these women as it had been for their mothers. However, they thought that the norm of early marriage should be changed, and they, like other second-generation Moroccan women, postponed marriage to a later age than had been common among the immigrant generation (see chapter 2).

Alongside these transformations in ethnic norms regarding education, employment, and age of marriage, these women attempted to institute additional changes that turned the family and the home into an arena where strategies and often struggles for mobility were carried out. Within the family, the women sought to change the ethnic-based norm regarding the division of household labor from one in which wives were expected to be the homemakers and the husbands the providers to one in which domestic duties would be divided equally between the spouses. This change was intended to free them to pursue their educational and mobility goals. In this way, the women wanted their husbands to become partners in their mobility. From a theoretical perspective, these women sought to transform their spousal gendered relationship from one rooted in a segregated division of family labor into one less differentiated and more fluid and malleable. Ruth wanted to initiate this change not only because it would enable her to pursue her ambition to rise within the middle class, but also because it coincided with her image of Ashkenazi spousal gender relationships, which she imagined were egalitarian.

Why did the husbands agree or acquiesce under pressure to their wives' expectations or demands that they change the division of household labor? One possible explanation is that they did not feel that their patriarchal position as head of household was threatened by their wives' low middle-class position. Another is that they saw the financial benefits of their wives' salaries for themselves and their families, even though the women earned only slightly more than minimum wage.

The women sought additional equality in the household by being the dominant partner in family financial decisions. This was evident from the recurrent use of the word *I* when speaking about the process of financial decision making within their family. This dominant position stemmed from their belief that their salary was important to their family regardless of the actual amount of their income.

## *Motherhood*

Motherhood continued to be as important to these women as it had been to their mothers. However, they wanted to have smaller families than the Moroccan immigrant generation had had (see chapter 2) so that they could devote more time and energy to advancing in their semiprofession and therefore in their class position.

The most striking aspect of their construction of motherhood was that they turned this role into a site for advancing not only their own mobility but also that of their children. They felt that limiting the number of children they had would enable them to invest more resources in fewer children and thereby promote their mobility. These women constructed a motherhood convergent with middle-class definitions of mothering that emphasize their children's educational success as their major mothering project.[16] Ruth equated middle-class mothering with her image of Ashkenazi mothering.

The women differed in the extent to which they saw parenthood as a joint project shared by themselves and their husband. However, from the narratives of both women in the low segment of the middle class, it was evident that producing a middle-class child was a struggle. These women began this process early by entrusting their children to early-childhood professionals. They sent them to day care and nursery school because they believed that professionals trained in early-childhood development could give their children a head start.

According to the women, their salaries contributed to advancing their children's mobility in two ways. One was by financing educational supplements to their children's schooling and the second was by initiating residential mobility into better neighborhoods than the ones they lived in. The major attraction of these new neighborhoods was that they offered better schools.

Although these women were employed full time throughout their child-rearing years, none saw employment and their goal of mobility as contradicting good mothering. Perhaps one reason these women did not see a conflict between the two was because, as kindergarten teachers' assistants, they worked hours that coincided with their children's schedules in nursery and elementary school.

## *The Body*

Ruth brought the site of the body into the process of mobility through her perception of differences between the working-class Moroccan feminine body and the middle-class Ashkenazi woman's body. Thus she made great efforts to divest herself of the "markers"[17] of her ethnic, working-class body and to assume those of her image of the ideal middle-class woman, an Ashkenazi woman from the hegemonic group, in a kind of regendering of her body that included dressing, makeup, speech, and posture. She was willing to make this transformation in her appearance and deportment even though she, personally, considered the Moroccan female body to be superior, more feminine, than the Ashkenazi female body. In other words, she was willing to trade one form of "corporeal capital"[18] for another because it was more profitable for mobility.

## *Emotions*

Emotions become a site where feelings about class and mobility are created and played out. In fact, specific feelings are associated with being in a particular class. For example, Steedman, in her book describing her working-class mother, wrote about the "structure of feeling" that accompanied her mother's working-class position and about her "longing and wanting" the luxuries that middle-class women enjoyed.[19] Others wrote of the strong feelings that working-class girls and women experience in the process of mobility into the middle class, including guilt and shame about wanting to leave the working class and yearning for the respectability that derives from belonging to the middle class. They showed that the contradictory emotions of alienation from one's former class and from one's new class amount to feelings of always being in limbo.[20] Valerie Hey reported the positive feelings her interviewees felt that accompanied their mobility, but these, too, were tinged with the psychological pain involved in crossing the class divide.[21]

However, these studies do not adequately reflect the heady, powerful emotions of increased self-esteem, autonomy, self-empowerment, and pride that were so evident in the narratives of the women in the low segment of the middle class—emotions that brought them to embrace wholeheartedly the upward mobility they had accomplished, without any concomitant feelings of being torn between class allegiances or ambivalence. But while their stories exuded a feeling of satisfaction about their class attainments, they also emitted a sense of anxiety about holding on to the middle-class position they had attained and enabling their children to advance further. This combination of satisfaction at having achieved one's goal and anxiety about losing it may be particularly characteristic of women who have entered only the low segment of the middle class, and it emphasizes that a link exists between a specific emotional configuration and women's position in a particular segment of the middle class.

As the narratives showed, the women in the low segment overcame the obstacle of their initial low structural position as daughters of working-class Moroccan immigrants in the Israeli class hierarchy with great difficulty. Although they had made investments in multiple sites to reach the middle class, by midlife they had not found ways to totally overcome this early disadvantage and rise above the low segment of the middle class.

## High-Ranking Clerical Workers: The Middle Segment of the Middle Class

Like the women in the low segment of the middle class, those in the middle segment came from poor working-class families. Sharon's father was a manual laborer, as was her mother, who worked as a cleaner. Sara's father was also a manual laborer, and her mother was a housewife, and thus she, too, belonged to the working class. However, while there were certain similarities between the women in the low and middle segments of the middle class, there were also some striking differences.

## *Education*

As was true for the women in the low segment of the middle class, the working-class origins of the women in the middle segment had a major impact on their schooling. Once again, this influence was revealed in an interaction between material and cultural factors. The poverty and low income of her parents led Sara to drop out of high school in order to help support her family, though she continued her high school studies in the evening. Parental cultural capital, which did not include support for her schooling, contributed to Sharon's dropping out of high school. While Sara completed her high school education and Sharon did not, neither did her post–high school matriculation examinations at the end of high school, as is expected, and therefore they could not continue to a university at the time.

However, as both these women's narratives showed, during their adult years they determined their own educational goals. They developed an unwavering belief in education as a site for mobility, an overwhelming desire to acquire an education, and they expended extraordinary efforts to improve their education. In their mature years they took their high school matriculation examinations and acquired a partial university education. Thus their ultimate educational achievements were definitely their own doing.

These women's sporadic education and their partial university education as adults meant that they, like the women in the low segment of the middle class, followed a nonmainstream path of education. Nevertheless, it was their partial university education that set them apart from those in the low segment because it increased their mobility resources.

## *Employment*

The women in the middle segment of the middle class had been socialized by their mothers to regard work rather than education as a means of "getting ahead." Furthermore, their mothers had stressed that their work should provide security and social status. Heeding their mother's advice, as adults they found work in the Municipal and National civil services. Within these large bureaucratic organizations, they rose from low-ranking clerical workers to their present high-ranking secretarial positions. Through their success in their work, their employment became an integral part of their feminine identity.

One of the benefits their employment framework offered was free programs during working hours to attend university preparatory courses, so that they could begin their university studies. Thus work became not only a site for mobility but also an arena for acquiring the educational credentials that enabled that mobility.

## *Marriage and Gendered Spousal Relationships*

The women in the middle segment of the middle class, like those in the low segment, had been socialized to ethnic feminine gender norms that included early marriage, early motherhood, and large families. However, they believed, because their life experiences had taught them, that these norms curtailed their educational and occupational advancement and therefore their mobility. In fact, Sara had ended her university studies because she complied with these norms. Consequently, she socialized her daughters to complete their education, including university studies, before marriage, which meant marrying later, and to have small families. Thereby, she constructed new ethnic feminine gender norms for a third generation of middle-class Moroccan women.

While the wives in the low segment of the middle class had successfully enlisted their husbands as partners in their mobility by instituting an egalitarian spousal relationship through the sharing of household labor, the women in the middle segment were unsuccessful in this pursuit. Their husbands rejected their attempts to establish such a relationship. These women had married Moroccan men, and they attributed their husbands' insistence on a traditional division of labor between spouses to their entrenched ethnic gender norms. The wives' attempts to transform spousal gendered relationships and the husbands' efforts to perpetuate them in their traditional segregated form exemplified how these relationships are contested, maintained, or redefined in the process of women's mobility into the middle class. This supports Edward Ransford and Jon Miller's contention that the upward mobility of women creates conflict between spouses because it challenges traditional gender roles.[22]

Why did the husbands of the women in the low segment of the middle class agree to be partners in their wives' mobility by sharing household duties, while these husbands did not? Perhaps for these husbands the threat to their patriarchal status by their wives' position in the middle segment of the middle class outweighed the financial benefits this mobility brought.

Sara made additional attempts to gain further equality in her spousal relationship by redefining the breadwinner role in the family. She considered herself a co-breadwinner, as equal a provider as her husband, because she earned a middle-class salary similar to his. Thus her income reduced somewhat the gender-specific roles within the household by blurring the distinctions between housewife and breadwinner. Sharon, the divorcée, was a single breadwinner, but her "good" salary and the supplements she earned from additional jobs gave her the feeling that her income was equal to that of a middle-class, male breadwinner. Furthermore, the organizational frameworks in which both women worked offered financial benefits that went beyond their salaries—advantages that men who were not employed in such a framework, such as Sara's husband, did not enjoy.

From what I could infer from her narrative, Sara's husband did not contest her attempts to redefine breadwinning as much as he did his wife's efforts to impose an egalitarian division of household labor. Why was he more accepting of her attempts to share his major masculine-gendered role, breadwinning, in the family than of her efforts to alter the division of household labor? One answer may lie in the fact that an increasing number of women in Israeli society, including second-generation Moroccan women, have entered the labor market,[23] and thus the normative distinction between the wife as homemaker and the husband as provider has weakened. This explanation concurs with findings that women's entry into the labor market transformed the norm of husbands as breadwinners and wives as homemakers among several first- and second-generation immigrant groups.[24]

## *Motherhood*

Like those in the low segment of the middle class, the women in the middle segment used motherhood as an arena to accomplish mobility not only for themselves but also for their children. They, too, rationalized the size of their families so that they could devote more time and energy to their work and invest more resources in fewer children.

However, these women were more explicit in their unanimous rejection of Moroccan mothering than were the women in the low segment. In its place, they constructed a motherhood that coincided with their perception of middle-class mothering as exemplified by Ashkenazi mothers. In their opinion, Israeli society values education and mobility, and a good mother supports these values by encouraging her children's educational and professional attainments—in short, their entrance into the middle class. These women's views reinforce scholarly claims that definitions of good mothering are determined by societal norms and social class,[25] and according to these women, by ethnicity as well.

Like the women in the low segment of the middle class, these women began rearing their children for mobility early by sending them to day care to encourage their intellectual development. Because they felt their children were well cared for while they worked full time, they did not see a conflict between their maternal role and their own mobility ambitions.

These mothers, like those in the low segment of the middle class, felt that they were the dominant parent in preparing their children for mobility. Besides being the one who inculcated in their children the values that would lead to their upward mobility, such as studying in order to acquire a middle-class profession, they felt they were the parent who made the major financial investment in creating a middle-class child. They did this by devoting their earnings to promoting their children's education. Here, again, their employment in the Municipal and National civil services was an advantage; they were able to finance these educational activities through special discounts and easy repayment plans that were available to civil service employees, but were not available to the women in the low segment of the middle class who did not work in such frameworks or, perhaps, to women who work for small private employers who cannot afford providing such opportunities for their employees. Since these women earned more than those in the low segment, they also had larger sums to devote to this purpose. Their greater earnings also enabled them to initiate a move to better neighborhoods than the women in the low segment could afford. These new areas offered larger apartments and provided each child with his and her own bedroom within which to study and prepare homework. These new neighborhoods also had better schools and, in Sharon's opinion, social networks composed of Ashkenazi children who would motivate her children to reach greater academic achievements.

## *The Body*

Like Ruth, the kindergarten teacher's assistant in the low segment of the middle class, Sara, too, was aware of the significance of the body as representing class and ethnicity. Like her, she also regarded the Moroccan body as superior, as more feminine, than the Ashkenazi middle-class woman's body. However, basing her opinion on her experience, she came to the conclusion that Moroccan women's corporeal capital loses its value because in contrast to Ashkenazi women's cultural capital it depreciates with age.

### *Emotions*

In contrast to the women in the low segment of the middle class, who evinced anxiety about their ability to remain in the middle class and to position their children within it, the women in the middle segment displayed confidence in their ability to maintain their middle-class position for themselves and their children. The obvious source of these women's sense of confidence was their employment in the civil services, which offered them job security, orderly advancement up the job hierarchy, financial benefits, and status. This noticeable difference in the sense of security between these two groups of women is important because it is further evidence that different emotions are linked to different positions in the middle class.

The women in the middle segment of the middle class were better able to overcome the constraints of their working-class origins than were those in the low segment. This was largely due to their steadfast ambition to be upwardly mobile as well as to their partial university education. It was this higher human capital that most distinguished them from the women in the lower segment of the middle class. Attaining this education was facilitated by the support offered by their employment frameworks that was not available to the women in the low segment. However, for reasons associated with Moroccan feminine ethnic norms, neither of the women in the middle segment completed their university studies, and this lack of a full academic degree was a barrier to their additional mobility.

## The Academic Professionals: The High Segment of the Middle Class

If the narratives of the women in the low and middle segments of the middle class told about the mobility of second-generation Moroccan women *into* the middle class, the narratives of the women in the high segment told about these women's mobility *within* the middle class. Essentially, the narratives of movement into the middle class may be considered "improvement narratives"[26] in that they told of self-improvements women born into the working class felt they needed to make to achieve their goal of middle-class mobility. To this end, their stories were infused with efforts devoted to "generating, accruing and/or displaying"[27] middle-class resources for themselves and their children. In contrast, the narratives of the women within the middle class can be considered "solidifying narratives" because they told of the efforts women born into that class made to fortify their position within it as well as to continue their own and their children's mobility. These two different types of narratives reflect the fact that these groups of women were and are in different structural positions within the Israeli class hierarchy.

## *Education*

Just as the material and cultural characteristics of the parents of the women in the two lower segments of the middle class interacted to affect the life chances of their daughters, so the material and cultural characteristics of the parents of the women in the high segment intertwined to create privileged opportunities for their daughters. The most obvious benefit of these parents' material resources was that they could more easily afford tuition and could provide their daughters with a full education, including university studies.

As among the women in the lower segments of the middle class, cultural factors such as parental values regarding education and the type and quality of this education molded parental attitudes and actions regarding their daughters' schooling. First and foremost, these parents instilled their daughters with the belief that education had intrinsic value. Furthermore, they took it for granted and articulated the idea that high academic achievement should be their daughters' primary endeavor in childhood and young adulthood and, consequently, freed them from all family responsibilities, particularly the need to help support their families. In addition, they made it clear that their daughters' education must include university studies; lesser attainments were not an option. I contend that these explicit educational objectives—as opposed to the vague ideas about, or lack of appreciation for, the importance of schooling for mobility that characterized the attitudes of most parents of the women in the lower segments of the middle class—contributed to the fact that these women did attain academic degrees.

The parents' own cultural capital also influenced their attitudes toward their daughters' schooling. Because the parents had acquired what at the time was considered a high-level education, they were able to oversee their daughters' education on a daily basis. Furthermore, they did not consider ethnic feminine gender norms to be a constraint on their educational goals for their daughters.

Unlike the women in the low and middle segments of the middle class, who followed a nonmainstream path to acquire their education, the women in the high segment followed the mainstream path. Like other women who come from advantageous backgrounds,[28] they, too, moved from one educational level to the next in a sequential age-appropriate progression and acquired a continuous, complete education that included elementary school, high school, and university—an academic institution with high social status.

The university provided them with a liberal and professional education and granted them degrees that enabled them to pursue academic professional work.

While the privileged background these women enjoyed from birth gave them preferential access to an academic education that led to their position in the high segment of the middle class, they themselves were also active in advancing their education. Both Naomi and Colette earned two academic degrees as well as teaching certificates. They regarded education as an accomplishment with intrinsic value and as a path to self-fulfillment, though its instrumental aspect was not totally absent.

If for the women in the two lower segments of the middle class education was a site for accomplishing mobility beyond the class position into which they were born, this was also true for the women in the high segment. However, these women acquired a higher level of education that was well above the postsecondary nonacademic, and partial university educations that typified the women in the low and middle segments of the middle class. In fact, these women's academic education—their higher human capital—was an outstanding factor that differentiated between them and the women in the lower segments. The importance of education for these women's class mobility supports findings that the longer women stay in the educational system, the greater their mobility.[29]

## *Employment*

For the women in the high segment of the middle class, as for those in the two lower segments, their employment was another arena for accomplishing mobility. They, too, chose to work within the female sector of the labor market, specifically in the academic professional labor market, as high school teachers. This choice of occupation reflects the trend among mothers, even those with academic professional qualifications, to opt for employment in this sector because it enables them to combine work and motherhood more easily than in the male sector of the academic professional labor market.[30] This compatibility between these women's choice of work and their mothering roles facilitated their full-time employment while their children were growing up.

Research has shown that one significant consequence of women's concentration in the female sector of the labor market is the limited range of incomes this sector provides.[31] This trend was evident in the salaries of the women in the three segments of the middle class: the semiprofessionals earned slightly more than minimum wage, while both the high-ranking clerical workers and the academic professionals received middle-class salaries, even though the latter had higher educational attainments. Through their incomes, the women in the high segment, like those in the lower segments, felt that they made a significant financial contribution to their families.

Both in acquiring their high educational levels and through academic professional work outside the home, the women in the high segment of the middle class continued a process that began among middle-class Jewish women in Morocco, but these Israeli-born women achieved more advanced schooling and entered higher segments of the labor market than had many of their predecessors both in Morocco and in Israel (see chapter 2). For these women, ethnic feminine gender norms already included education and employment and thus did not require the extensive reconstruction of such norms that was initiated among the women in the lower segments of the middle class.

## *Marriage and Gendered Spousal Relationships*

In contrast to the women in the low and middle segments of the middle class, the narratives of the women in the high segment suggested that class more than ethnicity influenced their constructions of both wifehood and motherhood. They spoke less of ethnic influences on their lives, such as being socialized to conform to ethnic feminine gender norms, than the women in the low and middle segments did. For example, marriage and motherhood seemed to be a lifestyle choice more than an ethnic dictate. Having married, the women took it for granted that wifehood included education and employment.

These women's efforts to turn their homes into a site where their strategies for mobility would be supported by their husbands were not successful; their spouses refused to be partners in their mobility aspirations by sharing the household division of labor so that the wives could devote time to advancing in their occupations. These wives could not renegotiate what they defined as their husband's entrenched ethnic patriarchal gender norms that advocated male authority and a gendered division of household labor. As mentioned earlier, the husbands of the women in the low segment did agree or acquiesce to being partners in their wives' mobility aspirations, while those in the middle segment did not. I suggest that the husbands' agreement or opposition was associated with their wives' position within the middle class; the higher the wives rose in the middle-class hierarchy, the more the husbands felt that their patriarchal position was threatened and the greater their unwillingness to accede to their wives' wishes. Since I did not interview the husbands, my explanation of their behavior is speculation, but because their willingness or refusal to be partners in their wives' upward mobility was important to the women, husbands' attitudes toward their spouse's mobility is worthy of in-depth study.

While these wives were not successful in enlisting their husbands as partners in their mobility, they were also less dependent upon them for this purpose because they hired domestic help in lieu of their husbands' participation in household labor. The women in the low segment of the middle class did not need to hire domestic help because their husbands shared household duties and they also gave the impression that allocating money for this purpose was not part of their lifestyle. Although the women in the middle segment did need help, they also gave the impression that hiring help was not an option (except Sharon, the high-ranking secretary, who hoped one day to be able to afford such help). In contrast, the women in the high segment of the middle class both needed this help and felt that it was a worthwhile expense. They seemed to take hiring domestic help for granted as part of the lifestyle of the segment of the middle class to which they belonged.

Like the women in the middle segment of the middle class, these women, too, blurred the dichotomy of homemaker and breadwinner even though they knew that their husbands earned more than they did. Again, these women's evaluation of their breadwinner role was a subjective expression of the importance they attached to their financial contribution to their family, rather than an objective appraisal of their addition to their family's finances.

## *Motherhood*

The women in the high segment of the middle class, like those in the lower segments, limited the size of their families in order to be able to invest more resources in their own mobility and in that of each child. Thus they had small- to moderate-sized families. However, unlike most of the women in the lower segments, these women did not consider Ashkenazi middle-class mothering as superior to their own mothering. Middle-class mothering was not a norm these women had to adopt or strive for; they did not need to trade one construction of motherhood for another because this was the only kind of motherhood they knew.

In practice, they were the epitome of middle-class mothering depicted by scholars.[32] They began their children's education in elementary school and it included university studies. Like their parents, who had set explicit, concrete educational goals for them, they set specific educational goals for their children. Indeed, all their children internalized their parents' wishes and were either doing their university studies or had completed them.

These women, like those in the lower segments of the middle class, viewed themselves as the principal and dominant parent in their children's education. They, too, used their incomes to further their children's education. This was expressed primarily in financing residential mobility so that they could provide their children with more comfortable living conditions, such as their own rooms in which to study, which would facilitate their educational achievements. These women moved into spacious houses in better neighborhoods, in contrast to the mothers in the lower segments of the middle class, who accomplished their residential mobility by moving into larger apartments.

### *Emotions*

Emotions related to class and mobility differed between the women in the low and middle segments and those in the high segment. While the stories of the women in the lower segments emphasized constraints to their mobility, a sense of wanting, of a struggle to overcome a variety of barriers in their move into the middle class, the narratives of the women in the high segment exuded a sentiment akin to elitism, a feeling of material security and privilege and of having the luxury of choices, opportunities, and alternatives about who and what they wanted to be. In fact, they appeared oblivious to many of the barriers to upward mobility the women in the lower segments of the middle class experienced, and they seemed to take for granted the advantageous access to the mobility resources they possessed. They also seemed unaware that they belonged to a minority among second-generation Moroccan immigrant women.

## Classed and Ethnicized Feminine Identities

Having compared the paths of mobility of the women in the three segments of the middle class, I focus now on the classed and ethnicized feminine identities they constructed through their mobility and how these affected their perception of their subordinate position vis-à-vis the hegemonic Ashkenazi women. While in real life these identities overlapped and were lived and experienced simultaneously by these women, I discuss them separately because they are different sources of identity.

For all the women in this study, being middle-class women involved not only being women but also being specific kinds of women; it involved constructing specific feminine identities that they associated with the middle class. Through their efforts they exemplified Reay's contention that women's class positions (and, I add, identities) are determined not only by economic factors but also by a "complicated mixture of the material, the discursive, psychological predispositions, and sociological dispositions."[33] Through this mixture these women "did"[34] middle-class femininities on a daily basis. Moreover, they strove to create consistency in these identities; they wanted to possess not just some, but all of the attributes they associated with being "complete," feminine middle-class women. Thus they acquired an education that would entitle them to a middle-class occupation, most strove to create gendered spousal relationships that conformed with their image of middle-class marital relationships, they practiced middle-class mothering, and some transformed the appearance of their bodies to coincide with their image of middle-class bodies. By "doing" middle-class femininities, they showed that feminine identities differ by class and in some aspects also by segments of the middle class.

The women used their own mobility resource—primarily their occupation—in determining their middle-class identities. Most began acquiring their occupation and the requisite education before they married, others acquired them after they married, and they all continued adding to these attainments throughout their lives. For the women in the middle and high segments of the middle class, their incomes added to their middle-class identity. Perhaps these women used their occupational/class ranking to determine their class position because they had invested so much effort in acquiring it that using it gave legitimacy to their investment.

The women also possessed middle-class values and culture that were central to their middle-class feminine identities. Primarily, these were directed to bringing about their own mobility and socializing their children toward mobility by instilling in them motivation for educational achievements and acquiring a profession. The importance of this type of influence on children has been corroborated in numerous studies that showed that mothers' education and occupation significantly influence and predict children's occupational mobility, especially those of daughters.[35] Emily Beller discovered that this influence existed even when mothers were unemployed housewives.[36] By their socializing influences, these mothers created a middle-class culture in their homes and were "critical agents in the production of family class and in the work of class mobility."[37] Through this "work of class mobility," they set the stage for the mobility of the third generation of Moroccans into and within this class and thereby enlarged the number of Moroccans in the middle class.

It is interesting that the women used a different criterion for determining their own class position, those of their husbands, and those of their families.

As mentioned, they measured their own class position primarily by their occupational attainments. In contrast, they measured their husband's class position by his income. Furthermore, they used both their own income and their husband's middle-class incomes in order to place their families within the middle class. This means that in the context of the debate about whether wives use their own, their husband's, or both of their class resources to determine the class position of their family (divorced women use their own),[38] these women's approach coincided with those of scholars who advocated using both spouses' resources when determining the class position of families.[39]

Although almost all of the husbands had lower educational attainments than their wives, they earned higher salaries, mostly because they were employed in the male sector of the labor market. These higher salaries enabled their families to enjoy the material benefits of a middle-class lifestyle (what Robert Erikson has called the "market situation" of the household[40]) that they would not have been able to afford on the basis of their wives' incomes alone.

In light of research indicating that Israelis tend to marry people with similar levels of education,[41] why did these women marry men with lower educational levels than their own? I contend that the answer lies in the intertwining of education and ethnic relations in Israeli society. The latest available statistics show that many second-generation Moroccan immigrant women have higher educational attainments than many second-generation Moroccan men.[42] Therefore, in the "marriage squeeze"[43] that ensues when these women search for educated Moroccan men, this "pool" is depleted quickly and Moroccan educated women have to "make do" with less educated Moroccan men—some who nevertheless offer middle-class incomes—or remain single. Theoretically, these women could have chosen Ashkenazi men, whom some preferred as husbands, with educations similar to theirs. However, their life experiences had taught them they would be rejected as spouses by Ashkenazi males because they are Moroccan. Therefore, marrying less educated Moroccan men offered these women both a middle-class income and shelter from ethnic discrimination and added to the attractiveness of Moroccan men as husbands.

The middle-class feminine identities these women constructed were not created in a vacuum, nor were they rooted in an abstract notion of class, but for most were formed against the backdrop of the subordinate and hegemonic relationship between them and Ashkenazi women. They were aware of the subordinate position they held in Israeli society vis-à-vis Ashkenazi women but were active in resisting attempts to define them as inferior and diligent in acquiring those attributes that would prevent others from defining them as such. Nevertheless, the feeling that Israeli society ascribes a subordinate position to Moroccan women was so palpable in all their narratives that I could not ignore the thought that their life stories would undoubtedly have been different had they belonged to the hegemonic group.

Theories about subordinate and hegemonic relationships between members of different groups, as well as critiques of these theories, have been dealt with thoroughly by others, both in a general context[44] and in the Israeli context regarding the relationship between Ashkenazim and Mizraḥim,[45] so there is no need for me to discuss them here. However, I do want to present three critiques that are particularly relevant to the topic of this study. My first argues against the assumption that resistance to dominant values by members of a subordinate group is inevitable. From the narratives of the women in this study, it was clear that they did not rebel against one of the dominant values or norms in Israeli society—that is, mobility through education and professionalization. On the contrary, they voluntarily and consciously adopted this norm because of the advantages it offered: self-fulfillment, self-empowerment, and a middle-class position in society. This critique supports Lawler's contention that the conclusions in research on subordinate/hegemonic relationships that present a "romanticized picture"[46] of "resistance and refusal"[47] and conjure up images of "a revolutionary stance, a sort of guerilla warfare against 'dominant' values'"[48] are not always justified.

My second critique argues that one should not assume that subordinate and hegemonic groups possess opposing characteristics, that they are either/or. The narratives in this study show that theories about subordination and hegemony should be more discriminating. They need to identify the areas in which members of subordinate groups (in this case, Moroccan women) consider themselves to be inferior to those in the hegemonic group (Ashkenazi women) and the areas in which they do not, because subordinate women may not feel that the hegemonic women are superior to them in all their attributes. For example, almost all the Moroccan women in this study considered their education, professional achievements, mothering, and how they conducted gendered spousal relationships to be inferior to those of Ashkenazi women because they were less conducive for mobility. However, they considered themselves equal to Ashkenazi women in their ethnic affiliation and superior to Ashkenazi women in their corporeal capital, as "better" or more feminine. Furthermore, Ruth, the kindergarten teacher's assistant, thought that Moroccan women were morally superior (less "lazy") to Ashkenazi women. Thus adopting a more differentiated approach to analyzing subordinate and hegemonic relationships may lead us to a more nuanced understanding of these relationships than the more simplistic approach of seeing them as opposites. This argument for a more discriminating approach has also been advocated by Harvey Goldberg and Chen Bram, who faulted subordination/hegemony theories for presenting subordinate and hegemonic groups as being too binary.[49]

My third critique also relates to adopting a more differentiated approach in analyzing subordinate/hegemonic relationships. The narratives showed that different structural locations within the middle-class hierarchy affect the relationship between subordinate and hegemonic women. Almost all of the women in the low and middle segments compared themselves to Ashkenazi women, who served as role models in defining the content of their middle-classed femininities. In contrast, the women in the high segment of the middle class did not make such comparisons. It was striking that their narratives included no explicit or implicit references to Ashkenazi women as superior to them. In fact, they regarded themselves as equals in terms of their mobility accomplishments—like Ashkenazi women, they were academic professionals in a high middle-class position and they maintained a middle-class lifestyle. Apparently, they also felt that their corporeal capital was equal to that of Ashkenazi women, because they did not compare their bodies with those of Ashkenazi women or find their own bodies inferior. This finding suggests that theories of subordination and hegemony need to specify not only the areas in which subordinate women feel that hegemonic women have superior traits but also in the eyes of whom. This also implies that under conditions of mobility, the perception of who is subordinate and who is hegemonic becomes dynamic; women who have acquired the traits of hegemonic women may feel they are no longer inferior in their mobility resources and that they are equal to hegemonic women.

If previously we saw how femininity is classed, we can now see how class is ethnicized, for these women constructed a new ethnic feminine identity in place of the more traditional one. They became part of a growing number of Moroccan women who identify themselves as middle-class and of middle-class women who identify themselves as Moroccan. Thereby they contributed to an ethnically diverse middle class composed not only of Ashkenazi women but also of a substantial number of Moroccan women, though Ashkenazi women still remained the dominant group within the middle class (see chapter 2, table 2.2).

The women in the low and middle segments of the middle class initiated major revisions in the constructions of their traditional ethnic femininity in the process of their mobility, while those in the high segment carried out significant but less extensive reconstructions. I argue that the changes in ethnic femininity these women initiated are central to Moroccan culture, because gender is at the core of culture and the social order.[50] Thus changes in ethnic femininity bring about changes in ethnic culture. These women's reconstruction of Moroccan femininity testifies to the dynamic and flexible nature of both ethnic femininity and ethnic culture that change according to social and historical contexts and women's desires.

This new femininity entailed a process of transition from ethnicity lived on a daily basis to one practiced on special occasions, essentially a symbolic ethnicity. Herbert Gans and others[51] claimed that ethnic identity among working-class immigrants in the United States is common, but by the third and fourth generation this identity becomes a matter of individual choice that is not expressed in everyday life, but in "ethnic behavior"[52] that assumes only symbolic value among the upwardly mobile. These changes ensue because "the old ethnic cultures serve no useful function for third generation ethnics."[53] Therefore, third and fourth generation ethnics "look for easy and intermittent ways"[54] of expressing their ethnic identity that do not interfere with other areas of their lives.

The women in this study made the transition in ethnic femininity from one lived on a daily basis to one expressed occasionally, to a symbolic ethnicity, because they concluded that their traditional femininity "served no useful function";[55] it was incompatible with their mobility goals. Thus, while the process of disengagement from everyday ethnicity and the transition to a symbolic ethnicity may be more characteristic of third- and fourth-generation immigrants, these narratives suggest that the desire to be mobile accelerates this process.

The symbolic practices these women preserved were, in Moroccan culture, gender specific to women, and therefore I contend that these women practiced not only a symbolic ethnicity but also a feminized symbolic ethnicity. For them, perpetuating these activities was one of the components of being a feminine Moroccan woman. These practices involved such activities as preparing Moroccan food for special occasions and holidays, such as the *Mimuna*, and arranging ceremonies like the *Henna*, the Moroccan engagement party that the mother of the bride organizes. The institution of this feminized symbolic ethnicity underlines the fact that women can function both as "keepers of the culture,"[56] as one of the social groups that are "social carriers" of ethnicity[57] and as agents of change.

While all the women in the study practiced this feminized symbolic ethnicity, they differed in their attachment to Moroccan culture. Irvin Long Child, in analyzing second-generation Italian Americans' individual ties to their ethnic identity, noted three psychological reactions among his respondents.[58] One was the "rebel reaction," in which his informants denied their own ethnicity and preferred an American identity. The second was an "in-group reaction," in which his respondents preferred their Italian identity and culture. The third, "apathetic reaction," typified those who were indifferent to both their Italian and American cultural identities. The reactions of the women in the present study to their ethnic identity cut across the three segments of the middle class; in other words, they were unaffected by the women's position in the middle class; some evinced a "rebel reaction" and some were apathetic, but none preferred their ethnic identity and culture to that of the wider Israeli society.

What sociological/anthropological factors, as opposed to psychological factors, affected these women's attachment to their ethnic culture? One influence was related to their socialization to Moroccan culture. As we learned from Sara's narrative (the high-ranking secretary), she was the only woman in the study who had been socialized by her mother to love her ethnic culture, and she continued to do so despite the changes she initiated in her ethnic feminine identity in order to accomplish mobility. The other women did not mention an active or intentional socialization to their Moroccan culture. This may partly explain why they did not express a positive affective attachment to their ethnicity.

I argue that these women's attachment to their ethnic culture was also determined by the costs they had to pay for identifying with their Moroccan ethnicity. Indeed, in the context of Israeli society, choosing a Moroccan ethnicity has real consequences that prevent such a choice from being "profitable." For almost all the women, such costs started early in life and were instilled in childhood through parents' stories of discrimination following their immigration and through their own experiences growing up. Later experiences, on the more intimate level of being rejected as potential marriage partners for Ashkenazi men, intensified the feeling that belonging to a subordinate ethnic group, rather than the hegemonic group, had drawbacks. Furthermore, choosing a Moroccan identity had costs in the workplace and hence for the occupational/class mobility of those women in the high segment of the middle class with further mobility aspirations. This implies that the costs are less for those who are content with their mobility achievements than for those with additional aspirations. For the women in this latter group, the cost of their ethnic identity is greater than that of their feminine gender identity. In other words, for such women the ethnic glass ceiling is more impenetrable than the gendered glass ceiling. The negative stereotypes and negative labeling that exist in Israeli society about Moroccan women add to the disadvantage of choosing a Moroccan feminine identity. These costs create an ethnic awareness of the "social distance"[59] that separates subordinate women from those in the hegemonic group. The costs of choosing a Moroccan feminine identity confirm the contention[60] that the freedom to choose one's ethnic identity or "ethnic options" is limited by structural factors, such as discrimination, which impose an ascribed identity, constrain this choice, and highlight the fact that "all ethnicities are not equal."[61] Together these costs prevent "being Moroccan" from being a "dime-store ethnicity,"[62] a cavalier ethnic identity that can be adopted or shed at will with little emotional involvement. This is particularly true because, according to these women, ethnicity, or being a Moroccan woman, still matters in Israeli society.

Social scientists have claimed that choosing an ethnic identity is a dual process of self-ascription and of ascription by others.[63] Portes and Rumbaut maintained that the process of self-identification among the second generation is more complex than that of the first because it often involves managing competing allegiances.[64] For the women in the current study, ethnic identity was determined first by others and then by self; most followed a pattern of being ascribed an identity by others, resistance or apathy, and then acceptance and self-ascription.

As Waters pointed out, at the same time that structural forces limit ethnic options, they may also sustain claims to an ethnic identity through the ideology of cultural pluralism.[65] Indeed, the shift from a melting pot ideology to one of cultural pluralism that occurred in Israel (see chapter 2) has sustained and supported claims to an ethnic identity and has led to expressions of ethnic culture that have increasingly been performed in public.[66] Such public displays have been more evident among the Mizraḥi groups than the Ashkenazi ones, which may indicate that the "cost" of expressing a subordinate ethnic identity in Israel has lessened. For Moroccans, the cost of claiming such an identity may have lessened even further in light of the fact that individual Moroccans have accomplished upward mobility, which has led to ethnic pride. This exemplifies the way external factors that occur in the wider society and internal factors that transpire within an immigrant group may affect the inclination to claim an ethnic identity.[67]

However, even though cultural pluralism made preserving ethnic identity acceptable and desirable, these second-generation immigrant women did not claim a dual identity or a hyphenated identity, as do some immigrant groups in the United States.[68] They were not concerned with how to be both Moroccan and Israeli; they showed a clear preference for an Israeli identity. They had a sense of belonging to the wider Israeli society through their identification with the same goals and concerns that they believe characterize other middle-class Israeli women outside their ethnic group, especially Ashkenazi middle-class women—the wish to study, to work, and to be mobile; the need and desire to contribute to their family's income; and the effort to create egalitarian spousal relationships. But what is most telling about their identification with Israeli society is their identification with a dominant norm of that society—upward mobility through education and professionalization.

As Portes pointed out, one should not assume that all immigrant groups or individuals identify with, and want to be, integrated into the wider society.[69] Some express separatist tendencies either by contributing toward the creation and perpetuation of ethnic enclaves or by practicing a reactive ethnicity.[70] However, these women's disapproval of such tendencies and their wholehearted desire to be part of mainstream Israeli society by identifying with one of its dominant norms serves as a force that integrates them into Israeli society. At the same time, this desire, and the fact that they could fulfill it, creates positive emotions toward the society,[71] strengthens its social cohesion, and limits the feelings of alienation and social schisms that in the past have led to demonstrations and violent protests among those first- and second-generation Mizraḥi immigrants, including Moroccan immigrants, who felt their mobility was blocked.[72]

## Human Agency, Structure, and Mobility

These women's use of various sites and social structures to achieve mobility, while, at the same time, constructing new classed and ethnicized feminine identities, exemplifies how in late modernity and postmodernity human agents interact with opportunities and constraints in the social structure to create new identities in order to achieve her goals.[73] Discussing the relationship between agency and structure, Ulrich Beck argued that when modernization reaches a certain level, individuals assert their agency to become "released" from traditional structural constraints in order to realize their unique self and through "the dynamic of individualization" create a "life of their own."[74] He contended that this desire to create a new identity is felt most by women who want to cast off ascribed roles and traditional expectations. However, he also pointed out that even with these new possibilities, women are not entirely free to choose their identities, for they are bound by new structural constraints that limit their choices and thereby their agency.

Indeed, the narratives of the women in this study revealed their efforts to loosen the hold of tradition, especially ethnic tradition, on their femininity in order to forge a new feminine identity that would enable them to achieve mobility. This process was more evident among the women in the low and middle segments of the middle class than among the women in the high segment, because the latter belonged to a social class that had already begun "detraditionalization"[75] in Morocco and so were at a more advanced stage of the process. However, the women in the low and middle segments did not have boundless options for creating a new feminine identity because their choices were dictated by their image of the classed and ethnicized femininity of the bulk of the women in the middle class, that is, Ashkenazi women. Thus, of the femininities from which these women could choose, they were limited to those they felt typified these hegemonic women. In essence, they exchanged one set of structural constraints for another. In contrast, the women in the high segment resembled Ashkenazi women more, but those who had additional mobility aspirations also faced the structural constraint of discrimination because of their ethnicity. These findings regarding the women in all segments of the middle class reinforce Beck's contention that even in late and postmodernity, human agents are limited by structural constraints of one kind or another.[76]

What accounts for these women's agency? A combination of explanations may explain this characteristic among Moroccan women in general. One explanation suggests that these women's agency received some license from the structure of patriarchal relationships common in Middle Eastern societies. I base this contention on research on Middle Eastern women that has claimed that while men have formal patriarchal authority over women, especially outside the home, women balance this authority by being dominant, exerting their agency, within the home.[77] What was unique about the women in this study was that they translated their dominance within the home into processes that had repercussions beyond the home; it facilitated their and their children's mobility.

A second explanation is economic and is based on the financial power that immigrant women have acquired as a result of entering the labor market. This explanation relies on research that claims that these women's greater contribution to the family budget through their work outside the home has usually given them greater equality in the home, including decisions regarding family finances.[78] Such immigrant women may have then socialized their daughters to exercise their own agency. This explanation applies more to mothers who worked after their immigration to Israel than to those who did not.

A third explanation, a cultural one, is rooted in Israeli society and refers to the ideology of popular feminism that has been prevalent in Israeli public discourse during these women's lifetime and aims at freeing women to assert their individuality. In their narratives, most of the women used concepts familiar to feminist discourse, such as having equal opportunities to study and work and expectations of having an egalitarian spousal relationship in order to fulfill themselves, in this context, by accomplishing mobility.

But are there additional explanations, more specific to these second-generation Moroccan immigrant women, that account for their ability to assert their agency in order to enter and to move upward within the middle class? Undoubtedly some psychological factors are at play, but these are not within the scope of this study. From a sociological and anthropological perspective, one explanation is their ability to identify a dominant norm in Israeli society that places great value on mobility acquired through education and a profession and their ability to identify the knowledge and skills required to achieve this goal.

Another explanation suggests that these women possessed a sense of more or stronger agency than other women have. Janet Saltzman Chafetz argued that perceptions about the extent of agency vary among women within a society.[79] She maintained that some categories of women—those in specific income, occupation, or racial and ethnic groups, or subcategories of the women in these groups—perceive that they have more "agenic power" and "agenic freedom" than others; they have "enhanced agency."[80] Applying Chafetz's theory to the women in this study leads to the conclusion that although they belonged to a subordinate ethnic group, they all felt they had greater agenic freedom and power than other women in their ethnic group, that they had more control over their ability to create "a life of their own"[81] in order to be mobile.

Focusing on what characterized the agency of these mobile women can lead us to speculate about what limited the agency of those who were nonmobile. Did they not identify with the norm of mobility through education and professionalization? Did they identify with it but feel unable to acquire the necessary knowledge and skills needed to achieve this goal? Stephen Steinberg, who addressed these questions in his study on race, ethnicity, and class in the United States, concluded that many immigrant groups identified with the American Dream of upward mobility but encountered different opportunity structures and obstacles to realizing that Dream and thus had different mobility outcomes.[82] Ann Swidler, in her discussion of the significance of culture and values on behavior (that I think applies to norms as well), stated that identifying or sharing values or norms is an insufficient explanation of behavior.[83] She argued that people may share values and aspirations, but may not have the "structural circumstances"[84] to acquire the knowledge and skills to achieve the goals that are valued.

In this study, Miriam, the kindergarten teacher's assistant, explained the tension between identifying with norms, but feeling that one does not have the agency to use "structural circumstances"[85] to turn these norms into action, when she said, "Maybe some Moroccans feel that 'their backs are up against a wall.' That they can't do what they want, that they can't send their children to the schools they want." In other words, nonmobiles may have the same values and norms as mobiles, but may feel that both their agency and their structural opportunities are limited.

In applying their agenic freedom and power, the women in this study used their agency and various social structures in new ways to achieve their mobility. In this sense they may be considered what Beck, as well as Mustafa Emirbayer and Ann Misch, referred to as innovators and pioneers,[86] because they sought to create new paths that others like them can follow. When these new paths are adopted by many—when they are used by increasing numbers of second-generation Moroccan immigrant women to enter and be mobile within the middle class—they become an institutionalized path by which women who belong to a subordinate group can accomplish middle-class mobility.

## A Comparative Perspective

There are two main areas in which the findings from this Israeli research have implications for a comparative approach to the study of mobility into and within the middle class among second-generation immigrant women from subordinate ethnic groups in other Western societies. The first has to do with the issues that proved to be significant in these women's upward mobility. These included the multiple sites the women used to achieve their mobility, the classed and ethnicized femininities they constructed in the process, the comparisons they made between their place in Israeli society and that of the women in the hegemonic group that had implications for their mobility accomplishments, and the appropriate age at which to determine their ultimate class achievements. While I maintain that these issues are equally meaningful in studies on the middle-class mobility of second-generation immigrant women from subordinate groups in other Western societies, additional research on this topic may raise other issues that may be equally meaningful or more so.

The second area that has implications for a comparative approach to studying the middle-class mobility of second-generation immigrant women from a subordinate group is almost a converse of the first. While I argue that the theoretical framework that derived from this Israeli study is applicable to second-generation immigrant women from subordinate groups in other Western societies, I am aware that one could claim that the Israeli case is unique. That is, one might argue that Moroccan women's mobility should be understood within the wider context that considers all Jewish immigrants—by virtue of their common ancestry, religion, and sense of peoplehood they share with all Jewish Israelis (the overwhelming majority)—as belonging to Israeli society despite their different ethnic/cultural origins.[87] Continuing this argument, one might claim that this a priori common denominator legitimizes Jewish immigrants' demands for acceptance, inclusion, and equal mobility opportunities and predisposes Israeli society to offer them membership and acceptance within it. However, as these women's narratives showed, in practice, this ideological stance did not eliminate the obstacles and constraints in their paths to their mobility and therefore does not detract from their impressive mobility attainments.

But how does a sense of belonging affect the mobility of second-generation immigrant women from a subordinate group in other Western societies? These multicultural societies, with their diverse racial, religious, and ethnic immigrants who differ from the hegemonic or native-born group, may not offer second-generation immigrant women from subordinate groups the feeling of inclusion and legitimacy to pursue their upward mobility goals as those that exist for Moroccan women in Israel. In fact, one often gets the impression from public discourse that while these societies support multiculturalism as an ideology or social program, they regard many immigrant groups as intruders, as strangers, in the deepest sense of the word. If so, will subordinate women's use of their agency over multiple social sites, their manipulation of social structures, and the classed and ethnicized femininities they create produce the same mobility results as those of the Moroccan women in this study? To be sure, multiculturalism is different in the United States and in Western Europe, as well as among the societies that compose the latter large bloc,[88] and the connection between mobility and multiculturalism is not the subject of this book. Nevertheless, these are legitimate questions to raise in light of the multiculturalism that does exist in these societies and in light of the constraints some second-generation immigrants from subordinate groups have experienced in several of these societies that have been expressed in alienation and riots when these immigrants have felt their upward mobility was blocked. These questions invite us to conduct additional research on the middle-class mobility of second-generation immigrant women from subordinate groups that can substantiate, elaborate, or qualify the theoretical conclusions of this study.

# *Methodology Appendix*
## Classifying the Women

I used Robert Erikson and John Goldthorpe's full-version class schema[1] to define class categories rather than the collapsed seven-class schema, because the collapsed version compressed the class categories in such a way that I "lost" some class distinctions that were important to this study. This is also the reason I did not use John Goldthorpe, Meir Yaish, and Vered Kraus's collapsed seven-class version of the Erikson and Goldthorpe class schema that they adjusted to Israeli society.[2]

Erikson and Goldthorpe's full-version class schema is as follows:

> Class I—higher-grade professionals, administrators, and officials; managers in large industrial establishments; and large proprietors. Class II—lower-grade professionals, administrators, and officials; higher-grade technicians; managers in small industrial establishments; and supervisors of non-manual employees. Class IIIa—routine non-manual employees and higher grade (administration and commerce). Class IIIb—routine non-manual employees and lower grade (sales and services). Classes IVa—small proprietors, artisans, etc., with employees. Class IVb—small proprietors, artisans, etc., without employees. Classes IVc—includes farmers and smallholders and other self-employed workers in primary production. Class V—lower-grade technicians and supervisors of manual workers. Class VI—skilled manual workers. Class VIIa—semi- and unskilled manual workers (not in agriculture, etc.). Class VIIb—agricultural and other workers in primary production.[3]

I also used Erikson and Goldthorpe's full-version class schema to assign the women into hierarchical class positions. While this schema is based on types of employment relationships and the different benefits that these relationships generate, rather than primarily on the people filling these positions, I think that using it as I have does not lead to distortions of their approach. This view is based on Erikson and Goldthorpe's observation that while "the schema is intended ultimately to apply to *positions* . . . rather than to *persons* . . . it is difficult to avoid referring to actual incumbents,"[4] as well as on their comment that though their schema is not a hierarchical model, "good grounds" could be made for introducing a "three-fold hierarchical division" into the schema.[5] Because this schema is an ideal-type model that I thought did not always reflect the class positions of the women in this study, I also referred to education, a major mobility attainment, to gain a fuller, more complete guide to placing the women in their class positions. In addition, I referred to the latest version of the Israeli government's Standard Classification of Occupations for a more detailed breakdown of the occupations that I included in the middle class.[6] This classification is more specific than the Erikson and Goldthorpe schema and is adapted to Israeli society.

In my study I placed those women who were academic professionals in the high segment of the middle class. These were women who were high school teachers with two academic degrees and teaching certificates. Their position corresponded to the upper level of Class II in the Erikson and Goldthorpe schema. I placed high-ranking secretaries in the middle segment of the middle class. In my research these were women who held high-ranking clerical positions in the Municipal and National civil services and were not only secretaries but also performed administrative duties. They had high school matriculation certificates and a partial academic education. Their position corresponded with what I considered the upper level of Class IIIa in the schema. I placed the semiprofessionals in the low segment of the middle class. In my study these were women who were kindergarten teachers' assistants. They had a partial or complete high school education and may or may not have had a matriculation certificate, but they had taken courses of two or three years in a postsecondary, nonacademic institution that granted them accreditation certificates to work in their field. Their position corresponded to what I considered low-level positions in Class IIIa. They are referred to as associate professionals in the Israeli government's Standard Classification of Occupations.[7]

In allocating the women into the various segments of the middle class, two dilemmas arose. One was in regard to the class position of high-ranking clerical workers. According to the Israeli government's Standard Classification of

Occupations and to research on clerical work,[8] this category includes a wide range of positions. Some are simple clerical jobs, and the women employed in them do elementary clerical work in small offices; they may have a complete high school education and perhaps a high school matriculation certificate and earn a minimum wage. But others, also defined as clerical workers, hold secretarial positions with a great deal of autonomy, authority, and administrative/managerial responsibilities in large bureaucratic organizations, such as the Municipal and National civil services, corporations, and the like. As Erikson and Goldthorpe argued, these are positions in which employees "exercise *delegated authority* or *specialized knowledge and expertise* in the interests of their employing organization."[9] Since the women I found in clerical occupations who suited the criteria for this study were high-ranking secretaries in the Municipal and National civil service, with matriculation certificates, and some academic education, and since they filled administrative duties, I solved this dilemma by placing them in the middle sector of the middle class.

The second dilemma concerned the class position of semiprofessionals. Again, according to the Israeli government's Standard Classification of Occupations, this category, too, includes a variety of occupations. It includes work that perhaps does not require a high school matriculation certificate, but usually does require a postsecondary nonacademic education of two or three years for accreditation. Since the women I found who suited my criteria for inclusion in the study were kindergarten teachers' assistants who had full or almost full high school educations, but did not have a matriculation certificate and were required to study at a nonacademic postsecondary institution for two years, as well as take part in continuing education courses in order to improve their professional knowledge, I classified them as belonging to the low segment of the middle class.

# *Notes*

## CHAPTER 1

1. Clifford Geertz, *After the Fact: Two Countries, Four Decades, One Anthropologist* (Cambridge, MA: Harvard University Press, 1995), 61.

2. Floya Anthias and Gabriella Lazaridis, "Introduction: Women on the Move in Southern Europe," in *Gender and Migration in Southern Europe*, ed. Floya Anthias and Gabriella Lazaridis (Oxford and New York: Berg, 2000), 1–15; Stephen Castles and Mark J. Miller, *The Age of Migration* (Houndsmills, Basingtoke, Hampshire, and London: Macmillan, 1993); Eleonore Kofman, "Female 'Birds of Passage' a Decade Later: Gender and Immigration in the European Union," *International Migration Review* 33, no. 2 (1999): 269–300.

3. *Demographic and Social Statistics* (New York: United Nations, 2008).

4. Anthias and Lazaridis, "Introduction"; Pierrette Hondagneu-Sotelo, "Gender and Immigration," in *Gender and U.S. Immigration*, ed. Pierrette Hondagneu-Sotelo (Berkeley: University of California Press, 2003), 3–20; Janet Salaff and Arent Greve, "Women That Move: International Migration from the PRC to Canada and the Negotiation of Gendered Job Opportunities," 2002, http://homes.chass.utoronto.ca/~salaff/PRC_GenMig.PDF.

5. Maurice Crul and Hans Vermeulen, "The Second Generation in Europe," *International Migration Review* 37, no. 4 (2003): 965–86; Yaacov Nahon, "Women: Education, Occupation, and Salary," in *Ethnic Communities in Israel: Socio-Economic Status*, ed. S. N. Eisenstadt, Moshe Lissak, and Yaacov Nahon (Jerusalem: Jerusalem Institute for Israel Studies, 1993), 90–103 (Hebrew); Larissa Remennick, "Providers, Caregivers, and Sluts: Women with a Russian Accent in Israel," *Nashim*, no. 8 (Fall 2004): 87–115; Marta Tienda and Karen Booth, "Gender, Migration, and Social Change," *International Sociology* 6, no. 1 (1991): 51–72.

6. Max Weber, "Class, Status, Party," in *Economy and Society*, vol. 2, ed. Gunther Roth and Claus Wittich (New York: Bedminster Press, 1968), 927.

7. Andrew Sayer, *The Moral Significance of Class* (Cambridge: Cambridge University Press, 2005).

8. I am indebted to Turner for his idea of a connection between emotions and the social structure.

9. E.g., M. Sharon Jeannotte, Dick Stanley, Ravi Pendakur, Bruce Jamieson, Maureen Williams, and Amanda Aizelwood, *Buying In or Dropping Out: The Public Policy Implications of Social Cohesion Research* (Ottawa: Department of Canadian Heritage, 2002); Jane Jensen, *Mapping Social Cohesion: The State of Canadian Research* (Ottawa: Canadian Policy Research Networks, 1998); Andrew Markus and Arunachalam Dharmalingam, "Attitudinal Divergence in a Melbourne Region of High Immigrant Concentration: A Case Study," *People and Place* 15, no. 4 (2007): 38–48.

10. Pat Mahony and Christine Zmroczek, eds., *Class Matters: "Working-Class" Women's Perspectives on Social Class* (London and Bristol, PA: Taylor and Francis, 1997); Beverley Skeggs, *Formations of Class and Gender* (London and Thousand Oaks, CA: Sage, 1997); Carolyn Kay Steedman, *Landscape for a Good Woman: A Story of Two Lives* (New Brunswick, NJ: Rutgers University Press, 1997); Valerie Walkerdine, "Reclassifying Upward Mobility: Femininity and the Neo-liberal Subject," *Gender and Education* 15, no. 3 (2003): 237–48.

11. Steph Lawler, *Mothering the Self* (London and New York: Routledge, 2000), 79.

12. Ibid., 121.

13. Walkerdine, "Reclassifying Upward Mobility," 238.

14. Lawler, *Mothering the Self*; Diane Reay, "A Risky Business? Mature Working-Class Women Students and Access to Higher Education," *Gender and Education* 15, no. 3 (2003): 301–19; Skeggs, *Formations of Class and Gender*.

15. Louise Archer and Carole Leathwood, "New Times—Old Inequalities: Diverse Working-Class Femininities in Education," *Gender and Education* 15, no. 3 (2003): 227–35.

16. Suki Ali, "'To Be a Girl': Culture and Class in Schools," *Gender and Education* 2, no. 3 (2003): 269–84.

17. Herbert J. Gans, "Symbolic Ethnicity: The Future of Ethnic Groups and Cultures in America," *Ethnic and Racial Studies* 2, no. 1 (1979): 5.

18. E.g., Nathan Glazer and Daniel Patrick Moynihan, *Beyond the Melting Pot: The Negroes, Puerto Ricans, Jews, Italians, and Irish of New York City* (Cambridge, MA: MIT Press, 1963); Howard F. Stein and Robert F. Hill, *The Ethnic Imperative: Examining the New White Movement* (University Park: Pennsylvania State University Press, 1977); Mary C. Waters, *Ethnic Options* (Berkeley: University of California Press, 1990).

19. Josephine Beoku-Betts, "We Got Our Way of Cooking Things," *Gender and Society* 9 (1995): 535–55; Janet Mancini Billson, *Keepers of Culture* (New York: Lexington, 1995); Beverly Mizrachi, "The Henna-Maker: A Moroccan Immigrant Woman Entrepreneur in an Ethnic Revival," in *Research in the Sociology of Work*, vol. 15, ed. Lisa A. Keister (Amsterdam: Elsevier, 2005), 257–79; Rachel Sharaby, *The Mimuna Holiday: From Periphery to the Center* (Tel Aviv: Hakibbutz Hameuchad, 2009) (Hebrew).

20. Ann Swidler, "Culture in Action: Symbols and Strategies," *American Sociological Review* 51 (1986): 273.

21. Georgina Tsolidis, *Educating Voula: A Report on Non-English-Speaking Background Girls and Education* (Melbourne: Victorian Ministerial Advisory Committee on Multicultural and Migrant Education, 1986).

22. Maurice Crul and Jeroen Doomernik, "The Turkish and Moroccan Second Generation in the Netherlands: Divergent Trends between and Polarization within the Two Groups," *International Migration Review* 37, no. 4 (2003): 1039–64.

23. I am aware that the terms *hegemonic* and *subordinate* come from the field of colonialism studies, but they have been used in other contexts that refer to relationships of superiority and inferiority. I use them here in the latter context. See Floya Anthias and Nira Yuval-Davis, "Contextualizing Feminism: Gender, Ethnic, and Class Divisions," *Feminist Review* 15 (1983): 62–75; Harriet Bradley, *Fractured Identities: Changing Patterns of Inequality* (Cambridge: Polity Press, 1996); Avtar Brah, "Time, Place, and Others: Discourses of Race, Nation, and Ethnicity," *Sociology* 28, no. 3 (1994): 805–13.

24. Skeggs, *Formations of Class and Gender*, 6.

25. Steedman, *Landscape for a Good Woman*, 20.

26. Richard D. Alba and Victor Nee, "Rethinking Assimilation Theory for a New Era of Immigration," *International Migration Review* 31, no. 4 (2003): 826–74; Crul and Doomernik, "The Turkish and Moroccan Second Generation in the Netherlands"; Crul and Vermeulen, "The Second Generation in Europe"; Jaap Dronkers and Fenella Fleischman, "The Effects of Social and Labour Market Policies of EU Countries on the Socio-Economic Integration of First and Second Generation Immigrants from Different Countries of Origin," paper presented at the Meeting of International Sociological Association Research Committee on Social Stratification and Mobility, Brno, Czech Republic, May 25–27, 2007; Philip Kasinitz, John H. Mollenkopf, and Mary C. Waters, eds., *Becoming New Yorkers* (New York: Russell Sage Foundation, 2004); Philip Kasinitz, John H. Mollenkopf, Mary C. Waters, and Jennifer Holdaway, *Inheriting the City: The Children of Immigrants Come of Age* (New York: Russell Sage Foundation; Cambridge, MA: Harvard University Press, 2008); Gretchen Livingston and Joan R. Kahn, "An American Dream Unfulfilled: The Limited Mobility of Mexican Americans," *Social Science Quarterly* 83, no. 4 (2002): 1003–13; Joel Perlmann and Roger Waldinger, "Second Generation Decline? Children of Immigrants, Past and Present: A Reconsideration," *International Migration Review* 31, no. 4 (1997): 893–922; Alejandro Portes, "Children of Immigrants: Segmented Assimilation and Its Determinants," in *The Economic Sociology of Immigration: Essays on Networks, Ethnicity, and Entrepreneurship*, ed. Alejandro Portes (New York: Russell Sage Foundation, 1995), 248–81; Alejandro Portes, ed., *The New Second Generation* (New York: Russell Sage Foundation, 1996); Alejandro Portes and Rubén G. Rumbaut, *Immigrant America: A Portrait*, 2nd ed. (Berkeley: University of California Press, 1996); Alejandro Portes and Min Zhou, "The New Second Generation: Segmented Assimilation and Its Variants," *Annals of American Academy of Political and Social Sciences* 530 (1993): 74–96; Christiane Timmerman, Els Vanderwaeren, and Maurice Crul, "The Second Generation in Belgium," *International Migration Review* 37, no. 4 (2003): 1065–89; Roger Waldinger and Joel Perlmann, "Second Generations: Past, Present, Future," *Journal of Ethnic and*

*Migration Studies* 24 (January 1998): 5–24; Mary C. Waters, "Ethnic and Racial Identities of Second-Generation Black Immigrants in New York City," in *The New Second Generation*, ed. Alejandro Portes (New York: Russell Sage Foundation, 1996), 170–97; Susanne Worbs, "The Second Generation in Germany: Between School and Labor Market," *The International Migration Review* 37, no. 4 (2003): 1020–39.

27. Julie Bettie, "Exceptions to the Rule: Upwardly Mobile White and Mexican American High School Girls," *Gender and Society* 16, no. 3 (2002): 403–22; Kimberly Goyette and Yu Xie, "Educational Expectations of Asian-American Youths: Determinants and Ethnic Differences," *Sociology of Education* 72, no. 1 (1999): 22–36; Grace Kao and Marta Tienda, "Optimism and Achievement: The Educational Performance of Immigrant Youth," *Social Science Quarterly* 76, no. 1 (1995): 1–20; Stacey J. Lee, "The Road to College: Hmong American Women's Pursuit of Higher Education," *Harvard Educational Review* 67, no. 4 (1997): 803–28; Vivian Louie, "Parents' Aspirations and Investment: The Role of Social Class in the Educational Experiences of 1.5 and Second-Generation Chinese Americans," *Harvard Educational Review* 71, no. 3 (2001): 438–74; Alejandro Portes and Rubén G. Rumbaut, *Legacies: The Story of the Immigrant Second Generation* (Berkeley: University of California Press; New York: Russell Sage Foundation, 2001).

28. Lyn Tett, "'I'm Working Class and Proud of It': Gendered Experiences of Non-Traditional Participants in Higher Education," *Gender and Education* 12, no. 2 (2000): 183–94.

29. Mizrachi, "The Henna-Maker."

30. Government of Israel, *Census* (Jerusalem: Central Bureau of Statistics, 1995) (Hebrew).

31. Ibid.; Government of Israel, *Census* (Jerusalem: Central Bureau of Statistics, 1983) (Hebrew); Henriette Dahan-Kalev, Niza Yanay, and Niza Berkovitch, eds., *Women of the South: Space, Periphery, and Gender* (Beer Sheva: Ben Gurion Research Institute, Ben Gurion University of the Negev, 2005) (Hebrew).

32. Rosemary Crompton and John Scott, "Introduction: The State of Class Analysis," in *Renewing Class Analysis*, ed. Rosemary Crompton, Fiona Devine, Mike Savage, and John Scott (Oxford and Malden, MA: Blackwell, 2000), 1–16; Robert Erikson and John H. Goldthorpe, *The Constant Flux* (Oxford: Clarendon Press, 1993); Geoff Payne and Pamela Abbott, *The Social Mobility of Women: Beyond Male Mobility Models* (London: Falmer, 1990).

33. Karl Mannheim, *Essays on the Sociology of Knowledge*, ed. Paul Kecskemeti (London: Routledge and Kegan Paul, 1952).

34. Simon Duncan, "Mothering, Class, and Rationality," *Sociological Review* 53, no. 1 (2005): 60.

35. E.g., Sami Shalom Chetrit, *The Mizrahi Struggle in Israel: Between Oppression and Liberation, Identification and Alternative, 1948–2003* (Tel Aviv: Am Oved, 2004) (Hebrew); Hannan Hever, Yehouda Shenhav, and Pnina Motzafi-Haller, eds., *Mizrahim in Israel: A Critical Observation into Israel's Ethnicity* (Jerusalem and Tel Aviv: Van Leer Jerusalem Institute and Hakibbutz Hameuchad, 2002) (Hebrew); Yehouda Shenhav, *The Arab Jews: Nationalism, Religion, and Ethnicity* (Tel Aviv: Am Oved, 2004) (Hebrew).

36. Leslie McCall, "The Complexity of Intersectionality," *Signs* 30, no. 3 (2005): 1771–800.

37. Zygmunt Bauman, "Figures of Modernity," in *The Bauman Reader*, ed. Peter Beilharz (Malden, MA: Blackwell, 2001), 200–230; Ulrich Beck, *Risk Society: Towards a New Modernity* (London: Sage, 1992); Mary Brinton, *Women and the Economic Miracle* (Berkeley: University of California Press, 1993); Anthony Giddens, *Modernity and Self-Identity: Self and Society in the Late Modern Age* (Stanford, CA: Stanford University Press, 1991).

38. Barney G. Glaser and Anselm Strauss, *The Discovery of Grounded Theory* (Chicago: Aldine, 1971).

## CHAPTER 2

1. I have included 1956 in the period of the mass immigration because of the large number of Moroccan Jews who immigrated to Israel by that year.

2. Nancy Foner, "The Immigrant Family: Cultural Legacies and Cultural Changes," *International Migration Review* 31, no. 4 (1997): 962.

3. Moshe Lissak, *The Mass Immigration in the Fifties: The Failure of the Melting Pot Policy* (Jerusalem: Bialik Institute, 1999), 7 (Hebrew).

4. Ibid.

5. S. N. Eisenstadt, *Israeli Society* (New York: Basic Books, 1967), 62.

6. Amir Ben-Porat, *Where Are All Those Bourgeoisies? The History of the Israeli Bourgeoisie* (Jerusalem: Magnes Press, Hebrew University, 1999) (Hebrew); Henry Rosenfeld and Shulamit Carmi, "The Privatization of Public Means: The State-Made Middle Class and the Realization of Family Value in Israel," in *Kinship and Modernization in Mediterranean Society*, ed. Jean George Peristiany (Rome: Center for Mediterranean Studies, American Universities Field Staff, 1976), 131–59; Ronen Shamir, "Jewish Bourgeoisie in Colonial Palestine: Outline for a Research Agenda," *Israeli Sociology* 3, no. 1 (2000): 133–49 (Hebrew).

7. Lissak, *The Mass Immigration in the Fifties*, 7.

8. Ibid.

9. Eliezer Ben-Rafael and Stephen Sharot, *Ethnicity, Religion, and Class in Israeli Society* (Cambridge: Cambridge University Press, 1991); Harvey Goldberg and Chen Bram, "Sephardic/Mizrahi/Arab-Jews: Reflections on Critical Sociology and the Study of Middle Eastern Jewries within the Context of Israeli Society," *Studies in Contemporary Jewry* 22 (2007): 227–56.

10. Eisenstadt, *Israeli Society*; Michael Inbar and Chaim Adler, *Ethnic Integration in Israel: A Comparative Study of Moroccan Brothers Who Settled in France and Israel* (New Brunswick, NJ: Transaction Books, 1977).

11. Aziza Khazzoom, *Shifting Ethnic Boundaries and Inequality in Israel* (Stanford, CA: Stanford University Press, 2008).

12. Yossi Shavit, "Segregation, Tracking, and the Educational Attainments of Minorities: Arabs and Oriental Jews in Israel," *American Sociological Review* 55 (1990): 115–26; Abraham Yogev, Idit Livneh, and Oren Pizmony-Levy, "Non-Academic Post-Secondary Education in Israel: Separate but Equal?" *Israeli Sociology* 11, no. 2

(2010): 363–89 (Hebrew); Ephraim Yuchtman-Yaar, "Differences in Ethnic Patterns of Socioeconomic Achievements in Israel: A Neglected Aspect of Structured Inequality," *International Review of Modern Sociology* 15 (1985): 99–116.

13. Deborah Bernstein and Shlomo Swirski, "The Rapid Economic Development of Israel and the Emergence of the Ethnic Division of Labour," *British Journal of Sociology* 33, no. 1 (1982): 64–85; Lissak, *The Mass Immigration in the Fifties*; Sammy Smooha, *Israel: Pluralism and Conflict* (Berkeley: University of California Press, 1978).

14. Yinon Cohen and Yitchak Haberfeld, "Second-Generation Jewish Immigrants in Israel: Have the Ethnic Gaps in Schooling and Earnings Declined?" *Ethnic and Racial Studies* 21, no. 3 (1998): 507–29; Momi Dahan, "Inequality in Israel: The Role of Education," *Economic Quarterly* 51, no. 2 (2004): 187–98 (Hebrew).

15. Moshe Semyonov and Noah Lewin-Epstein, "The Impact of Parental Transfers on Living Standards of Married Children," *Social Indicators Research* 54, no. 2 (2001): 115–25.

16. Vered Kraus, "Social Segregation in Israel as a Function of Objective and Subjective Attributes of the Ethnic Groups," *Sociology and Social Research* 69, no. 1 (1984): 50–71; Seymour Spilerman and J. Habib, "Development Towns in Israel: The Role of Community in Creating Ethnic Disparities in Labor Force Characteristics," *American Journal of Sociology* 81 (1976): 781–812.

17. Deborah Bernstein, "Conflict and Protest: The Case of the Black Panthers of Israel," *Youth and Society* 16, no. 2 (1984): 129–52; Yoav Peled, "Towards a Redefinition of Jewish Nationalism in Israel? The Enigma of *Shas*," *Ethnic and Racial Studies* 21, no. 4 (1998): 703–28.

18. Beverly Mizrachi, "Elite Educational Institutions and the Recruitment of Women into National Elite Positions in Israel," *Israel Social Science Research* 12, no. 2 (1997): 93–109.

19. Sami Shalom Chetrit, *The Mizrahi Struggle in Israel: Between Oppression and Liberation, Identification and Alternative, 1948–2003* (Tel Aviv: Am Oved, 2004) (Hebrew); Henriette Dahan-Kalev, "You're So Pretty: You Don't Look Moroccan," *Israel Studies* 6, no. 1 (2001): 1–13; Khazzoom, *Shifting Ethnic Boundaries and Inequality in Israel*; Pnina Motzafi-Haller, "Scholarship, Identity, and Power: Mizrachi Women in Israel," *Signs* 26, no. 3 (2001): 697–735; Edward W. Said, *Orientalism* (London: Penguin Books, 1995).

20. E.g., Cohen and Haberfeld, "Second-Generation Jewish Immigrants in Israel."

21. Yinon Cohen and Yitchak Haberfeld, "Gender, Ethnic, and National Earnings Gaps in Israel: The Role of Rising Inequality," Discussion Paper No. 5-2003 (Tel Aviv: Tel Aviv University, The Pinhas Sapir Center for Development, 2003), 2.

22. Cohen and Haberfeld, "Second-Generation Jewish Immigrants in Israel"; Noah Lewin-Epstein and Moshe Semyonov, "Ethnic Group Mobility in the Israeli Labor Market," *American Sociological Review* 51, no. 3 (1986): 342–51; Sammy Smooha and Vered Kraus, "Ethnicity as a Factor in Status Attainment in Israel," *Research in Social Stratification and Mobility* 4 (1985): 151–75.

23. Deborah Bernstein, "Oriental and Ashkenazi Jewish Women in the Labor Market," in *Calling the Equality Bluff: Women in Israel*, ed. Barbara Swirski and

Marilyn P. Safir (New York: Pergamon Press, 1991), 192–97; Yaacov Nahon, "Women: Education, Occupation, and Salary," in *Ethnic Communities in Israel: Socio-Economic Status*, ed. S. N. Eisenstadt, Moshe Lissak, and Yaacov Nahon (Jerusalem: Jerusalem Institute for Israel Studies, 1993), 90–103 (Hebrew).

24. Bernstein, "Oriental and Ashkenazi Jewish Women in the Labor Market"; Nahon, "Women: Education, Occupation, and Salary."

25. Ben-Rafael and Sharot, *Ethnicity, Religion, and Class in Israeli Society*; Peled, "Towards a Redefinition of Jewish Nationalism in Israel?"

26. Ben-Rafael and Sharot, *Ethnicity, Religion, and Class in Israeli Society*, 33; Peled, "Towards a Redefinition of Jewish Nationalism in Israel?" 710.

27. Meir Yaish, "Class Structure in a Deeply Divided Society: Class and Ethnic Inequality in Israel," *British Journal of Sociology* 52, no. 3 (2001): 409–38.

28. Hanna Ayalon, Eliezer Ben-Rafael, and Stephen Sharot, "The Impact of Stratification: Assimilation or Ethnic Solidarity," *Research in Social Stratification and Mobility* 7 (1988): 305–26; Ben-Rafael and Sharot, *Ethnicity, Religion, and Class in Israeli Society*; Smooha, *Israel: Pluralism and Conflict.*

29. Sammy Smooha, "Class, Ethnic, and National Cleavages and Democracy in Israel," in *Israeli Democracy under Stress*, ed. Ehud Sprinzak and Larry Diamond (Boulder, CO: Lynne Rienner, 1993), 324.

30. Dan Horowitz and Moshe Lissak, *Trouble in Utopia* (Albany: State University of New York Press, 1989).

31. Chetrit, *The Mizrahi Struggle in Israel.*

32. Bernstein, "Conflict and Protest"; Shlomo Hasson, *Urban Social Movements in Jerusalem: The Protest of the Second Generation* (Jerusalem: State University of New York Press, in cooperation with the Jerusalem Institute for Israeli Studies, 1993).

33. Peled, "Towards a Redefinition of Jewish Nationalism in Israel?"

34. Chetrit, *The Mizrahi Struggle in Israel.*

35. Yariv Zfati, "The Ethnic Genie in Israel: In the Bottle on a Low Flame," *Megamot: Social Science Quarterly* 40, no. 1 (1999): 5–30 (Hebrew).

36. Yochanan Peres, "Ethnic Relations in Israel," *American Journal of Sociology* 76, no. 6 (1971): 1021–47.

37. Harvey Goldberg, "Historical and Cultural Dimensions of Ethnic Phenomena in Israel," in *Studies in Israeli Ethnicity*, ed. Alex Weingrod (New York: Gordon and Breach, 1985), 179–200; Judith L. Goldstein, "Iranian Identity in Israel: The Performance of Identity," in *Immigration to Israel*, ed. Elazar Leshem and Judith T. Shuval (New Brunswick, NJ: Transaction Publishers, 1998), 387–407; Moshe Lissak, *The Mass Immigration in the Fifties: The Failure of the Melting Pot Policy* (Jerusalem: Bialik Institute, 1999); Beverly Mizrachi, "The Henna-Maker: A Moroccan Immigrant Woman Entrepreneur in an Ethnic Revival," in *Research in the Sociology of Work*, vol. 15, ed. Lisa A. Keister (Amsterdam: Elsevier, 2005), 257–79; Alex Weingrod, "Recent Trends in Israeli Ethnicity," *Ethnic and Racial Studies* 2, no. 1 (1979): 55–65.

38. Hanna Ayalon, Eliezer Ben-Rafael, and Stephen Sharot, "Class Consciousness in Israel," *International Journal of Comparative Sociology* 28, nos. 3–4 (1987): 158–73; Amir Ben-Porat, "Class Structure in Israel: From Statehood to the 1980s,"

*British Journal of Sociology* 43, no. 2 (1992): 225–38; Eisenstadt, *Israeli Society*; Tally Katz-Gerro and Yossi Shavit, "Lifestyle and Social Class in Israel," *Israeli Sociology* 1, no. 1 (1998): 91–115 (Hebrew); Moshe Lissak, *Social Mobility in Israeli Society* (Jerusalem: Israel Universities Press, 1969) (Hebrew); Smooha, "Class, Ethnic, and National Cleavages and Democracy in Israel"; Ephraim Yaar, "Private Entrepreneurship as a Path to Socio-Economic Mobility: An Additional Look at Ethnic Stratification in Israel," in *Stratification in Israeli Society: Ethnic, National, and Class Cleavages*, vol. 1, ed. Moshe Lissak (Tel Aviv: Open University of Israel, 1989), 386–428 (Hebrew); Yaish, "Class Structure in a Deeply Divided Society."

39. Uri Cohen and Nissim Leon, "Concerning the Question of the Mizraḥi Middle Class," *Alpayim* 32 (2008): 83–101 (Hebrew).

40. Smooha, "Class, Ethnic, and National Cleavages and Democracy in Israel," 313.

41. Abraham Yogev and Rina Shapira, "Ethnicity, Meritocracy, and Credentialism in Israel: Elaborating the Credential Society Thesis," *Research in Social Stratification and Mobility* 6 (1987): 187–212.

42. Lissak, *The Mass Immigration in the Fifties*, 9.

43. Anthropologists have been drawn to studying Moroccans in Israel somewhat more than have sociologists. The few sociological studies on Moroccans in Israel can be found in Eliezer Ben-Rafael, *The Emergence of Ethnicity* (Westport, CT: Greenwood Press, 1982); Inbar and Adler, *Ethnic Integration in Israel*; Khazzoom, *Shifting Ethnic Boundaries and Inequality in Israel.*

44. Ben-Rafael, *The Emergence of Ethnicity*; Horowitz and Lissak, *Trouble in Utopia.*

45. Government of Israel, *Census* (Jerusalem: Central Bureau of Statistics, 1983) (Hebrew).

46. Ibid.

47. Government of Israel, *Census* (Jerusalem: Central Bureau of Statistics, 1995) (Hebrew).

48. Pamela Abbott and Roger Sapsford, *Women and Social Class* (London: Tavistock, 1987), 1.

49. Michel Abitbol, "Morocco and Its Jews," in *Morocco*, ed. Haim Saadon (Jerusalem: Ministry of Education and Culture, Government of Israel and Ben-Zvi Institute for Research on Jewish Communities in the East, 2004), 12 (Hebrew).

50. Yaron Tsur, *A Torn Community: The Jews of Morocco and Nationalism, 1943–1954* (Tel Aviv: Am Oved, 2001), 30 (Hebrew).

51. Michael M. Laskier, *The Alliance Israélite Universelle and the Jewish Communities of Morocco: 1862–1962* (Albany: State University of New York Press 1983), 8. Statistics on the size of the Moroccan Jewish community are often incomplete and contradictory; see Tsur, *A Torn Community*, 30.

52. Tsur, *A Torn Community*, 31.

53. Elias Canetti, *Voices from Marrakech* (Jerusalem: Carmel Press, 2000) (Hebrew).

54. Tsur, *A Torn Community*, 1.

55. Ibid., 30.

56. Eliezer Bashan, *The Jews of Morocco: Their Past and Culture* (Tel Aviv: Hakibbutz Hameuchad, 2000) (Hebrew).

57. Ibid.

58. Laskier, *The Alliance Israélite Universelle and the Jewish Communities of Morocco*, 270.

59. Shlomo Deshen, "Women in the Jewish Family in Pre-Colonial Morocco," *Anthropological Quarterly* 53, no. 3 (1983): 134–45.

60. Doris Donat, "Emancipation of the Jewish Woman in Morocco," *In the Dispersion* (1963): 127–37.

61. Bashan, *The Jews of Morocco*.

62. Ibid.

63. Donat, "Emancipation of the Jewish Woman in Morocco."

64. Bashan, *The Jews of Morocco*; Kenneth Brown, "Mellah and Medina: A Moroccan City and Its Jewish Quarter (Sale ca. 1880–1930)," in *Studies in Judaism and Islam*, ed. Shlomo Morag, Issachar Ben Ami, and Norman Stillman (Jerusalem: Magnes Press, Hebrew University, 1981), 253–76.

65. Donat, "Emancipation of the Jewish Woman in Morocco."

66. Aron Rodrigue, *Images of Sephardi and Eastern Jewries in Transition* (Seattle: University of Washington Press, 1993), 7.

67. Ibid., 71.

68. Laskier, *The Alliance Israélite Universelle and the Jewish Communities of Morocco*.

69. Ibid., 37.

70. Laskier, *The Alliance Israélite Universelle and the Jewish Communities of Morocco*; idem, "Education," in *Morocco*, ed. Haim Saadon (Jerusalem: Ministry of Education and Culture, Government of Israel and Ben-Zvi Institute for Research on Jewish Communities in the East, 2004), 129–44 (Hebrew).

71. Tsur, *A Torn Community*, 30.

72. Ben-Rafael, *The Emergence of Ethnicity*, 36.

73. Tsur, *A Torn Community*, 37.

74. Rodrigue, *Images of Sephardi and Eastern Jewries in Transition*.

75. Ibid., 18–19.

76. Laskier, *The Alliance Israélite Universelle and the Jewish Communities of Morocco*.

77. Ibid.

78. Brown, "Mellah and Medina."

79. Ibid., 266.

80. Inbar and Adler, *Ethnic Integration in Israel*, estimated that about 50 percent of Jewish women were illiterate.

81. Donat, "Emancipation of the Jewish Woman in Morocco"; Laskier, *The Alliance Israélite Universelle and the Jewish Communities of Morocco*; Elisheva Shitreet, "Jewish Women's Work in the Traditional Society of Marrakech," in *The Work of Her Hands: Women, Work, and Family*, ed. Tova Cohen (Ramat Gan, Israel: Bar-Ilan University, 2001), 35–41 (Hebrew); Tsur, *A Torn Community*.

82. Donat, "Emancipation of the Jewish Woman in Morocco"; Laskier, *The Alliance Israélite Universelle and the Jewish Communities of Morocco*; Tsur, *A Torn Community*.

83. Yaron Tsur and Hagar Hillel, *The Jews of Casablanca: Studies in the Modernization of the Political Elite in a Colonial Community* (Tel Aviv: Open University of Israel, 1995) (Hebrew).

84. Haim Saadon, "The Immigration of Moroccan Jewry: Stages and Characteristics," in *Morocco*, ed. Haim Saadon (Jerusalem: Ministry of Education and Culture, Government of Israel, and Ben Zvi Institute for Research on Jewish Communities in the East, 2004), 93–95 (Hebrew).

85. Inbar and Adler, *Ethnic Integration in Israel*; Saadon, "The Immigration of Moroccan Jewry"; Tsur, *A Torn Community*.

86. Robert Erikson and John H. Goldthorpe, *The Constant Flux* (Oxford: Clarendon Press, 1993).

87. Government of Israel, *Census*, 1995.

88. Ibid.

89. Ibid.

90. Vered Kraus, *Secondary Breadwinners: Israeli Women in the Labor Force* (Westport, CT: Praeger, 2002); Linda Wirth, *Breaking through the Glass Ceiling* (Geneva: International Labour Office, 2001).

91. Kraus, *Secondary Breadwinners*.

92. Bernstein, "Oriental and Ashkenazi Jewish Women in the Labor Market"; Kraus, *Secondary Breadwinners*.

93. Government of Israel, *Census*, 1983.

94. Ibid.

95. Government of Israel, *Census*, 1995.

96. Government of Israel, *Census*, 1983.

97. Ibid.

98. Government of Israel, *Census*, 1995.

99. Ibid.

100. Bashan, *The Jews of Morocco*.

101. Douglas B. Downey, "When Bigger Is Not Better: Family Size, Parental Resources, and Children's Educational Performance," *American Sociological Review* 60, no. 5 (1995): 746–61; Reuven Gronau, "The Effects of Children on the Housewife's Value of Time," *Journal of Political Economy* 81, no. 2 (1973): 168–99.

102. Dov Friedlander, Zvi Eisenbach, and Calvin Goldscheider, "Family-Size Limitation and Birth Spacing: The Fertility Transition of African and Asian Immigrants in Israel," *Population and Development Review* 6, no. 4 (1980): 581–94.

103. Government of Israel, *Compulsory Education Law* (Jerusalem: Government of Israel, 1949) (Hebrew).

104. The two notable exceptions are Esther Schely-Newman's study on Tunisian immigrant women (*Our Lives Are but Stories: Narratives of Tunisian-Israeli Women* [Detroit: Wayne State University Press, 2002]) and Lisa Gilad's book on Yemenite women (*Ginger and Salt: Yemeni Jewish Women in an Israeli Town* [Boulder, CO: Westview Press, 1989]).

105. Moshe Semyonov and Tamar Lerenthal, "Country of Origin, Gender, and the Attainment of Socioeconomic Status: A Study of Stratification in the Jewish Population in Israel," *Research in Social Stratification and Mobility* 10 (1991): 325–43.

106. Esther Goshen-Gottstein, *Marriage and First Pregnancy: Cultural Influences on Attitudes of Israeli Women* (London: Tavistock, 1966).

107. Shoshana Sharni, *Characteristics of Moroccan and Yemenite Women with 0–8 Years of Schooling* (Jerusalem: Center for Demography, Prime Minister's Office, Government of Israel, 1973) (Hebrew).

108. Rahel Wasserfall, "Menstruation and Identity: The Meaning of Niddah for Moroccan Women Immigrants to Israel," in *People of the Body: Jews and Judaism from an Embodied Perspective*, ed. Howard Eilberg-Schwartz (Albany: State University of New York Press, 1992), 309–29.

109. Doli Benhabib, "Margalit, My Homeland: Gender and Ethnicity in Sami Michael's Transit Camp *(Ma'abarot)* Novels," *Theory and Criticism* 20 (2002): 243–59 (Hebrew).

110. Ibid.

111. Yael Katzir, "Yemenite Jewish Women in Israeli Rural Development: Female Power vs. Male Authority," *Economic Development and Cultural Change* 32, no. 1 (1983): 45–61.

112. Orly Lubin, "From Territory to Site: The Oriental Woman in the Film 'Jacky,' *Criticism and Interpretation* 34 (1991): 177–93 (Hebrew); Ella Shohat, "Making the Silences Speak in the Israeli Cinema," in *Calling the Equality Bluff: Women in Israel*, ed. Barbara Swirski and Marilyn P. Safir (New York: Pergamon Press, 1991), 31–41.

## CHAPTER 3

1. Vivian Louie, "Parents' Aspirations and Investment: The Role of Social Class in the Educational Experiences of 1.5 and Second-Generation Chinese Americans," *Harvard Educational Review* 71, no. 3 (2001): 438–74.

2. Grace Kao and Marta Tienda, "Optimism and Achievement: The Educational Performance of Immigrant Youth," *Social Science Quarterly* 76, no. 1 (1995): 1–20.

3. Philip Kasinitz, John H. Mollenkopf, Mary C. Waters, and Jennifer Holdaway, *Inheriting the City: The Children of Immigrants Come of Age* (New York: Russell Sage Foundation; Cambridge, MA: Harvard University Press, 2008); Peter Kwong, *The New Chinatown* (New York: Noonday Press, 1996).

4. Bruria Feigenbaum, personal communication to author, January 5, 2005.

5. Government of Israel, *Census* (Jerusalem: Central Bureau of Statistics, 1995) (Hebrew).

6. Ibid.

7. Sandra E. Black, "Do Better Schools Matter? Parental Evaluation of Elementary Education," *Quarterly Journal of Economics* (May 1999): 577–600; Kasinitz et al., *Inheriting the City*.

8. Jay MacLeod, "Ain't No Makin' It: Leveled Aspirations in a Low-Income Neighborhood," in *Social Stratification in Sociological Perspective*, ed. David B. Grusky (Boulder, CO: Westview Press, 1994), 347–59; Stephen C. Wright, Donald M. Taylor, and Fathali M. Moghaddam, "Responding to Membership in a Disadvantaged Group: From Acceptance to Collective Protest," *Journal of Personality and Social Psychology* 58, no. 6 (1990): 994–1003.

9. Carolyn Britton and Arthur Baxter, "Becoming a Mature Student: Gendered Narratives of the Self," *Gender and Education* 11, no. 2 (1999): 182.

10. Ibid., 186.

11. Zygmunt Bauman, "Figures of Modernity," in *The Bauman Reader*, ed. Peter Beilharz (Malden, MA: Blackwell, 2001), 200–230.

12. Richard Sennett and Jonathan Cobb, *The Hidden Injuries of Class* (New York: Norton, 1972).

## CHAPTER 4

1. Yossi Shavit, "Segregation, Tracking, and the Educational Attainments of Minorities: Arabs and Oriental Jews in Israel," *American Sociological Review* 55 (1990): 115–26; Yossi Yona and Yitzhak Sporta, "Pre-Vocational Education and the Creation of the Working Class in Israel," in *Mizrahim in Israel: A Critical Observation into Israel's Ethnicity*, ed. Hannan Hever, Yehouda Shenhav, and Pnina Motzafi-Haller (Tel Aviv and Jerusalem: Van Leer Jerusalem Institute and Hakibbutz Hameuchad, 2002), 68–105 (Hebrew).

2. Jane Gaskell, "Course Enrollment in the High School: The Perspective of Working Class Females," *Sociology of Education* 58 (January 1985): 48–59.

3. Carolyn Britton and Arthur Baxter, "Becoming a Mature Student: Gendered Narratives of the Self," *Gender and Education* 11, no. 2 (1999): 179–93; Diane Reay, "A Risky Business? Mature Working-Class Women Students and Access to Higher Education," *Gender and Education* 15, no. 3 (2003): 301–19.

4. Sara Ruddick, *Maternal Thinking: Towards a Politics of Peace* (London: The Women's Press, 1989).

5. Steph Lawler, *Mothering the Self* (London and New York: Routledge, 2000), 1.

6. Daphna Birenbaum-Carmeli, *Tel Aviv North: The Makings of a New Israeli Middle Class* (Jerusalem: Magnes Press, Hebrew University, 2000) (Hebrew); Nili Mark, "Ethnic Gaps in Israel in Incomes and Consumption," *Economic Quarterly* 41, no. 1 (1994): 55–77 (Hebrew); Beverly Mizrachi, "Elite Educational Institutions and the Recruitment of Women into National Elite Positions in Israel," *Israel Social Science Research* 12, no. 2 (1997): 93–109; Moshe Semyonov and Noah Lewin-Epstein, "The Impact of Parental Transfers on Living Standards of Married Children," *Social Indicators Research* 54, no. 2 (2001): 115–25.

7. Robyn Dowling, "Gender, Class, and Home Ownership: Placing the Connections," *Housing Studies* 13, no. 4 (1998): 474.

8. E.g., Suki Ali, "'To Be a Girl': Culture and Class in Schools," *Gender and Education* 2, no. 3 (2003): 269–84; Pierre Bourdieu, *Distinction* (Cambridge, MA: Harvard University Press, 1984); Anthony Giddens, *Modernity and Self-Identity: Self and Society in the Late Modern Age* (Stanford, CA: Stanford University Press, 1991); Judith Lorber and Lisa Jean Moore, *Gendered Bodies: Feminist Perspectives* (Los Angeles: Roxbury, 2007); Maeve O'Brien, "Girls and Transition to Second-Level Schooling in Ireland: 'Moving On' and 'Moving Out,'" *Gender and Education* 15, no. 3 (2003): 249–68; Beverley Skeggs, *Formations of Class and Gender* (London: Sage, 1997).

9. Hillary Radner, *Shopping Around: Feminine Culture and the Pursuit of Pleasure* (London: Routledge, 1995), xii.
10. Ibid., 157.
11. Skeggs, *Formations of Class and Gender*, 74.
12. Ibid., 102.
13. Yen Le Espiritu, "'We Don't Sleep Around Like White Girls Do': Family Culture, Culture, and Gender in Filipina American Lives," in *Gender and U.S. Immigration*, ed. Pierrette Hondagneu-Sotelo (Berkeley: University of California Press, 2003), 280.
14. Britton and Baxter, "Becoming a Mature Student," 188.
15. Ibid., 189.
16. Ibid.
17. Ibid.

## CHAPTER 5

1. Morris Altman and Louise Lamontagne, "On the Natural Intelligence of Women in a World of Constrained Choice: How the Feminization of Clerical Work Contributed to Gender Pay Equality in Early Twentieth Century Canada," *Journal of Economic Issues* 37, no. 4 (2003): 1045–74; Joshua G. Behr, "Black and Female Municipal Employment: A Substantive Benefit of Minority Political Incorporation," *Journal of Urban Affairs* 22, no. 3 (2000): 243–64; Ileen A. DeVault, *Sons and Daughters of Labor: Class and Clerical Work in Turn-of-the-Century Pittsburgh* (Ithaca, NY: Cornell University Press, 1990).
2. Behr, "Black and Female Municipal Employment"; Robert Erikson and John H. Goldthorpe, *The Constant Flux* (Oxford: Clarendon Press, 1993); Beverly Mizrachi, "Elite Educational Institutions and the Recruitment of Women into National Elite Positions in Israel," *Israel Social Science Research* 12, no. 2 (1997): 93–109.
3. Behr, "Black and Female Municipal Employment," 250.
4. E.g., Rosemary Crompton and Gareth Jones, *White-Collar Proletariat: Deskilling and Gender in Clerical Work* (London and Basingstoke: Macmillan, 1984); Evelyn Nakano Glenn and Roslyn L. Feldberg, "Degraded and Deskilled: The Proletarianization of Clerical Work," *Social Problems* 25, no. 1 (1977): 52–64.
5. Behr, "Black and Female Municipal Employment"; Sharon Strom, *Beyond the Typewriter: Gender, Class, and the Origins of Modern American Office Work* (Urbana: University of Illinois Press, 1992).
6. Beverley Skeggs, *Formations of Class and Gender* (London: Sage, 1997), 102.
7. Beverly Mizrachi, "The Henna-Maker: A Moroccan Immigrant Woman Entrepreneur in an Ethnic Revival," in *Research in the Sociology of Work*, vol. 15, ed. Lisa A. Keister (Amsterdam: Elsevier, 2005), 257–79; Rachel Sharaby, *The Mimuna Holiday: From Periphery to the Center* (Tel Aviv: Hakibbutz Hameuchad, 2009) (Hebrew).
8. Nancy Foner, "The Immigrant Family: Cultural Legacies and Cultural Changes," *International Migration Review* 31, no. 4 (1997): 961.

## CHAPTER 6

1. E.g., Nancy Foner, "The Immigrant Family: Cultural Legacies and Cultural Changes," *International Migration Review* 31, no. 4 (1997): 961–74; Yael Katzir, "Yemenite Jewish Women in Israeli Rural Development: Female Power vs. Male Authority," *Economic Development and Cultural Change* 32, no. 1 (1983): 45–61; Nazli Kibria, "Power, Patriarchy, and Gender Conflict in a Vietnamese Community," *Gender and Society* 4, no. 1 (1990): 9–24; Marta Tienda and Karen Booth, "Gender, Migration, and Social Change," *International Sociology* 6, no. 1 (1991): 51–72.

2. Sylvia Fogiel-Bijaoui, "Families in Israel: Between Familism and Post-Modernity," in *Sex, Gender, Politics: Women in Israel*, ed. Dafna N. Izraeli, Henriette Dahan-Kalev, Sylvie Fogiel-Bijaoui, Hanna Herzog, Manar Hasan, and Hannah Naveh (Tel Aviv: Hakibbutz Hameuchad, 1999), 107–67 (Hebrew).

3. Yochanan Peres and Ruth Katz, "Stability and Centrality: The Nuclear Family in Modern Israel," *Social Forces* 59 (1981): 687–704.

4. Shlomo Swirski, Vered Kraus, Etty Konor-Attias, and Anat Herbst, "Solo Mothers in Israel," *Equality Monitor* 12 (2003): 3.

5. Ibid., 14.

6. Ibid., 29.

7. Ibid., 30.

8. Anat Herbst, "We Support the Law for Single-Parent Families, Poor Things," *National Insurance* 80 (August 2009): 25–58 (Hebrew); Karen Seccombe, Delores James, and Kimberly Battle Walters, "'They Think You Ain't Much of Nothing': The Social Construction of the Welfare Mother," *Journal of Marriage and the Family* 60 (1998): 849–65; Ruth Sidel, *Unsung Heroines* (Berkeley: University of California Press, 2006).

9. Swirski et al., "Solo Mothers in Israel," 14.

10. Government of Israel, *Single Parent Family Law* (Jerusalem: Government of Israel, 1992) (Hebrew).

11. Herbst, "We Support the Law for Single-Parent Families"; Seccombe, James, and Walters, "They Think You Ain't Much of Nothing"; Sidel, *Unsung Heroines.*

12. Robyn Dowling, "Gender, Class, and Home Ownership: Placing the Connections," *Housing Studies* 13, no. 4 (1998): 474.

13. Noah Lewin-Epstein, Yuval Elmelech, and Moshe Semyonov, "Ethnic Inequality in Home Ownership and the Value of Housing: The Case of Immigrants in Israel," *Social Forces* 75, no. 4 (1997): 1439–63, at 1447.

14. Ibid., 1449.

15. Ruth Madigan, Moira Munro, and Susan J. Smith, "Gender and the Meaning of Home," *International Journal of Urban and Regional Research* 14, no. 4 (1990): 625–47.

16. Dowling, "Gender, Class, and Home Ownership."

17. Randall Collins, *Sociological Insight* (Oxford: Oxford University Press, 1992); Bonnie Smith, *Ladies of the Leisure Class* (Princeton, NJ: Princeton University Press, 1981).

18. Smith, *Ladies of the Leisure Class*, 6.

19. Katherine Grier, *Culture and Comfort: Parlor Making and the Middle-Class Identity, 1850–1930* (Washington, DC: Smithsonian Institution Press, 1997).

20. Peter Gay, *Pleasure Wars* (New York: Norton, 1998).

21. Floya Anthias, "Metaphors of Home: Gendering New Migrations to Southern Europe," in *Gender and Migration in Southern Europe*, ed. Floya Anthias and Gabriella Lazaridis (Oxford and New York: Berg, 2000), 15–49; Beverly Mizrachi, "Elite Educational Institutions and the Recruitment of Women into National Elite Positions in Israel," *Israel Social Science Research* 12, no. 2 (1997): 93–109.

22. Sidel, *Unsung Heroines*.

23. Herbst, "We Support the Law for Single-Parent Families"; Deborah J. Jones, Rex Forehand, Gene Brody, and Lisa Armistead, "Psychosocial Adjustment of African American Children in Single-Mother Families: A Test of Three Risk Models," *Journal of Marriage and Family* 64 (February 2002): 105–15.

24. Julie Bettie, "Exceptions to the Rule: Upwardly Mobile White and Mexican American High School Girls," *Gender and Society* 16, no. 3 (2003): 409.

25. Eliezer Ben-Rafael and Stephen Sharot, *Ethnicity, Religion, and Class in Israeli Society* (Cambridge: Cambridge University Press, 1991); Vered Kraus, "Social Segregation in Israel as a Function of Objective and Subjective Attributes of the Ethnic Groups," *Sociology and Social Research* 69, no. 1 (1984): 50–71.

26. Richard Sennett and Jonathan Cobb, *The Hidden Injuries of Class* (New York: Norton, 1972).

27. Sidel, *Unsung Heroines*, 60.

28. Ibid., 103.

## CHAPTER 7

1. Katherine Grier, "Childhood Socialization and Companion Animals: United States, 1820–1870," *Society and Animals* 7, no. 2 (1999): 95.

2. Government of Israel, *Census* (Jerusalem: Central Bureau of Statistics, 1983) (Hebrew).

3. Michael M. Laskier, *The Alliance Israélite Universelle and the Jewish Communities of Morocco: 1862–1962* (Albany: State University of New York Press, 1983); Aron Rodrigue, *Images of Sephardi and Eastern Jewries in Transition* (Seattle: University of Washington Press, 1993).

4. Aziza Khazzoom, *Shifting Ethnic Boundaries and Inequality in Israel* (Stanford, CA: Stanford University Press, 2008), 76.

5. Ibid., 150.

6. Alejandro Portes and Rubén G. Rumbaut, *Legacies: The Story of the Immigrant Second Generation* (Berkeley: University of California Press; New York: Russell Sage Foundation, 2001).

7. Ibid., 62.

8. Peter Kwong, *The New Chinatown* (New York: Noonday Press, 1996); Vivian Louie, "Parents' Aspirations and Investment: The Role of Social Class in the Educational Experiences of 1.5 and Second-Generation Chinese Americans," *Harvard Educational Review* 71, no. 3 (2001): 438–74.

9. Audrey Addi-Raccah and Hanna Ayalon, "Gender Inequality in Leadership Positions of Teachers," *British Journal of Education* 23, no. 2 (2002): 157–78.

10. Central Bureau of Statistics, *Statistical Abstract of Israel* (Jerusalem: Government of Israel, 2005), No. 56, Tables 8.33, 8.34.

11. Audrey Addi-Raccah, "Gender, Ethnicity, and School Principalship in Israel: Comparing Two Organizational Cultures," *International Journal of Inclusive Education* 9, no. 3 (2005): 82.

12. Ina Fuchs, "Teaching Images and Socio-Economic Status of Teachers in Four Sectors of the Israeli Educational System," *Megamot: Social Science Quarterly* 38, no. 2 (1997): 226–46 (Hebrew); Stephen Steinberg, *The Ethnic Myth* (Boston: Beacon Press, 2001).

13. Sheila Cunnsion, "Gender Joking in the Staffroom," in *Teachers, Gender, and Careers*, ed. Sandra Acker (East Sussex: Falmer Press, 1989), 151–71.

14. Dahlia Moore and Abraham Gobi, "Role Conflict and Perceptions of Gender Roles (The Case of Israel)," *Sex Roles* 32, no. 3/4 (1995): 251–71.

15. Lya Kremer-Hayon and Zahava Goldstein, "The Inner World of Israeli Secondary School Teachers: Work, Centrality, Job Satisfaction, and Stress," *Comparative Education* 26, no. 3/4 (1990): 285–99.

16. See also Beverley Skeggs, *Formations of Class and Gender* (London: Sage, 1997).

17. Andrew J. Cherlin, "The Deinstitutionalization of Marriage," *Journal of Marriage and Family* 66 (November 2004): 848–61; idem, *The Marriage-Go-Round* (New York: Random House, 2009).

18. Cherlin, "The Deinstitutionalization of Marriage," 855.

19. Gary S. Becker, *A Treatise on the Family* (Cambridge, MA: Harvard University Press, 1991).

20. Sylvia Fogiel-Bijaoui, "Families in Israel: Between Familism and Post-Modernity," in *Sex, Gender, Politics: Women in Israel*, ed. Dafna N. Izraeli, Henriette Dahan-Kalev, Sylvie Fogiel-Bijaoui, Hanna Herzog, Manar Hasan, and Hannah Naveh (Tel Aviv: Hakibbutz Hameuchad, 1999), 107–67 (Hebrew); Yochanan Peres and Ruth Katz, "Stability and Centrality: The Nuclear Family in Modern Israel," *Social Forces* 59 (1981): 687–704.

21. Government of Israel, *Census* (Jerusalem: Central Bureau of Statistics, 1995) (Hebrew).

22. Floya Anthias, "Metaphors of Home: Gendering New Migrations to Southern Europe," in *Gender and Migration in Southern Europe*, ed. Floya Anthias and Gabriella Lazaridis (Oxford and New York: Berg, 2000), 15–49; Beverly Mizrachi, "Elite Educational Institutions and the Recruitment of Women into National Elite Positions in Israel," *Israel Social Science Research* 12, no. 2 (1997): 93–109.

23. Robyn Dowling, "Gender, Class, and Home Ownership: Placing the Connections," *Housing Studies* 13, no. 4 (1998): 476.

24. Pierre Bourdieu, *Distinction* (Cambridge, MA: Harvard University Press, 1984).

25. Ian Munt, "The 'Other' Postmodern Tourism: Culture, Travel, and the New Middle Classes," *Theory, Culture, and Society* 11 (1994): 101–23.

26. Mary C. Waters, *Ethnic Options* (Berkeley: University of California Press, 1990).

27. Shlomo Deshen, "Political Ethnicity and Cultural Ethnicity in Israel during the 1960s," in *Urban Ethnicity*, ed. Abner Cohen (London: Tavistock, 1974), 281–311; Harvey Goldberg, "Historical and Cultural Dimensions of Ethnic Phenomena in Israel," in *Studies in Israeli Ethnicity*, ed. Alex Weingrod (New York: Gordon and Breach, 1985), 179–200; idem, "The Changing Meaning of Ethnic Affiliation," *Jerusalem Quarterly* 44 (1987): 39–50; Beverly Mizrachi, "The Henna-Maker: A Moroccan Immigrant Woman Entrepreneur in an Ethnic Revival," in *Research in the Sociology of Work*, vol. 15, ed. Lisa A. Keister (Amsterdam: Elsevier, 2005), 257–79; see also chapter 2 of the current volume.

28. Alex Weingrod, "Recent Trends in Israeli Ethnicity," *Ethnic and Racial Studies* 2, no. 1 (1979): 55–65.

29. Zygmunt Bauman, "Figures of Modernity," in *The Bauman Reader*, ed. Peter Beilharz (Malden, MA: Blackwell, 2001), 218.

30. Ibid., 221.

## CHAPTER 8

1. Ian Munt, "The 'Other' Postmodern Tourism: Culture, Travel, and the New Middle Classes," *Theory, Culture, and Society* 11 (1994): 101–23.

2. Deniz Kandiyoti, "Bargaining with Patriarchy," *Gender and Society* 2, no. 3 (1988): 274–90.

3. Constantina Safilios-Rotschild and Marcellinus Dijkers, "Handling Unconventional Asymmetries," in *Working Couples*, ed. Rhona Rapoport and Robert N. Rapoport (London: Routledge and Kegan Paul, 1978), 62–74.

4. Henriette Dahan-Kalev, "Illusions in Assimilation," in *The Flying Camel*, ed. Loolwa Khazzoom (New York: Seal Press, 2003), 157.

5. Shas, as a political party, does in fact attract Mizraḥim from the lower socioeconomic strata. Yoav Peled, "Towards a Redefinition of Jewish Nationalism in Israel? The Enigma of *Shas*," *Ethnic and Racial Studies* 21, no. 4 (1998): 703–28.

6. E.g., Joan Acker, *Doing Comparable Worth: Gender, Class, and Pay Equity* (Philadelphia: Temple University Press, 1989); Audrey Addi-Raccah and Hanna Ayalon, "Gender Inequality in Leadership Positions of Teachers," *British Journal of Education* 23, no. 2 (2002): 157–78; Carolyn Riehl and Mark A. Byrd, "Gender Differences among New Recruits to School Administration: Cautionary Footnotes to an Optimistic Tale," *Educational Evaluation and Policy Analysis* 19, no. 1 (1997): 45–64.

7. Addi-Raccah and Ayalon, "Gender Inequality in Leadership Positions of Teachers"; Riehl and Byrd, "Gender Differences among New Recruits to School Administration."

8. Patricia Anne Banks, "The Essential Leadership Model," *National Association of Secondary School Principals Bulletin* 90, no. 4 (2006): 4–18.

9. Audrey Addi-Raccah, "Gender, Ethnicity, and School Principalship in Israel: Comparing Two Organizational Cultures," *International Journal of Inclusive Education* 9, no. 3 (2005): 71–93.

10. Addi-Raccah and Ayalon, "Gender Inequality in Leadership Positions of Teachers."

11. Addi-Raccah, "Gender, Ethnicity, and School Principalship in Israel."

12. Mary C. Waters, *Ethnic Options* (Berkeley: University of California Press, 1990).

13. Jay MacLeod, "Ain't No Makin' It: Leveled Aspirations in a Low-Income Neighborhood," in *Social Stratification in Sociological Perspective*, ed. David B. Grusky (Boulder, CO: Westview Press, 1994), 347–59.

14. Janet Salaff and Arent Greve, "Women That Move: International Migration from the PRC to Canada and the Negotiation of Gendered Job Opportunities," 2002, http://homes.chass.utoronto.ca/~salaff/PRC_GenMig.PDF.

## CHAPTER 9

1. Rosemary Crompton, "The Gendered Restructuring of the Middle Classes: Employment and Caring," in *Renewing Class Analysis*, ed. Rosemary Crompton, Fiona Devine, Mike Savage, and John Scott (Oxford and Malden, MA: Blackwell, 2000), 165–84; Simon Duncan, "Mothering, Class, and Rationality," *Sociological Review* 53, no. 1 (2005): 50–76; Carol Vincent, Stephen J. Ball, and Sophie Kemp, "The Social Geography of Childcare: Making Up a Middle-Class Child," *British Journal of Sociology of Education* 25, no. 2 (2004): 229–45; Yi-Lee Wong, "A Unified Middle Class or Two Middle Classes? A Comparison of Career Strategies and Intergenerational Mobility Strategies between Teachers and Managers in Contemporary Hong Kong," *British Journal of Sociology* 55, no. 2 (2004): 167–87.

2. S. N. Eisenstadt, *Israeli Society* (New York: Basic Books, 1967); Dan Horowitz and Moshe Lissak, *Trouble in Utopia* (Albany: State University of New York Press, 1989); Abraham Yogev and Rina Shapira, "Ethnicity, Meritocracy, and Credentialism in Israel: Elaborating the Credential Society Thesis," *Research in Social Stratification and Mobility* 6 (1987): 187–212.

3. Carolyn Britton and Arthur Baxter, "Becoming a Mature Student: Gendered Narratives of the Self," *Gender and Education* 11, no. 2 (1999): 179–93.

4. My use of the term *life chances* derives from Max Weber, "Class, Status, and Party," in *Economy and Society*, vol. 2, ed. Gunther Roth and C. Wittich (New York: Bedminster Press, 1968), 926–40.

5. Louise Archer and Carole Leathwood, "New Times—Old Inequalities: Diverse Working-Class Femininities in Education," *Gender and Education* 15, no. 3 (2003): 234.

6. Fiona Devine, "Talking about Class in Britain," in *Social Inequalities in Comparative Perspective*, ed. Fiona Devine and Mary C. Waters (Malden, MA: Blackwell, 2004), 210.

7. Archer and Leathwood, "New Times."

8. Sammy Smooha, "Class, Ethnic, and National Cleavages and Democracy in Israel," in *Israeli Democracy under Stress*, ed. Ehud Sprinzak and Larry Diamond (Boulder, CO: Lynne Rienner, 1993), 293–343.

9. E.g., Philip Kasinitz, John H. Mollenkopf, Mary C. Waters, and Jennifer Holdaway, *Inheriting the City: The Children of Immigrants Come of Age* (New York:

Russell Sage Foundation; Cambridge, MA: Harvard University Press, 2008); Vivian Louie, "Parents' Aspirations and Investment: The Role of Social Class in the Educational Experiences of 1.5 and Second-Generation Chinese Americans," *Harvard Educational Review* 71, no. 3 (2001): 438–74; Alejandro Portes and Rubén G. Rumbaut, *Legacies: The Story of the Immigrant Second Generation* (Berkeley: University of California Press; New York: Russell Sage Foundation, 2001); Stephen Steinberg, *The Ethnic Myth* (Boston: Beacon Press, 2001).

10. Kasinitz et al., *Inheriting the City*.

11. Beverly Mizrachi, "Non-Mainstream Education, Limited Mobility, and the Second Generation of Moroccan Immigrant Women: The Case of the Kindergarten Teacher's Assistant," *Nashim* 8 (Fall 2004): 50–73.

12. Uri Shwed and Yossi Shavit, "The Occupational and Economic Attainments of College and University Graduates in Israel," *European Sociological Review* 22, no. 4 (2006): 431–42; Alex Trillo, "Somewhere between Wall Street and El Barrio: Community College as a Second Chance for Second-Generation Latino Students," in *Becoming New Yorkers*, ed. Philip Kasinitz, John H. Mollenkopf, and Mary C. Waters (New York: Russell Sage Foundation, 2004), 57–79.

13. See chapter 2, table 2.2. See also Elisheva Shitreet, "Jewish Women's Work in the Traditional Society of Marrakech," in *The Work of Her Hands: Women, Work, and Family*, ed. Tova Cohen (Ramat Gan, Israel: Bar-Ilan University, 2001), 35–41 (Hebrew).

14. Vered Kraus, *Secondary Breadwinners: Israeli Women in the Labor Force* (Westport, CT: Praeger, 2002); Linda Wirth, *Breaking through the Glass Ceiling* (Geneva: International Labour Office, 2001).

15. Karen Aschaffenbur, "Rethinking Images of the Mobility Regime: Making a Case for Women's Mobility," *Research in Social Stratification and Mobility* 4 (1995): 201–35.

16. Duncan, "Mothering, Class, and Rationality"; Steph Lawler, *Mothering the Self* (London and New York: Routledge, 2000); Vincent, Ball, and Kemp, "The Social Geography of Childcare."

17. Beverley Skeggs, *Formations of Class and Gender* (London: Sage, 1997), 88.

18. Ibid., 102.

19. Carolyn Kay Steedman, *Landscape for a Good Woman: A Story of Two Lives* (New Brunswick, NJ: Rutgers University Press, 1997), 6.

20. Helen Lucey, June Melody, and Valerie Walkerdine, "Uneasy Hybrids: Psychological Aspects of Becoming Educationally Successful for Working-Class Young Women," *Gender and Education* 15, no. 3 (2003): 285–301; Skeggs, *Formations of Class and Gender*.

21. Valerie Hey, "Joining the Club? Academic and Working-Class Femininities," *Gender and Education* 15, no. 3 (2003): 319–35.

22. H. Edward Ransford and Jon Miller, "Race, Sex, and Feminist Outlooks," *American Sociological Review* 48 (1983): 46–59.

23. See chapter 2, table 2.2; see also Kraus, *Secondary Breadwinners*.

24. James A. Geschwender, "Ethgender, Women's Waged Labor, and Economic Mobility," *Social Problems* 39, no. 1 (1992): 1–17.

25. Duncan, "Mothering, Class, and Rationality"; Lawler, *Mothering the Self*; Vincent, Ball, and Kemp, "The Social Geography of Childcare."

26. Skeggs, *Formations of Class and Gender*, 82.

27. Ibid., 82.

28. Beverly Mizrachi, "Elite Educational Institutions and the Recruitment of Women into National Elite Positions in Israel," *Israel Social Science Research* 12, no. 2 (1997): 93–109; idem, "Non-Mainstream Education, Limited Mobility, and the Second Generation of Moroccan Immigrant Women."

29. Pamela Abbott and Roger Sapsford, *Women and Social Class* (London: Tavistock, 1987).

30. Mary Blair-Loy, *Competing Devotions: Career and Family among Women Executives* (Cambridge, MA: Harvard University Press, 2003); Christine Percheski, "Opting Out? Cohort Differences in Professional Women's Employment Rates from 1960 to 2005," *American Sociological Review* 73, no. 3 (2008): 497–517.

31. Yinon Cohen and Yitchak Haberfeld, "Gender, Ethnic, and National Earnings Gaps in Israel: The Role of Rising Inequality," Discussion Paper No. 5-2003 (Tel Aviv: Tel Aviv University, The Pinhas Sapir Center for Development, 2003).

32. E.g., Duncan, "Mothering, Class, and Rationality"; Lawler, *Mothering the Self*; Vincent, Ball, and Kemp, "The Social Geography of Childcare."

33. Diane Reay, "Rethinking Social Class: Qualitative Perspectives on Class and Gender," *Sociology* 32, no. 2 (1998): 259.

34. Candace West and Don Zimmerman, "Doing Gender," *Gender and Society* 1, no. 2 (1987): 125–51.

35. Emily Beller, "Bringing Intergenerational Social Mobility Research into the Twenty-First Century: Why Mothers Matter," *American Sociological Review* 74, no. 4 (2009): 507–28; Aziza Khazzoom, "The Impact of Mother's Occupations on Children's Occupational Destinations," *Research in Stratification and Mobility* 15 (1997): 57–89; Sylvia A. Korupp, Harry B. G. Ganzeboom, and Tanja van der Lippe, "Do Mothers Matter? A Comparison of Models of Influence of Mothers' and Fathers' Educational and Occupational Status on Children's Educational Attainment," *Quality and Quantity* 36, no. 1 (2002): 17–42.

36. Beller, "Bringing Intergenerational Social Mobility Research into the Twenty-first Century."

37. Nancy Abelmann, "Women's Class Mobility and Identities in South Korea: A Gendered, Transnational, Narrative Approach," *Journal of Asian Studies* 56, no. 2 (1997): 400.

38. Robert Erikson, "Social Class of Men, Women, and Families," *Sociology* 18, no. 4 (1984): 500–514; John H. Goldthorpe, "Women and Class Analysis: In Defense of the Conventional View," *Sociology* 17, no. 4 (1983): 465–88; John H. Goldthorpe and Gordon Marshall, "The Promising Future of Class Analysis: A Response to Recent Critiques," *Sociology* 26, no. 3 (1992): 381–400; John H. Goldthorpe and Clive Payne, "On the Class Mobility of Women: Results from Different Approaches to the Analysis of Recent British Data," *Sociology* 20, no. 4 (1986): 531–55; Michelle Stanworth, "Women and Class Analysis: A Reply to John Goldthorpe," *Sociology* 18, no. 2 (1984): 159–70.

39. Nancy J. Davis and Robert V. Robinson, "Do Wives Matter? Class Identities of Wives and Husbands," *Social Forces* 76, no. 3 (1988): 1063–86; Bernadette Hayes and F. I. Jones, "Class Identification among Australian Couples: Are Wives' Characteristics Irrelevant?" *British Journal of Sociology* 43 (1992): 462–83; Annette Sørenson, "Women, Family, and Class," *Annual Review of Sociology* 20 (1994): 27–47.

40. Erikson, "Social Class of Men, Women, and Families," 500.

41. Haya Stier and Yossi Shavit, "Age at Marriage, Sex Ratios, and Ethnic Heterogamy," *European Sociological Review* 10, no. 1 (1994): 79–84.

42. Government of Israel, *Census* (Jerusalem: Central Bureau of Statistics, 1995) (Hebrew).

43. Stier and Shavit, "Age at Marriage, Sex Ratios, and Ethnic Heterogamy," 80.

44. E.g., James C. Scott, *Domination and the Arts of Resistance* (New Haven, CT: Yale University Press, 1990).

45. Sami Shalom Chetrit, *The Mizrahi Struggle in Israel: Between Oppression and Liberation, Identification and Alternative, 1948–2003* (Tel Aviv: Am Oved, 2004) (Hebrew); Hannan Hever, Yehouda Shenhav, and Pnina Motzafi-Haller, eds., *Mizrahim in Israel: A Critical Observation into Israel's Ethnicity* (Jerusalem and Tel Aviv: Van Leer Jerusalem Institute and Hakibbutz Hameuchad, 2002) (Hebrew).

46. Lawler, *Mothering the Self*, 169.

47. Ibid., 168.

48. Ibid.

49. Harvey Goldberg and Chen Bram, "Sephardic/Mizrahi/Arab-Jews: Reflections on Critical Sociology and the Study of Middle Eastern Jewries within the Context of Israeli Society," *Studies in Contemporary Jewry* 22 (2007): 227–56.

50. Judith Lorber and Susan Farrell, eds., *The Social Construction of Gender* (Newbury Park, CA: Sage, 1994); West and Zimmerman, "Doing Gender."

51. Herbert J. Gans, "Symbolic Ethnicity: The Future of Ethnic Groups and Cultures in America," *Ethnic and Racial Studies* 2, no. 1 (1979): 1–21; Nathan Glazer and Daniel Patrick Moynihan, *Beyond the Melting Pot: The Negroes, Puerto Ricans, Jews, Italians, and Irish of New York City* (Cambridge, MA: MIT Press, 1963); Howard F. Stein and Robert F. Hill, *The Ethnic Imperative: Examining the New White Movement* (University Park: Pennsylvania State University Press, 1977); Mary C. Waters, *Ethnic Options* (Berkeley: University of California Press, 1990).

52. Gans, "Symbolic Ethnicity," 5.

53. Ibid., 6.

54. Ibid., 8.

55. Ibid., 6.

56. Janet Mancini Billson, *Keepers of Culture* (New York: Lexington, 1995).

57. S. N. Eisenstadt and Bernhard Giesen, "The Construction of Collective Identity," *Archives Europeennes de Sociologie* 36 (1995): 77.

58. Irvin Long Child, *Italian or American? The Second Generation in Conflict* (New Haven, CT: Yale University Press, 1943).

59. Alejandro Portes, "The Rise of Ethnicity: Determinants of Ethnic Perceptions among Cuban Exiles in Miami," *American Sociological Review* 49 (1984): 383–97.

60. Joane Nagel, "Constructing Ethnicity: Creating and Recreating Ethnic Identity and Culture," *Social Problems* 41, no. 1 (1994): 152–76; Jonathan Y. Okamura, "Situational Ethnicity," *Ethnic and Racial Studies* 4, no. 4 (1981): 452–66; Waters, *Ethnic Options.*

61. Waters, *Ethnic Options*, 160.

62. Stein and Hill, *The Ethnic Imperative.*

63. Fredrik Barth, "Introduction," in *Ethnic Groups and Boundaries*, ed. Fredrik Barth (Bergen-Oslo: Universitets Forlagt; London: Allen and Unwin, 1969), 7–9; Nagel, "Constructing Ethnicity."

64. Portes and Rumbaut, *Legacies.*

65. Waters, *Ethnic Options.*

66. Harvey Goldberg, "Historical and Cultural Dimensions of Ethnic Phenomena in Israel," in *Studies in Israeli Ethnicity*, ed. Alex Weingrod (New York: Gordon and Breach, 1985), 179–200; Judith L. Goldstein, "Iranian Identity in Israel: The Performance of Identity," in *Immigration to Israel*, ed. Elazar Leshem and Judith T. Shuval (New Brunswick, NJ: Transaction Publishers, 1998), 387–407; Beverly Mizrachi, "The Henna-Maker: A Moroccan Immigrant Woman Entrepreneur in an Ethnic Revival," in *Research in the Sociology of Work*, vol. 15, ed. Lisa A. Keister (Amsterdam: Elsevier, 2005), 257–79; Alex Weingrod, "Recent Trends in Israeli Ethnicity," *Ethnic and Racial Studies* 2, no. 1 (1979): 55–65.

67. Nagel, "Constructing Ethnicity."

68. Richard D. Alba, *Ethnic Identity: The Transformation of White America* (New Haven, CT: Yale University Press, 1990); Philip Kasinitz, John H. Mollenkopf, and Mary C. Waters, eds. *Becoming New Yorkers* (New York: Russell Sage Foundation, 2004); Waters, *Ethnic Options.*

69. Portes, "The Rise of Ethnicity: Determinants of Ethnic Perceptions among Cuban Exiles in Miami."

70. Ibid.; Portes and Rumbaut, *Legacies.*

71. Jonathan H. Turner, *Human Emotions: A Sociological Theory* (London and New York: Routledge, 2007).

72. Deborah Bernstein, "Conflict and Protest: The Case of the Black Panthers of Israel," *Youth and Society* 16, no. 2 (1984): 129–52; Chetrit, *The Mizrahi Struggle in Israel*; Shlomo Hasson, *Urban Social Movements in Jerusalem: The Protest of the Second Generation* (Albany: State University of New York Press, in cooperation with the Jerusalem Institute for Israeli Studies, 1993); Horowitz and Lissak, *Trouble in Utopia.*

73. Zygmunt Bauman, "Figures of Modernity," in *The Bauman Reader*, ed. Peter Beilharz (Malden, MA: Blackwell, 2001), 200–230; Ulrich Beck, *Risk Society: Towards a New Modernity* (London: Sage, 1992); S. N. Eisenstadt, "Frameworks of the Great Revolutions: Culture, Social Structure, History, and Human Agency," *International Social Science Journal* 133, no. 44 (1992): 385–403; Mustafa Emirbayer and Ann Misch, "What Is Agency?" *American Journal of Sociology* 103, no. 4 (1998): 962–1023; Anthony Giddens, *The Constitution of Society* (Berkeley: University of California Press, 1984); idem, *Modernity and Self-Identity: Self and Society in the Late Modern Age* (Stanford, CA: Stanford University Press, 1991).

74. Beck, *Risk Society*, 105.
75. Ibid., 87.
76. Ibid.
77. Yael Katzir, "Yemenite Jewish Women in Israeli Rural Development: Female Power vs. Male Authority," *Economic Development and Cultural Change* 32, no. 1 (1983): 45–61; Leonora Peets, *Women of Marrakech* (London: Hurst, 1988); Rahel Wasserfall, "Menstruation and Identity: The Meaning of Niddah for Moroccan Women Immigrants to Israel," in *People of the Body: Jews and Judaism from an Embodied Perspective*, ed. Howard Eilberg-Schwartz (Albany: State University of New York Press, 1992), 309–29.
78. Nancy Foner, "The Immigrant Family: Cultural Legacies and Cultural Changes," *International Migration Review* 31, no. 4 (1997): 961–74; Katzir, "Yemenite Jewish Women in Israeli Rural Development"; Marta Tienda and Karen Booth, "Gender, Migration, and Social Change," *International Sociology* 6, no. 1 (1991): 51–72.
79. Janet Saltzman Chafetz, "Structure, Consciousness, Agency, and Social Change in Feminist Sociological Theories," *Current Perspectives in Social Theory* 19 (1999): 145–64.
80. Ibid., 147.
81. Beck, *Risk Society*, 120.
82. Steinberg, *The Ethnic Myth*.
83. Ann Swidler, "Culture in Action: Symbols and Strategies," *American Sociological Review* 51 (1986): 273–86.
84. Ibid., 278.
85. Ibid.
86. Beck, *Risk Society*; Emirbayer and Misch, "What Is Agency?"
87. For some thoughts on the upward mobility of Arab Israeli women, see Mizrachi, "Elite Educational Institutions and the Recruitment of Women into National Elite Positions in Israel."
88. Agnes Heller, "The Many Faces of Multiculturalism," in *The Challenge of Diversity*, ed. Rainer Bauböck, Agnes Heller, and Aristide R. Zolberg (Aldershot, England: Avebury, 1996), 43–67.

## METHODOLOGY APPENDIX

1. Robert Erikson and John H. Goldthorpe, *The Constant Flux* (Oxford: Clarendon Press, 1993).
2. John H. Goldthorpe, Meir Yaish, and Vered Kraus, "Class Mobility in Israeli Society," *Research in Stratification and Mobility* 15 (1997): 3–28.
3. Erikson and Goldthorpe, *The Constant Flux*, 38–39.
4. Ibid., 37.
5. Ibid., 45.
6. Government of Israel, *Standard Classification of Occupations* (Jerusalem: Central Bureau of Statistics, 1994) (Hebrew).
7. Ibid.

8. Ibid.; Joshua G. Behr, "Black and Female Municipal Employment: A Substantive Benefit of Minority Political Incorporation," *Journal of Urban Affairs* 22, no. 3 (2000): 243–64; Ileen A. DeVault, *Sons and Daughters of Labor: Class and Clerical Work in Turn-of-the-Century Pittsburgh* (Ithaca, NY: Cornell University Press, 1990); Erikson and Goldthorpe, *The Constant Flux*; Sharon Strom, *Beyond the Typewriter: Gender, Class, and the Origins of Modern American Office Work* (Urbana: University of Illinois Press, 1992).

9. Erikson and Goldthorpe, *The Constant Flux*, 42.

# *Bibliography*


Abelmann, Nancy. "Women's Class Mobility and Identities in South Korea: A Gendered, Transnational, Narrative Approach." *Journal of Asian Studies* 56, no. 2 (1997): 398–420.

Abbott, Pamela, and Roger Sapsford. *Women and Social Class*. London: Tavistock, 1987.

Abitbol, Michel. "Morocco and Its Jews." In *Morocco*, edited by Haim Saadon, 9–22. Jerusalem: Ministry of Education and Culture, Government of Israel and Ben-Zvi Institute for Research on Jewish Communities in the East, 2004. Hebrew.

Acker, Joan. *Doing Comparable Worth: Gender, Class, and Pay Equity*. Philadelphia: Temple University Press, 1989.

Addi-Raccah, Audrey. "Gender, Ethnicity, and School Principalship in Israel: Comparing Two Organizational Cultures." *International Journal of Inclusive Education* 9, no. 3 (2005): 71–93.

Addi-Raccah, Audrey, and Hanna Ayalon. "Gender Inequality in Leadership Positions of Teachers." *British Journal of Education* 23, no. 2 (2002): 157–78.

Alba, Richard D. *Ethnic Identity: The Transformation of White America*. New Haven, CT: Yale University Press, 1990.

Alba, Richard D., and Victor Nee. "Rethinking Assimilation Theory for a New Era of Immigration." *International Migration Review* 31, no. 4 (2003): 826–74.

Ali, Suki. "'To Be a Girl': Culture and Class in Schools." *Gender and Education* 2, no. 3 (2003): 269–84.

Altman, Morris, and Louise Lamontagne. "On the Natural Intelligence of Women in a World of Constrained Choice: How the Feminization of Clerical Work Contributed to Gender Pay Equality in Early Twentieth Century Canada." *Journal of Economic Issues* 37, no. 4 (2003): 1045–74.

Anthias, Floya. "Metaphors of Home: Gendering New Migrations to Southern Europe." In *Gender and Migration in Southern Europe*, edited by Floya Anthias and Gabriella Lazaridis, 15–49. Oxford and New York: Berg, 2000.

Anthias, Floya, and Gabriella Lazaridis. "Introduction: Women on the Move in Southern Europe." In *Gender and Migration in Southern Europe*, edited by Floya Anthias and Gabriella Lazaridis, 1–15. Oxford and New York: Berg, 2000.

Anthias, Floya, and Nira Yuval-Davis. "Contextualizing Feminism: Gender, Ethnic, and Class Divisions." *Feminist Review* 15 (1983): 62–75.

Archer, Louise, and Carole Leathwood. "New Times—Old Inequalities: Diverse Working-Class Femininities in Education." *Gender and Education* 15, no. 3 (2003): 227–35.

Aschaffenbur, Karen. "Rethinking Images of the Mobility Regime: Making a Case for Women's Mobility." *Research in Social Stratification and Mobility* 4 (1995): 201–35.

Ayalon, Hanna, Eliezer Ben-Rafael, and Stephen Sharot. "Class Consciousness in Israel." *International Journal of Comparative Sociology* 28, nos. 3–4 (1987): 158–73.

———. "The Impact of Stratification: Assimilation or Ethnic Solidarity." *Research in Social Stratification and Mobility* 7 (1988): 305–26.

Banks, Patricia Anne. "The Essential Leadership Model." *National Association of Secondary School Principals Bulletin* 90, no. 4 (2006): 4–18.

Barth, Fredrik. 1969. "Introduction." In *Ethnic Groups and Boundaries*, edited by Fredrik Barth, 7–9. Bergen-Oslo: Universitets Forlagt; London: Allen and Unwin.

Bashan, Eliezer. 2000. *The Jews of Morocco: Their Past and Culture.* Tel Aviv: Hakibbutz Hameuchad. Hebrew.

Bauman, Zygmunt. "Figures of Modernity." In *The Bauman Reader*, edited by Peter Beilharz, 200–230. Malden, MA: Blackwell, 2001.

Beck, Ulrich. *Risk Society: Towards a New Modernity.* London: Sage, 1992.

Becker, Gary S. *A Treatise on the Family.* Cambridge, MA: Harvard University Press, 1991.

Behr, Joshua G. "Black and Female Municipal Employment: A Substantive Benefit of Minority Political Incorporation." *Journal of Urban Affairs* 22, no. 3 (2000): 243–64.

Beller, Emily. "Bringing Intergenerational Social Mobility Research into the Twenty-First Century: Why Mothers Matter." *American Sociological Review* 74, no. 4 (2009): 507–28.

Ben-Porat, Amir. "Class Structure in Israel: From Statehood to the 1980s." *British Journal of Sociology* 43, no. 2 (1992): 225–38.

———. *Where Are All Those Bourgeoisies? The History of the Israeli Bourgeoisie.* Jerusalem: Magnes Press, Hebrew University, 1999. Hebrew.

Ben-Rafael, Eliezer. *The Emergence of Ethnicity.* Westport, CT: Greenwood Press, 1982.

Ben-Rafael, Eliezer, and Stephen Sharot. *Ethnicity, Religion, and Class in Israeli Society.* Cambridge: Cambridge University Press, 1991.

Benhabib, Doli. "Margalit, My Homeland: Gender and Ethnicity in Sami Michael's Transit Camp (*Ma'abarot*) Novels." *Theory and Criticism* 20 (2002): 243–59. Hebrew.

Beoku-Betts, Josephine. "We Got Our Way of Cooking Things." *Gender and Society* 9 (1995): 535–55.

Bernstein, Deborah. "Conflict and Protest: The Case of the Black Panthers of Israel." *Youth and Society* 16, no. 2 (1984): 129–52.

———. "Oriental and Ashkenazi Jewish Women in the Labor Market." In *Calling the Equality Bluff: Women in Israel*, edited by Barbara Swirski and Marilyn P. Safir, 192–97. New York: Pergamon Press, 1991.

Bernstein, Deborah, and Shlomo Swirski. "The Rapid Economic Development of Israel and the Emergence of the Ethnic Division of Labour." *British Journal of Sociology* 33, no. 1 (1982): 64–85.

Bettie, Julie. "Exceptions to the Rule: Upwardly Mobile White and Mexican American High School Girls." *Gender and Society* 16, no. 3 (2002): 403–22.

Billson, Janet Mancini. *Keepers of Culture.* New York: Lexington, 1995.

Birenbaum-Carmeli, Daphna. *Tel Aviv North: The Makings of a New Israeli Middle Class.* Jerusalem: Magnes Press, Hebrew University, 2000. Hebrew.

Black, Sandra E. "Do Better Schools Matter? Parental Evaluation of Elementary Education." *Quarterly Journal of Economics* (May 1999): 577–600.

Blair-Loy, Mary. *Competing Devotions: Career and Family among Women Executives.* Cambridge, MA: Harvard University Press, 2003.

Bourdieu, Pierre. *Distinction.* Cambridge, MA: Harvard University Press, 1984.

Bradley, Harriet. *Fractured Identities: Changing Patterns of Inequality.* Cambridge: Polity Press, 1996.

Brah, Avtar. "Time, Place, and Others: Discourses of Race, Nation, and Ethnicity." *Sociology* 28, no. 3 (1994): 805–13.

Brinton, Mary. *Women and the Economic Miracle.* Berkeley: University of California Press, 1993.

Britton, Carolyn, and Arthur Baxter. "Becoming a Mature Student: Gendered Narratives of the Self." *Gender and Education* 11, no. 2 (1999): 179–93.

Brown, Kenneth. "Mellah and Medina: A Moroccan City and Its Jewish Quarter (Sale ca. 1880–1930)." In *Studies in Judaism and Islam*, edited by Shlomo Morag, Issachar Ben Ami, and Norman Stillman, 253–76. Jerusalem: Magnes Press, Hebrew University, 1981.

Canetti, Elias. *Voices from Marrakech.* Jerusalem: Carmel Press, 2000. Hebrew.

Castles, Stephen, and Mark J. Miller. *The Age of Migration.* Houndsmills, Basingtoke, Hampshire: Macmillan, 1993.

Central Bureau of Statistics. *Statistical Abstract of Israel.* Jerusalem: Government of Israel, 2005.

Chafetz, Janet Saltzman. "Structure, Consciousness, Agency, and Social Change in Feminist Sociological Theories." *Current Perspectives in Social Theory* 19 (1999): 145–64.

Cherlin, Andrew J. "The Deinstitutionalization of Marriage." *Journal of Marriage and Family* 66 (November 2004): 848–61.

———. 2009. *The Marriage-Go-Round.* New York: Random House.

Chetrit, Sami Shalom. *The Mizrahi Struggle in Israel: Between Oppression and Liberation, Identification and Alternative, 1948–2003.* Tel Aviv: Am Oved, 2004. Hebrew.

Child, Irvin Long. *Italian or American? The Second Generation in Conflict*. New Haven, CT: Yale University Press, 1943.

Cohen, Uri, and Nissim Leon. "Concerning the Question of the Mizrahi Middle Class." *Alpayim* 32 (2008): 83–101. Hebrew.

Cohen, Yinon, and Yitchak Haberfeld. "Gender, Ethnic, and National Earnings Gaps in Israel: The Role of Rising Inequality." Discussion Paper No. 5-2003. Tel Aviv: Tel Aviv University, The Pinhas Sapir Center for Development, 2003.

———. "Second-Generation Jewish Immigrants in Israel: Have the Ethnic Gaps in Schooling and Earnings Declined?" *Ethnic and Racial Studies* 21, no. 3 (1998): 507–29.

Collins, Randall. *Sociological Insight*. Oxford: Oxford University Press, 1992.

Crompton, Rosemary. "The Gendered Restructuring of the Middle Classes: Employment and Caring." In *Renewing Class Analysis*, edited by Rosemary Crompton, Fiona Devine, Mike Savage, and John Scott, 165–84. Oxford and Malden, MA: Blackwell, 2000.

Crompton, Rosemary, and Gareth Jones. *White-Collar Proletariat: Deskilling and Gender in Clerical Work*. London: Macmillan, 1984.

Crompton, Rosemary, and John Scott. "Introduction: The State of Class Analysis." In *Renewing Class Analysis*, edited by Rosemary Crompton, Fiona Devine, Mike Savage, and John Scott, 1–16. Oxford and Malden, MA: Blackwell, 2000.

Crul, Maurice, and Jeroen Doomernik. "The Turkish and Moroccan Second Generation in the Netherlands: Divergent Trends between and Polarization within the Two Groups." *International Migration Review* 37, no. 4 (2003): 1039–64.

Crul, Maurice, and Hans Vermeulen. "The Second Generation in Europe." *International Migration Review* 37, no. 4 (2003): 965–86.

Cunnsion, Sheila. "Gender Joking in the Staffroom." In *Teachers, Gender, and Careers*, edited by Sandra Acker, 151–71. East Sussex: Falmer Press, 1989.

Dahan, Momi. "Inequality in Israel: The Role of Education." *Economic Quarterly* 51, no. 2 (2004): 187–98. Hebrew.

Dahan-Kalev, Henriette. "Illusions in Assimilation." In *The Flying Camel*, edited by Loolwa Khazzoom, 157–73. New York: Seal Press, 2003.

———. "You're So Pretty: You Don't Look Moroccan." *Israel Studies* 6, no. 1 (2001): 1–13.

Dahan-Kalev, Henriette, Niza Yanay, and Niza Berkovitch, eds. *Women of the South: Space, Periphery, and Gender*. Beer Sheva: Ben Gurion Research Institute, Ben Gurion University of the Negev, 2005. Hebrew.

Davis, Nancy J., and Robert V. Robinson. "Do Wives Matter? Class Identities of Wives and Husbands." *Social Forces* 76, no. 3 (1998): 1063–86.

Deshen, Shlomo. "Political Ethnicity and Cultural Ethnicity in Israel during the 1960s." In *Urban Ethnicity*, edited by Abner Cohen, 281–311. London: Tavistock, 1974.

———. "Women in the Jewish Family in Pre-Colonial Morocco." *Anthropological Quarterly* 53, no. 3 (1983): 134–45.

DeVault, Ileen A. *Sons and Daughters of Labor: Class and Clerical Work in Turn-of-the-Century Pittsburgh*. Ithaca, NY: Cornell University Press, 1990.

Devine, Fiona. "Talking about Class in Britain." In *Social Inequalities in Comparative Perspective*, edited by Fiona Devine and Mary C. Waters, 191–214. Malden, MA: Blackwell, 2004.

Donat, Doris. "Emancipation of the Jewish Woman in Morocco." *In the Dispersion* (1963): 127–37.

Dowling, Robyn. "Gender, Class, and Home Ownership: Placing the Connections." *Housing Studies* 13, no. 4 (1998): 471–86.

Downey, Douglas B. "When Bigger Is Not Better: Family Size, Parental Resources, and Children's Educational Performance." *American Sociological Review* 60, no. 5 (1995): 746–61.

Dronkers, Jaap, and Fenella Fleischman. "The Effects of Social and Labour Market Policies of EU Countries on the Socio-Economic Integration of First and Second Generation Immigrants from Different Countries of Origin." Paper presented at the Meeting of International Sociological Association Research Committee on Social Stratification and Mobility, Brno, Czech Republic, May 25–27, 2007.

Duncan, Simon. "Mothering, Class, and Rationality." *Sociological Review* 53, no. 1 (2005): 50–76.

Eisenstadt, S. N. "Frameworks of the Great Revolutions: Culture, Social Structure, History, and Human Agency." *International Social Science Journal* 133, no. 44 (1992): 385–403.

———. *Israeli Society*. New York: Basic Books, 1967.

Eisenstadt, S. N., and Bernhard Giesen. "The Construction of Collective Identity." *Archives Europeennes de Sociologie* 36 (1994): 72–102.

Emirbayer, Mustafa, and Ann Misch. "What Is Agency?" *American Journal of Sociology* 103, no. 4 (1998): 962–1023.

Erikson, Robert. "Social Class of Men, Women, and Families." *Sociology* 18, no. 4 (1984): 500–514.

Erikson, Robert, and John H. Goldthorpe. *The Constant Flux*. Oxford: Clarendon Press, 1993.

Espiritu, Yen Le. "'We Don't Sleep Around Like White Girls Do': Family Culture, Culture, and Gender in Filipina American Lives." In *Gender and U.S. Immigration*, edited by Pierrette Hondagneu-Sotelo, 263–87. Berkeley: University of California Press, 2003.

Fogiel-Bijaoui, Sylvia. "Families in Israel: Between Familism and Post-Modernity." In *Sex, Gender, Politics: Women in Israel*, edited by Dafna N. Izraeli, Henriette Dahan-Kalev, Sylvie Fogiel-Bijaoui, Hanna Herzog, Manar Hasan, and Hannah Naveh, 107–67. Tel Aviv: Hakibbutz Hameuchad, 1999. Hebrew.

Foner, Nancy. "The Immigrant Family: Cultural Legacies and Cultural Changes." *International Migration Review* 31, no. 4 (1997): 961–74.

Friedlander, Dov, Zvi Eisenbach, and Calvin Goldscheider. "Family-Size Limitation and Birth Spacing: The Fertility Transition of African and Asian Immigrants in Israel." *Population and Development Review* 6, no. 4 (1980): 581–94.

Fuchs, Ina. "Teaching Images and Socio-Economic Status of Teachers in Four Sectors of the Israeli Educational System." *Megamot: Social Science Quarterly* 38, no. 2 (1997): 226–46. Hebrew.

Gans, Herbert J. "Symbolic Ethnicity: The Future of Ethnic Groups and Cultures in America." *Ethnic and Racial Studies* 2, no. 1 (1979): 1–21.

Gaskell, Jane. "Course Enrollment in the High School: The Perspective of Working Class Females." *Sociology of Education* 58 (January 1985): 48–59.

Gay, Peter. *Pleasure Wars.* New York: Norton, 1998.

Geertz, Clifford. *After the Fact: Two Countries, Four Decades, One Anthropologist.* Cambridge, MA: Harvard University Press, 1995.

Geschwender, James A. "Ethgender, Women's Waged Labor, and Economic Mobility." *Social Problems* 39, no. 1 (1992): 1–17.

Giddens, Anthony. *The Constitution of Society.* Berkeley: University of California Press, 1984.

———. *Modernity and Self-Identity: Self and Society in the Late Modern Age.* Stanford, CA: Stanford University Press, 1991.

Gilad, Lisa. *Ginger and Salt: Yemeni Jewish Women in an Israeli Town.* Boulder, CO: Westview Press, 1989.

Glaser, Barney G., and Anselm Strauss. *The Discovery of Grounded Theory.* Chicago: Aldine, 1971.

Glazer, Nathan, and Daniel Patrick Moynihan. *Beyond the Melting Pot: The Negroes, Puerto Ricans, Jews, Italians, and Irish of New York City.* Cambridge, MA: MIT Press, 1963.

Glenn, Evelyn Nakano, and Roslyn L. Feldberg. "Degraded and Deskilled: The Proletarianization of Clerical Work." *Social Problems* 25, no. 1 (1977): 52–64.

Goldberg, Harvey. "The Changing Meaning of Ethnic Affiliation." *Jerusalem Quarterly* 44 (1987): 39–50.

———. "Historical and Cultural Dimensions of Ethnic Phenomena in Israel." In *Studies in Israeli Ethnicity*, edited by Alex Weingrod, 179–200. New York: Gordon and Breach, 1985.

Goldberg, Harvey, and Chen Bram. "Sephardic/Mizrahi/Arab-Jews: Reflections on Critical Sociology and the Study of Middle Eastern Jewries within the Context of Israeli Society." *Studies in Contemporary Jewry* 22 (2007): 227–56.

Goldstein, Judith L. "Iranian Identity in Israel: The Performance of Identity." In *Immigration to Israel*, edited by Elazar Leshem and Judith T. Shuval, 387–407. New Brunswick, NJ: Transaction Publishers, 1998.

Goldthorpe, John H. "Women and Class Analysis: In Defense of the Conventional View." *Sociology* 17, no. 4 (1983): 465–88.

Goldthorpe, John H., and Gordon Marshall. "The Promising Future of Class Analysis: A Response to Recent Critiques." *Sociology* 26, no. 3 (1992): 381–400.

Goldthorpe, John H., and Clive Payne. "On the Class Mobility of Women: Results from Different Approaches to the Analysis of Recent British Data." *Sociology* 20, no. 4 (1986): 531–55.

Goldthorpe, John H., Meir Yaish, and Vered Kraus. "Class Mobility in Israeli Society." *Research in Stratification and Mobility* 15 (1997): 3–28.

Goshen-Gottstein, Esther. *Marriage and First Pregnancy: Cultural Influences on Attitudes of Israeli Women.* London: Tavistock, 1966.

Government of Israel. *Census.* Jerusalem: Central Bureau of Statistics, 1983. Hebrew.

———. *Census.* Jerusalem: Central Bureau of Statistics, 1995. Hebrew.

———. *Compulsory Education Law.* Jerusalem: Government of Israel, 1949. Hebrew.

———. *Single Parent Family Law.* Jerusalem: Government of Israel, 1992. Hebrew.

———. *Standard Classification of Occupations.* Jerusalem: Central Bureau of Statistics, 1994. Hebrew.

Goyette, Kimberly, and Yu Xie. "Educational Expectations of Asian-American Youths: Determinants and Ethnic Differences." *Sociology of Education* 72, no. 1 (1999): 22–36.

Grier, Katherine. "Childhood Socialization and Companion Animals: United States, 1820–1870. *Society and Animals* 7, no. 2 (1999): 95–120.

——— *Culture and Comfort: Parlor Making and the Middle-Class Identity, 1850–1930.* Washington, DC: Smithsonian Institution Press, 1997.

Gronau, Reuven. "The Effects of Children on the Housewife's Value of Time." *Journal of Political Economy* 81, no. 2 (1973): 168–99.

Hasson, Shlomo. *Urban Social Movements in Jerusalem: The Protest of the Second Generation.* Albany: State University of New York Press, in cooperation with the Jerusalem Institute for Israeli Studies, 1993.

Hayes, Bernadette, and F. I. Jones. "Class Identification among Australian Couples: Are Wives' Characteristics Irrelevant?" *British Journal of Sociology* 43 (1992): 462–83.

Heller, Agnes. "The Many Faces of Multiculturalism." In *The Challenge of Diversity*, edited by Rainer Bauböck, Agnes Heller, and Aristide R. Zolberg, 43–67. Aldershot, England: Avebury, 1996.

Herbst, Anat. "We Support the Law for Single-Parent Families, Poor Things." *National Insurance* 80 (August 2009): 25–58. Hebrew.

Hever, Hannan, Yehouda Shenhav, and Pnina Motzafi-Haller, eds. *Mizrahim in Israel: A Critical Observation into Israel's Ethnicity.* Jerusalem and Tel Aviv: Van Leer Jerusalem Institute and Hakibbutz Hameuchad, 2002. Hebrew.

Hey, Valerie. "Joining the Club? Academic and Working-Class Femininities." *Gender and Education* 15, no. 3 (2003): 319–35.

Hondagneu-Sotelo, Pierrette. "Gender and Immigration." In *Gender and U.S. Immigration,* edited by Pierrette Hondagneu-Sotelo, 3–20. Berkeley: University of California Press, 2003.

Horowitz, Dan, and Moshe Lissak. *Trouble in Utopia.* Albany: State University of New York Press, 1989.

Inbar, Michael, and Chaim Adler. *Ethnic Integration in Israel: A Comparative Study of Moroccan Brothers Who Settled in France and Israel.* New Brunswick, NJ: Transaction Books, 1977.

Jeannotte, M. Sharon, Dick Stanley, Ravi Pendakur, Bruce Jamieson, Maureen Williams, and Amanda Aizelwood. *Buying In or Dropping Out: The Public Policy Implications of Social Cohesion Research.* Ottawa: Department of Canadian Heritage, 2002.

Jensen, Jane. *Mapping Social Cohesion: The State of Canadian Research.* Ottawa: Canadian Policy Research Networks, 1998.

Jones, Deborah J., Rex Forehand, Gene Brody, and Lisa Armistead. "Psychosocial Adjustment of African American Children in Single-Mother Families: A Test of Three Risk Models." *Journal of Marriage and Family* 64 (February 2002): 105–15.

Kandiyoti, Deniz. "Bargaining with Patriarchy." *Gender and Society* 2, no. 3 (1998): 274–90.

Kao, Grace, and Marta Tienda. "Optimism and Achievement: The Educational Performance of Immigrant Youth." *Social Science Quarterly* 76, no. 1 (1995): 1–20.

Kasinitz, Philip, John H. Mollenkopf, and Mary C. Waters, eds. *Becoming New Yorkers.* New York: Russell Sage Foundation, 2004.

Kasinitz, Philip, John H. Mollenkopf, Mary C. Waters, and Jennifer Holdaway. *Inheriting the City: The Children of Immigrants Come of Age.* New York: Russell Sage Foundation; Cambridge, MA: Harvard University Press, 2008.

Katz-Gerro, Tally, and Yossi Shavit. "Lifestyle and Social Class in Israel." *Israeli Sociology* 1, no. 1 (1998): 91–115. Hebrew.

Katzir, Yael. "Yemenite Jewish Women in Israeli Rural Development: Female Power vs. Male Authority." *Economic Development and Cultural Change* 32, no. 1 (1983): 45–61.

Khazzoom, Aziza. "The Impact of Mother's Occupations on Children's Occupational Destinations." *Research in Stratification and Mobility* 15 (1997): 57–89.

———. *Shifting Ethnic Boundaries and Inequality in Israel.* Stanford, CA: Stanford University Press, 2008.

Kibria, Nazli. "Power, Patriarchy, and Gender Conflict in a Vietnamese Community." *Gender and Society* 4, no. 1 (1990): 9–24.

Kofman, Eleonore. "Female 'Birds of Passage' a Decade Later: Gender and Immigration in the European Union." *International Migration Review* 33, no. 2 (1999): 269–300.

Korupp, Sylvia A., Harry B. G. Ganzeboom, and Tanja van der Lippe. "Do Mothers Matter? A Comparison of Models of Influence of Mothers' and Fathers' Educational and Occupational Status on Children's Educational Attainment." *Quality and Quantity* 36 (2002): 17–42.

Kraus, Vered. *Secondary Breadwinners: Israeli Women in the Labor Force.* Westport, CT: Praeger, 2002.

———. "Social Segregation in Israel as a Function of Objective and Subjective Attributes of the Ethnic Groups." *Sociology and Social Research* 69, no. 1 (1984): 50–71.

Kremer-Hayon, Lya, and Zahava Goldstein. "The Inner World of Israeli Secondary School Teachers: Work, Centrality, Job Satisfaction, and Stress." *Comparative Education* 26, no. 3/4 (1990): 285–99.

Kwong, Peter. *The New Chinatown.* New York: Noonday Press, 1996.

Laskier, Michael M. *The Alliance Israélite Universelle and the Jewish Communities of Morocco: 1862–1962.* Albany: State University of New York Press, 1983.

———. "Education." In *Morocco*, edited by Haim Saadon, 129–44. Jerusalem: Ministry of Education and Culture, Government of Israel and Ben-Zvi Institute for Research on Jewish Communities in the East, 2004. Hebrew.

Lawler, Steph. *Mothering the Self.* London and New York: Routledge, 2000.

Lee, Stacey J. "The Road to College: Hmong American Women's Pursuit of Higher Education." *Harvard Educational Review* 67, no. 4 (1997): 803–28.

Lewin-Epstein, Noah, Yuval Elmelech, and Moshe Semyonov. "Ethnic Inequality in Home Ownership and the Value of Housing: The Case of Immigrants in Israel." *Social Forces* 75, no. 4 (1997): 439–62.

Lewin-Epstein, Noah, and Moshe Semyonov. "Ethnic Group Mobility in the Israeli Labor Market." *American Sociological Review* 51, no. 3 (1986): 342–51.

Lissak, Moshe. *The Mass Immigration in the Fifties: The Failure of the Melting Pot Policy.* Jerusalem: The Bialik Institute, 1999. Hebrew.

———. *Social Mobility in Israeli Society.* Jerusalem: Israel Universities Press, 1969. Hebrew.

Livingston, Gretchen, and Joan R. Kahn. "An American Dream Unfulfilled: The Limited Mobility of Mexican Americans." *Social Science Quarterly* 83, no. 4 (2002): 1003–13.

Lorber, Judith, and Susan Farrell, eds. *The Social Construction of Gender.* Newbury Park, CA: Sage, 1994.

Lorber, Judith, and Lisa Jean Moore. *Gendered Bodies: Feminist Perspectives.* Los Angeles: Roxbury, 2007.

Louie, Vivian. "Parents' Aspirations and Investment: The Role of Social Class in the Educational Experiences of 1.5 and Second-Generation Chinese Americans." *Harvard Educational Review* 71, no. 3 (2001): 438–74.

Lubin, Orly. "From Territory to Site: The Oriental Woman in the Film 'Jacky.'" *Criticism and Interpretation* 34 (2000): 177–93. Hebrew.

Lucey, Helen, June Melody, and Valerie Walkerdine. "Uneasy Hybrids: Psychological Aspects of Becoming Educationally Successful for Working-Class Young Women." *Gender and Education* 15, no. 3 (2003): 285–301.

MacLeod, Jay. "Ain't No Makin' It: Leveled Aspirations in a Low-income Neighborhood." In *Social Stratification in Sociological Perspective*, edited by David B. Grusky, 347–59. Boulder, CO: Westview Press, 1994.

Madigan, Ruth, Moira Munro, and Susan J. Smith. "Gender and the Meaning of Home." *International Journal of Urban and Regional Research* 14, no. 4 (1990): 625–47.

Mahony, Pat, and Christine Zmroczek, eds. *Class Matters: "Working-Class" Women's Perspectives on Social Class.* London and Bristol, PA: Taylor and Francis, 1997.

Mannheim, Karl. *Essays on the Sociology of Knowledge*, edited by Paul Kecskemeti. London: Routledge and Kegan Paul, 1952.

Mark, Nili. "Ethnic Gaps in Israel in Incomes and Consumption." *Economic Quarterly* 41, no. 1 (1994): 55–77. Hebrew.

Markus, Andrew, and Arunachalam Dharmalingam. "Attitudinal Divergence in a Melbourne Region of High Immigrant Concentration: A Case Study." *People and Place* 15, no. 4 (2007): 38–48.

McCall, Leslie. "The Complexity of Intersectionality." *Signs* 30, no. 3 (2005): 1771–800.

Mizrachi, Beverly. "Elite Educational Institutions and the Recruitment of Women into National Elite Positions in Israel." *Israel Social Science Research* 12, no. 2 (1997): 93–109.

———. "The Henna-Maker: A Moroccan Immigrant Woman Entrepreneur in an Ethnic Revival." In *Research in the Sociology of Work*, vol. 15, edited by Lisa A. Keister, 257–79. Amsterdam: Elsevier, 2005.

———. "Non-Mainstream Education, Limited Mobility, and the Second Generation of Moroccan Immigrant Women: The Case of the Kindergarten Teacher's Assistant." *Nashim* 8 (Fall 2004): 50–73.

Moore, Dahlia, and Abraham Gobi. "Role Conflict and Perceptions of Gender Roles (The Case of Israel)." *Sex Roles* 32, no. 3/4 (1995): 251–71.

Motzafi-Haller, Pnina. "Scholarship, Identity, and Power: Mizrachi Women in Israel." *Signs* 26, no. 3 (2001): 697–735.

Munt, Ian. "The 'Other' Postmodern Tourism: Culture, Travel, and the New Middle Classes." *Theory, Culture, and Society* 11 (1994): 101–23.

Nagel, Joane. "Constructing Ethnicity: Creating and Recreating Ethnic Identity and Culture." *Social Problems* 41, no. 1 (1994): 152–76.

Nahon, Yaacov. "Women: Education, Occupation, and Salary." In *Ethnic Communities in Israel: Socio-Economic Status*, edited by S. N. Eisenstadt, Moshe Lissak, and Yaacov Nahon, 90–103. Jerusalem: Jerusalem Institute for Israel Studies, 1993. Hebrew.

O'Brien, Maeve. "Girls and Transition to Second-Level Schooling in Ireland: 'Moving On' and 'Moving Out'." *Gender and Education* 15, no. 3 (2003): 249–68.

Okamura, Jonathan Y. "Situational Ethnicity." *Ethnic and Racial Studies* 4, no. 4 (1981): 452–66.

Payne, Geoff, and Pamela Abbott. *The Social Mobility of Women: Beyond Male Mobility Models*. London: Falmer, 1990.

Peets, Leonora. *Women of Marrakech*. London: Hurst, 1998.

Peled, Yoav. "Towards a Redefinition of Jewish Nationalism in Israel? The Enigma of *Shas*." *Ethnic and Racial Studies* 21, no. 4 (1998): 703–28.

Percheski, Christine. "Opting Out? Cohort Differences in Professional Women's Employment Rates from 1960 to 2005." *American Sociological Review* 73, no. 3 (2008): 497–517.

Peres, Yochanan. "Ethnic Relations in Israel." *American Journal of Sociology* 76, no. 6 (1971): 1021–47.

Peres, Yochanan, and Ruth Katz. "Stability and Centrality: The Nuclear Family in Modern Israel." *Social Forces* 59 (1981): 687–704.

Perlmann, Joel, and Roger Waldinger. "Second Generation Decline? Children of Immigrants, Past and Present: A Reconsideration." *International Migration Review* 31, no. 4 (1997): 893–922.

Portes, Alejandro. "Children of Immigrants: Segmented Assimilation and Its Determinants." In *The Economic Sociology of Immigration: Essays on Networks, Eth-*

*nicity, and Entrepreneurship*, edited by Alejandro Portes, 248–81. New York: Russell Sage Foundation, 1995.

———. "The Rise of Ethnicity: Determinants of Ethnic Perceptions among Cuban Exiles in Miami." *American Sociological Review* 49 (1984): 383–97.

Portes, Alejandro, ed. *The New Second Generation.* New York: Russell Sage Foundation, 1996.

Portes, Alejandro, and Rubén G. Rumbaut. *Immigrant America: A Portrait*, 2nd ed. Berkeley: University of California Press, 1996.

———. *Legacies: The Story of the Immigrant Second Generation.* Berkeley: University of California Press; New York: Russell Sage Foundation, 2001.

Portes, Alejandro, and Min Zhou. "The New Second Generation: Segmented Assimilation and Its Variants." *Annals of American Academy of Political and Social Sciences* 530 (1993): 74–96.

Radner, Hillary. *Shopping Around: Feminine Culture and the Pursuit of Pleasure.* London: Routledge, 1995.

Ransford, H. Edward, and Jon Miller. "Race, Sex, and Feminist Outlooks." *American Sociological Review* 48 (1983): 46–59.

Reay, Diane. "Rethinking Social Class: Qualitative Perspectives on Class and Gender." *Sociology* 32, no. 2 (1998): 259–76.

———. "A Risky Business? Mature Working-Class Women Students and Access to Higher Education." *Gender and Education* 15, no. 3 (2003): 301–19.

Remennick, Larissa. "Providers, Caregivers, and Sluts: Women with a Russian Accent in Israel." *Nashim*, no. 8 (Fall 2004): 87–115.

Riehl, Carolyn, and Mark A. Byrd. "Gender Differences among New Recruits to School Administration: Cautionary Footnotes to an Optimistic Tale." *Educational Evaluation and Policy Analysis* 19, no. 1 (1997): 45–64.

Rodrigue, Aron. *Images of Sephardi and Eastern Jewries in Transition.* Seattle: University of Washington Press, 1993.

Rosenfeld, Henry, and Shulamit Carmi. "The Privatization of Public Means: The State-Made Middle Class and the Realization of Family Value in Israel." In *Kinship and Modernization in Mediterranean Society*, edited by Jean George Peristiany, 131–59. Rome: Center for Mediterranean Studies, American Universities Field Staff, 1976.

Ruddick, Sara. *Maternal Thinking: Towards a Politics of Peace.* London: The Women's Press, 1989.

Saadon, Haim. "The Immigration of Moroccan Jewry: Stages and Characteristics." In *Morocco*, edited by Haim Saadon, 109–29. Jerusalem: Ministry of Education and Culture, Government of Israel and Ben-Zvi Institute for Research on Jewish Communities in the East, 2004. Hebrew.

Safilios-Rotschild, Constantina, and Marcellinus Dijkers. "Handling Unconventional Asymmetries." In *Working Couples*, edited by Rhona Rapoport and Robert N. Rapoport, 62–74. London: Routledge and Kegan Paul, 1978.

Said, Edward W. *Orientalism.* London: Penguin Books, 1995.

Salaff, Janet, and Arent Greve. "Women That Move: International Migration from the PRC to Canada and the Negotiation of Gendered Job Opportunities," 2002. http://homes.chass.utoronto.ca/~salaff/PRC_GenMig.PDF.

Sayer, Andrew. *The Moral Significance of Class.* Cambridge: Cambridge University Press, 2005.

Schely-Newman, Esther. *Our Lives Are But Stories: Narratives of Tunisian-Israeli Women.* Detroit: Wayne State University Press, 2002.

Scott, James C. *Domination and the Arts of Resistance.* New Haven, CT: Yale University Press, 1990.

Seccombe, Karen, Delores James, and Kimberly Battle Walters. "'They Think You Ain't Much of Nothing': The Social Construction of the Welfare Mother." *Journal of Marriage and the Family* 60 (1998): 849–65.

Semyonov, Moshe, and Tamar Lerenthal. "Country of Origin, Gender, and the Attainment of Socioeconomic Status: A Study of Stratification in the Jewish Population in Israel." *Research in Social Stratification and Mobility* 10 (1991): 325–43.

Semyonov, Moshe, and Noah Lewin-Epstein. "The Impact of Parental Transfers on Living Standards of Married Children." *Social Indicators Research* 54, no. 2 (2001): 115–25.

Sennett, Richard, and Jonathan Cobb. *The Hidden Injuries of Class.* New York: Norton, 1972.

Shamir, Ronen. "Jewish Bourgeoisie in Colonial Palestine: Outline for a Research Agenda." *Israeli Sociology* 3, no. 1 (2000): 133–49. Hebrew.

Sharaby, Rachel. *The Mimuna Holiday: From Periphery to the Center.* Tel Aviv: Hakibbutz Hameuchad, 2009. Hebrew.

Sharni, Shoshana. *Characteristics of Moroccan and Yemenite Women with 0–8 Years of Schooling.* Jerusalem: Center for Demography, Prime Minister's Office, Government of Israel, 1973. Hebrew.

Shavit, Yossi. "Segregation, Tracking, and the Educational Attainments of Minorities: Arabs and Oriental Jews in Israel." *American Sociological Review* 55 (1990): 115–26.

Shenhav, Yehouda. *The Arab Jews: Nationalism, Religion, and Ethnicity.* Tel Aviv: Am Oved, 2004. Hebrew.

Shitreet, Elisheva. "Jewish Women's Work in the Traditional Society of Marrakech." In *The Work of Her Hands: Women, Work, and Family*, edited by Tova Cohen, 35–41. Ramat Gan, Israel: Bar-Ilan University, 2001. Hebrew.

Shohat, Ella. "Making the Silences Speak in the Israeli Cinema." In *Calling the Equality Bluff: Women in Israel*, edited by Barbara Swirski and Marilyn P. Safir, 31–41. New York: Pergamon Press, 1991.

Shwed, Uri, and Yossi Shavit. "The Occupational and Economic Attainments of College and University Graduates in Israel." *European Sociological Review* 22, no. 4 (2006): 431–42.

Sidel, Ruth. *Unsung Heroines.* Berkeley: University of California Press, 2006.

Skeggs, Beverley. *Formations of Class and Gender.* London: Sage, 1997.

Smith, Bonnie. *Ladies of the Leisure Class.* Princeton, NJ: Princeton University Press, 1981.

Smooha, Sammy. "Class, Ethnic, and National Cleavages and Democracy in Israel." In *Israeli Democracy under Stress*, edited by Ehud Sprinzak and Larry Diamond, 293–343. Boulder, CO: Lynne Rienner, 1993.

———. *Israel: Pluralism and Conflict.* Berkeley: University of California Press, 1978.

Smooha, Sammy, and Vered Kraus. "Ethnicity as a Factor in Status Attainment in Israel." *Research in Social Stratification and Mobility* 4 (1985): 151–75.

Sørenson, Annette. "Women, Family, and Class." *Annual Review of Sociology* 20 (1994): 27–47.

Spilerman, Seymour, and J. Habib. "Development Towns in Israel: The Role of Community in Creating Ethnic Disparities in Labor Force Characteristics." *American Journal of Sociology* 81 (1976): 781–812.

Stanworth, Michelle. "Women and Class Analysis: A Reply to John Goldthorpe." *Sociology* 18, no. 2 (1984): 159–70.

Steedman, Carolyn Kay. *Landscape for a Good Woman: A Story of Two Lives.* New Brunswick, NJ: Rutgers University Press, 1997.

Stein, Howard F., and Robert F. Hill. *The Ethnic Imperative: Examining the New White Movement.* University Park: Pennsylvania State University Press, 1977.

Steinberg, Stephen. *The Ethnic Myth.* Boston: Beacon Press, 2001.

Stier, Haya, and Yossi Shavit. "Age at Marriage, Sex Ratios, and Ethnic Heterogamy." *European Sociological Review* 10, no. 1 (1994): 79–84.

Strom, Sharon. *Beyond the Typewriter: Gender, Class, and the Origins of Modern American Office Work.* Urbana: University of Illinois Press, 1992.

Swidler, Ann. "Culture in Action: Symbols and Strategies." *American Sociological Review* 51 (1986): 273–86.

Swirski, Shlomo, Vered Kraus, Etty Konor-Attias, and Anat Herbst. "Solo Mothers in Israel." *Equality Monitor* 12 (2003): 1–36.

Tett, Lyn. "'I'm Working Class and Proud of It': Gendered Experiences of Non-Traditional Participants in Higher Education." *Gender and Education* 12, no. 2 (2000): 183–94.

Tienda, Marta, and Karen Booth. "Gender, Migration, and Social Change." *International Sociology* 6, no. 1 (1991): 51–72.

Timmerman, Christiane, Els Vanderwaeren, and Maurice Crul. "The Second Generation in Belgium." *International Migration Review* 37, no. 4 (2003): 1065–89.

Trillo, Alex. "Somewhere between Wall Street and El Barrio: Community College as a Second Chance for Second-Generation Latino Students." In *Becoming New Yorkers,* edited by Philip Kasinitz, John H. Mollenkopf, and Mary C. Waters, 57–79. New York: Russell Sage Foundation, 2004.

Tsolidis, Georgina. *Educating Voula: A Report on Non-English-Speaking Background Girls and Education.* Melbourne: Victorian Ministerial Advisory Committee on Multicultural and Migrant Education, 1986.

Tsur, Yaron. *A Torn Community: The Jews of Morocco and Nationalism, 1943–1954.* Tel Aviv: Am Oved, 2001. Hebrew.

Tsur, Yaron, and Hagar Hillel. *The Jews of Casablanca: Studies in the Modernization of the Political Elite in a Colonial Community.* Tel Aviv: Open University of Israel, 1995. Hebrew.

Turner, Jonathan H. *Human Emotions: A Sociological Theory.* London and New York: Routledge, 2007.

United Nations. *Demographic and Social Statistics*. New York: United Nations, 2008.

Vincent, Carol, Stephen J. Ball, and Sophie Kemp. "The Social Geography of Childcare: Making Up a Middle-Class Child." *British Journal of Sociology of Education* 25, no. 2 (2004): 229–45.

Waldinger, Roger, and Joel Perlmann. "Second Generations: Past, Present, Future." *Journal of Ethnic and Migration Studies* 24 (January 1998): 5–24.

Walkerdine, Valerie. "Reclassifying Upward Mobility: Femininity and the Neo-Liberal Subject." *Gender and Education* 15, no. 3 (2003): 237–48.

Wasserfall, Rahel. "Menstruation and Identity: The Meaning of Niddah for Moroccan Women Immigrants to Israel." In *People of the Body: Jews and Judaism from an Embodied Perspective*, edited by Howard Eilberg-Schwartz, 309–29. Albany: State University of New York Press, 1992.

Waters, Mary C. *Ethnic Options*. Berkeley: University of California Press, 1990.

———. "Ethnic and Racial Identities of Second-Generation Black Immigrants in New York City." In *The New Second Generation*, edited by Alejandro Portes, 170–97. New York: Russell Sage Foundation, 1996.

Weber, Max. "Class, Status, Party." In *Economy and Society*, vol. 2, edited by Gunther Roth and Claus Wittich, 926–40. New York: Bedminster Press, 1968.

Weingrod, Alex. "Recent Trends in Israeli Ethnicity." *Ethnic and Racial Studies* 2, no. 1 (1979): 55–65.

West, Candace, and Don Zimmerman. "Doing Gender." *Gender and Society* 1, no. 2 (1987): 125–51.

Wirth, Linda. *Breaking through the Glass Ceiling*. Geneva: International Labour Office, 2001.

Wong, Yi-Lee. "A Unified Middle Class or Two Middle Classes? A Comparison of Career Strategies and Intergenerational Mobility Strategies between Teachers and Managers in Contemporary Hong Kong." *British Journal of Sociology* 55, no. 2 (2004): 167–87.

Worbs, Susanne. "The Second Generation in Germany: Between School and Labor Market." *International Migration Review* 37, no. 4 (2003): 1020–39.

Wright, Stephen C., Donald M. Taylor, and Fathali M. Moghaddam. "Responding to Membership in a Disadvantaged Group: From Acceptance to Collective Protest." *Journal of Personality and Social Psychology* 58, no. 6 (1990): 994–1003.

Yaar, Ephraim. "Private Entrepreneurship as a Path to Socio-Economic Mobility: An Additional Look at Ethnic Stratification in Israel." In *Stratification in Israeli Society: Ethnic, National, and Class Cleavages*, vol. 1, edited by Moshe Lissak, 386–428. Tel Aviv: Open University of Israel, 1989. Hebrew.

Yaish, Meir. "Class Structure in a Deeply Divided Society: Class and Ethnic Inequality in Israel." *British Journal of Sociology* 52, no. 3 (2001): 409–38.

Yogev, Abraham, Idit Livneh, and Oren Pizmony-Levy. "Non-Academic Post-Secondary Education in Israel: Separate but Equal?" *Israeli Sociology* 11, no. 2 (2010): 363–89. Hebrew.

Yogev, Abraham, and Rina Shapira. "Ethnicity, Meritocracy, and Credentialism in Israel: Elaborating the Credential Society Thesis." *Research in Social Stratification and Mobility* 6 (1987): 187–212.

Yona, Yossi, and Yitzhak Sporta. "Pre-Vocational Education and the Creation of the Working Class in Israel." In *Mizrahim in Israel: A Critical Observation into Israel's Ethnicity*, edited by Hannan Hever, Yehouda Shenhav, and Pnina Motzafi-Haller, 68–105. Tel Aviv and Jerusalem: Van Leer Jerusalem Institute and Hakibbutz Hameuchad, 2002. Hebrew.

Yuchtman-Yaar, Ephraim. "Differences in Ethnic Patterns of Socioeconomic Achievements in Israel: A Neglected Aspect of Structured Inequality." *International Review of Modern Sociology* 15 (1985): 99–116.

Zfati, Yariv. "The Ethnic Genie in Israel: In the Bottle on a Low Flame." *Megamot: Social Science Quarterly* 40, no. 1 (1999): 5–30. Hebrew.

# *Index*


Abbott, Pamela, 18

academic professionals: among second-generation women, 98–99, 107, 112, 113, 115–18, 133–38, 142. *See also* teachers, Israeli

Addi-Raccah, Audrey, 117

agency: among nonmobile women, 148; among subordinate groups, 148, 150; limitations to, 146; of second-generation women, 1, 121, 146–49; and structure, 146

Alliance Israélite Universelle (AIU), 20–21, 95, 97, 107; and Zionism, 22

Arab Israeli women, upward mobility of, 177n87

Archer, Louise, 122, 123

Ashkenazim, Israeli: class position of, 61, 122; devaluation of Moroccan culture, 114; hegemony of, 113–14; intermarriage with Moroccans, 41–42; male stereotypes of, 54; marriage with Mizraḥim, 41–42, 54; modernity of, 55; relationship with Mizraḥim, 141; spousal relationships among, 54, 55, 126

Ashkenazi women, Israeli, 14–16; bodily traits of, 61, 62, 127, 132; class attainments of, 25, 26–29, 122; consumption practices of, 60; educational attainments of, 14, 24, 26, 27, 28–29, 122; education of children, 59–60; employment of, 26, 27, 122; family formation patterns of, 30; femininity of, 31, 76–77, 142, 147; first-generation, 26, 31; hegemony of, 15, 27, 64, 119, 123, 138, 140, 141; intelligence of, 62; in labor market, 15, 28–29, 31; middle-class, 27, 28, 119, 122, 142, 145–46; versus Moroccan women, 76; Moroccan women's view of, 141–42; motherhood of, 59–61, 75, 127, 131, 137; representations of, 32–33; as role models, 142; second-generation, 27, 28, 30; self-presentation of, 62, 63; stereotypes of, 32; working-class, 26, 27

Ayalon, Hanna, 117

Bauman, Zygmunt, 49, 106

Baxter, Arthur, 48, 52; on self-transformation, 66

Beck, Ulrich, 146, 149

Becker, Gary: *A Treatise on the Family*, 99

Behr, Joshua, 70

Beller, Emily, 139
Benhabib, Doli, 32–33
Ben-Harush, David, 15
Ben-Rafael, Eliezer, 162n43
Birenbaum-Carmeli, Daphna, 61
Black Panthers, Israeli, 15
body, feminine: of Ashkenazi women, 61, 62, 127, 132, 142; of Moroccan women, 61–62, 127, 132, 142; as site for mobility, 127, 132
Bourdieu, Pierre, 103
Britton, Carolyn, 48, 52; on self-transformation, 66

Chafetz, Janet Saltzman, 148
Cherlin, Andrew, 99
Child, Irvin Long, 143
children, Ashkenazi: education of, 59–60
children, Moroccan: of divorcees, 89–93; education of, 126–27, 138; mobility of, 122, 132, 133, 147; mothers' socialization of, 59, 78–79, 139, 147; parents' aspirations for, 36–37, 96–97, 144
Chinese Americans, parental aspirations among, 36
class: alienation from, 128; among Mizraḥim, 15, 17, 61; of Ashkenazim, 61, 122; determination of, 139–40; effect of motherhood on, 29; emotions concerning, 127–28; ethnicization of, 142; in feminine identity, 138–46; in Israeli society, 16–17, 33, 48, 61, 92. *See also* middle class
clerical workers: benefits for, 70, 132; specialized, 70; in Western societies, 69–70
clerical workers, Israeli: autonomy of, 153; in civil services, 66, 67, 69–70, 82; class position of, 152, 153; high-ranking, 128–32; second-generation women, 67, 69–70, 75
Cobb, Jonathan, 49
Cohen, Uri, 16–17
Colette (life history narrator): academic profession of, 107, 112, 113, 115–18; children of, 112–13; class position of, 107, 118; education of, 109–10, 111–12, 119, 135; ethnic identity of, 114–15, 117; experience of discrimination, 116, 117–18; gender identity of, 117; marriage of, 110–13, 117; motherhood of, 112–13; parents of, 107–9, 114; residential mobility of, 112–13; salary of, 118; travel abroad, 110
colonial studies, hegemony and subordination in, 157n23
cooking, Moroccan, 76–77, 104, 110
credentialism, mobility through, 17
culture, Moroccan: Ashkenazi devaluation of, 114; cooking in, 76–77, 104, 110; disengagement from, 115; divorce in, 82–83; feminine capital in, 76; French influences in, 103, 107, 114; gender roles in, 71–72, 78, 79, 83, 134; immigrants' loss of, 68; marriage in, 56–57, 71–72; pride in, 83; reading in, 74. *See also* femininity, ethnic Moroccan

Devine, Fiona, 122
Dijkers, Marcellinus, 112
division of labor, marital, 44; ethnic norms of, 126; in high middle class, 100–102, 136–37; in low middle class, 54–55, 137; in middle segment of middle class, 73, 77–78, 79, 84–85, 130–31; traditional, 100
division of labor, patriarchal, 66, 83, 126, 136
divorce, in Moroccan culture, 82–83
divorcees: benefits for, 85; in Israeli society, 81, 85; mobility of, 93–94; second-generation Moroccan, 80, 81–94; sense of loss, 93; stereotypes of, 86, 89
domesticity: middle-class, 95; rise of, 87

Donat, Doris, 19
Dror (Zionist organization), 22

economy, neoliberal: female labor in, 3
education: in access to middle class, 29, 46–47; among subordinate groups, 124; discrimination in, 52, 115–18; effect of gender norms on, 71; ethnic norms regarding, 29, 125, 133; in high middle class, 95, 97, 99, 104, 108, 109–12, 119, 135; human capital in, 135; immigrants' attitude toward, 124; in low middle class, 37, 52–53, 124; in middle sector of middle class, 68–69, 70–71, 72, 82, 90, 93–94, 129, 130; parental attitudes toward, 108, 134; role of cultural capital in, 134–35; as site of mobility, 3, 5, 8, 14, 46–47, 74, 79, 80, 90–91, 121, 123–24, 129, 130, 134–35, 152; vocational, 52
Elmelech, Yuval, 86
Emirbayer, Mustafa, 149
emotions: as site for mobility, 127–28, 133, 138; and social structure, 156n8
employment: of immigrant Moroccan women, 8–9, 23; role in class determination, 140; role in feminine identity, 130, 139; as site of mobility, 3, 5, 8, 14, 121, 124–25, 129–30, 135–36, 152
Erikson, Robert, 140; class schema of, 23, 151–53
Espiritu, Yen Le, 64
ethnicity: bodily representations of, 132; changes to, 143; gender norms of, 78, 83, 111; and hierarchical relationships, 6–7; in-group reaction to, 144; in Israeli society, 14–16, 144–45; Italian, 143–44; and marriage choices, 41–42; norms concerning education, 29, 125, 133; political, 105–6, 116; and respectability, 62; role in discrimination, 117–18; role in mobility, 4–5, 6, 119, 144; subordinate, 104; symbolic, 4, 143; Turkish, 5–6. *See also* femininity, ethnic; identity, feminine ethnic

family formation, mobility and, 29–33
femininity, ethnic, 57; Ashkenazi, 31, 76–77, 142, 147; changes to ethnic culture, 143; constraints of, 49; disengagement from, 143–44; and division of labor, 102; in-group differences in, 6; marriage norms of, 30, 56, 71–72, 111, 117, 130; Moroccan versus Ashekenazi, 76–77; motherhood in, 19, 43, 74; obstacles of, 64; and social mobility, 4–5, 149; superiority/inferiority in, 6; transitions in, 143. *See also* ethnicity; identity, feminine ethnic
femininity, ethnic Moroccan: Ashkenazi influence on, 147; education and, 29, 133; ethnic definitions of, 42–43; gender norms of, 71–72, 78, 79, 83, 134; reconstruction of, 143; role of cooking in, 76–77, 104, 110; role of employment in, 130; of second-generation immigrants, 4, 40, 138–46; symbolic, 143; traditional, 55–56, 142
femininity, Jewish: motherhood in, 19–20
feminism, Israeli, 55, 147–48
Foner, Nancy, 79–80

Gans, Herbert, 4
Geertz, Clifford, 1
gender: effect on mobility, 144; role in discrimination, 117–18
gender norms: effect on education, 71; ethnic-based, 78, 83, 111; Israeli, 57; in marriage, 111–12, 130–31; of modernity, 40; in Moroccan culture, 71–72, 78, 79, 83, 134; patriarchal, 136; for third-generation women, 130

gender relationships: Ashkenazi, 126; effect of immigration on, 33; in lower middle class, 125–26. *See also* division of labor, marital
Gobi, Abraham, 98
Goldberg, Harvey, 142
Goldstein, Zahava, 98
Goldthorpe, John: class schema of, 23, 151–53
Goshen-Gottstein, Esther, 32
Grier, Katherine, 87, 95

hegemony: of Ashkenazi women, 15, 27, 64, 119, 123; in colonial studies, 157n23; of immigrant women, 6–8; and marriage choices, 41
*Henna* (Moroccan engagement party), 65, 68, 77, 83, 105, 115, 143
Hey, Valerie, 128
Holocaust, Nazi, 22
home ownership, Israeli, 86–87

identity: bodily construction of, 61; Israeli, 145
identity, feminine ethnic, 64–65, 102, 138–46; Ashkenazi, 31; choice in, 145; construction of, 142; middle-class, 139; role of employment in, 130, 139; sources of, 138; subordinate, 145. *See also* ethnicity; femininity, ethnic
immigrants: activism among, 3; separatist, 146; social cohesion among, 3
immigrants, Israeli, 13–18; Ashkenazi, 14–16; from Europe, 13–14; Middle Eastern, 9–10; Mizraḥi, 14–17; North African, 13–14; optimism of, 36; shared traits of, 150. *See also* Ashkenazim, Israeli; Mizraḥim, Israel
immigrants, Moroccan, 11, 17; anthropological studies of, 162n43; attitude toward education, 124; cultural capital of, 124, 134–35; discrimination against, 64–65, 67, 83, 91–92, 104, 114, 116, 117–18, 140; ethnic identity of, 48; ethnic pride among, 105; family size of, 108; human capital of, 2, 97, 133, 135; importance of work for, 82; intermarriage with Ashkenazim, 41–42; male mobility among, 17, 18; middle-class, 95–97, 107–9; mobility of, 17, 18, 51, 65, 116; nonmobile, 122; numbers of, 159n1; to Palestine, 22; socialization of children, 68, 144; transit camps for, 51, 69; working-class, 21, 36, 81–82, 122, 123, 128. *See also* second-generation women, Moroccan
immigrant women: ethnic stereotyping of, 2; hegemonic relationships among, 6–8; human capital of, 2, 133; mobility of, 2; mothers, 7; in Netherlands, 5–6; Tunisian, 164n104; Turkish Muslim, 5–6; working-class, 2, 3. *See also* second-generation women
immigrant women, Moroccan: aspirations for children, 36–37; class position of, 23, 25; education of, 22, 23, 24–25, 26; family formation patterns among, 29, 31; financial power of, 147; hierarchies among, 12; housewives, 108; importance of work for, 85; insecurity among, 119; middle-class attainments of, 17–18, 23–26; obstacles facing, 36; occupations of, 8–9, 23; socialization of daughters, 147; stereotypes of, 1, 13, 32; view of Israeli establishment, 32; in working class, 36. *See also* Jewish Moroccan women; Mizraḥi women, Israeli; second-generation women, Moroccan
immigration: effect on gender relationships, 33; feminization of, 2
income: of second-generation Moroccan women, 73, 86, 118, 131, 135–36, 140; as site of mobility, 14

Israel: cultural pluralism in, 16, 105, 115, 145; European immigrants to, 13–14; feminism in, 55, 147–48; home ownership in, 86–87; Mapai Party, 16; Ministry for Social Welfare, 82; Ministry of Education, 39, 69, 74; Municipal civil service, 66, 67, 71, 73, 80, 132, 153; National civil service, 66, 82, 132, 153; National Insurance Institute, 85; Shas party, 15–16, 116, 171n5; single-parent families in, 85; Standard Classification of Occupations, 151–52; Western culture of, 14; women's military service in, 37–38, 48, 53, 78, 82, 109. *See also* middle class, Israeli; society, Israeli

Jerusalem: Armon neighborhood, 103; Basle neighborhood, 113; Bilu neighborhood, 45, 57; Gordon neighborhood, 45, 57, 73; Mizraḥi neighborhoods of, 57, 73, 91–92; Moroccan population of, 8; Nativ neighborhood, 103; Rechavia neighborhood of, 9, 91, 92
Jewish Moroccan women, 18–23; versus Ashkenazi women, 76; beauty of, 61–62, 75–76, 79; bodily traits of, 61–62, 127, 132; corporeal capital of, 76, 127, 132, 142; discrimination against, 67; education of, 20–21, 136; ethnic identity of, 118; French culture of, 21, 103, 107; gender construction of, 21; gender equality of, 102; housewives, 5, 28, 41, 69, 82, 108; marriage age for, 19, 41, 71–72, 78; middle-class discontentment among, 107, 118; mobility goals of, 122, 145, 150; self-confidence of, 76; self-presentation of, 61, 62, 63–64; self-transformations by, 51–66; stereotypes of, 68, 102, 144; symbolic ethnicity of, 143; third-generation, 130, 139; view of Ashkenazi women, 141–42; view of wifehood, 56; working-class, 21; work outside home, 125. *See also* immigrant women, Moroccan; Mizraḥi women; second-generation women, Moroccan
Jewish women: femininity of, 19; illiteracy among, 163n80; mothers, 19–20
Jews, Diaspora, 16
Jews, Moroccan: class differences among, 21–22; contact with modernity, 20; education of, 20–21; during French Protectorate, 18–22; urban, 18, 19; Zionist, 22–23, 95. *See also* immigrants, Moroccan

Khazzoom, Aziza, 95–96
kindergarten assistants, 9, 23, 35, 38–40, 57, 64; class position of, 152, 153; duties of, 39; training for, 38, 39, 47, 53, 125
Kraus, Vered, 151
Kremer-Hayon, Lya, 98

labor market, clerical, 69–70
labor market, Israeli: female sector of, 28–29, 31, 112–13, 125, 135; male sector of, 140; Mizraḥim in, 14–15; second-generation Moroccan women in, 28–29, 40; semiprofessional, 35–49, 135; teachers in, 97
Lawler, Steph, 3; on motherhood, 59
Leathwood, Carole, 122, 123
Leon, Nissim, 16–17
Lerenthal, Tamar, 32
Lewin-Epstein, Noah, 61, 86
life history narratives: empirical data from, 10; of Jewish Moroccan women, 9–12; qualitative methodology of, 9
Likud Party, Mizraḥi support for, 16
Louie, Vivian, 36

MacLeod, Jay, 118
Mannheim, Karl, 9
Mapai Party (Israel), 16
Mark, Nili, 61
marriage: age for, 19, 41, 71–72, 78, 125, 130; within education levels, 140; ethnic norms of, 30, 56, 71–72, 98, 111–12, 117, 130; gender norms of, 111–12, 130–31; *Henna* ceremony in, 65, 68, 77, 83, 105, 115, 143; in high middle class, 98–102, 110–13, 117; ideals of, 56–57; individual expression in, 99; interethnic, 41–42, 54, 144; intraethnic, 99, 105, 110; in lower middle class, 41–43, 44–46, 54–57, 125–26; in middle sector of middle class, 71–72, 78, 130, 131; self-fulfillment through, 100; as site of mobility, 30–31, 125–26, 130–31, 136–37. *See also* division of labor, marital
Michael, Sammy, 32, 33
middle class, domesticity of, 95
middle class, Israeli, 16; access through education, 29; Ashkenazim in, 61, 122; Ashkenazi women in, 27, 28, 119, 122, 142, 145–46; car ownership in, 87; division of labor in, 101; divorced women in, 81; domestic help in, 88, 102, 112, 137; ethnic diversity in, 142; feminine identity in, 139; formation of, 17; high, 8–9, 12, 95, 98, 103, 107, 109, 110, 133–38, 146–47, 151–52; home ownership by, 86–87; human capital in, 135; immobility in, 7–8; low, 8–9, 12, 123–28, 146–47; marital relationships of, 139; middle segment, 8–9, 12, 128–32; Mizraḥ im in, 15, 17; mobility within, 133; semiprofessionals in, 152, 153; third-generation Moroccans in, 139
middle class, Western: benefits of membership, 3
military service, Israeli women's, 37–38, 48, 53, 78, 82, 109
Miller, Jon, 130
Miriam (life history narrator): agency of, 148–49; autonomy of, 44–45; childhood of, 43; children of, 43–46, 47; choices available to, 48–49; education of, 37, 124; financial decisions by, 45–46; marriage of, 41–43, 44–46; mobility attainments of, 45–48, 80; motherhood of, 42–44; motivations of, 39; parents of, 35–37, 124; siblings of, 37
Misch, Ann, 149
Mizraḥim, Israeli, 14–17; activism of, 146; class position of, 15, 17, 61; education of, 52; family size of, 31; gender relationships among, 33; lower class, 171n5; male stereotypes of, 54; marriage with Ashkenazim, 54; neighborhoods of, 57, 73, 91–92; political parties of, 15–16; relationship with Ashkenazim, 141; social status of, 113–14; upwardly mobile, 45, 73, 103, 145
Mizraḥi women, Israeli: class attainments of, 16–17, 26; discrimination against, 117; educational attainments of, 14; in labor market, 14–15; in middle class, 15, 17; mobility among, 15; mothers, 39; second-generation, 15; stereotypes of, 32; subordinate position of, 15, 17, 32, 113–14, 119; teachers, 97. *See also* immigrant women, Moroccan; second-generation women, Moroccan
mobility, social: American Dream of, 148; among Arab Israeli women, 177n87; among male Moroccan immigrants, 17, 18, 96; among second-generation Mizraḥim, 15; comparative studies of, 149–50; of divorcees, 93–94; effect of gender on, 144; emotional rewards of, 49; emotions as site for, 127–28, 133,

138; employment as site of, 3, 5, 8, 14, 121, 124–25, 129–30, 135–36, 152; and ethnic femininity, 4–5, 149; family cooperation for, 80; and family formation patterns, 29–32; feminine body in, 127, 132; goals of, 122, 150; human agency in, 146–49; husbands' attitudes toward, 137; individual, 10; in Israeli society, 4, 38; marriage as site of, 30–31, 125–26, 130–31, 136–37; in modernity, 106; motherhood as site of, 43–44, 121, 126–27, 131–32, 137–38; motivations for, 12, 122; and multiculturalism, 150; residential, 57, 73, 91–92, 112–13, 121, 138; role in social cohesion, 3; role of education in, 3, 5, 8, 14, 46–47, 74, 79, 80, 90–91, 121, 123–24, 129, 130, 134–35, 152; role of ethnicity in, 4–6, 119, 144; role of work in, 51–52; through credentialism, 17; through professionalization, 17; in Western societies, 2; for working-class women, 3, 5; and Zionism, 95, 96
modernity: of Ashkenazim, 55; gender norms of, 40; mobility in, 106
Moore, Dahlia, 98
Morocco: detraditionalization in, 147; French influences in, 103, 107, 114; independence from France, 18; Jewish communities of, 11; Jewish women in, 18–23; *mellahs* of, 18, 21, 22, 51; school system of, 20–21; Zionist movement in, 22–23, 95
motherhood: Ashkenazi, 59–61, 75, 127, 131, 137; hierarchies in, 59; as identity, 58; immigrant women's, 7; in Jewish femininity, 19–20; middle-class, 74–75, 126–27, 139; Mizraḥi women's, 39; scientific, 20; as site of mobility, 43–44, 121, 126–27, 131–32, 137–38; socialization of children in, 59, 78–79, 139, 147; working-class, 128
motherhood, Moroccan: among second-generation women, 42–44, 58–59, 74–75; conspicuous consumption in, 60, 61; ethnic-based construction of, 74; in high middle class, 100, 112–13, 137–38; in low middle class, 42–44, 58–59, 126–27; in middle sector of middle class, 72, 74–75, 89–93, 131–32; rejection of, 131; role in occupational choices, 135; socialization of children, 59, 78–79, 139, 147; traditional, 59, 84
Munt, Ian, 103

Naomi (life history narrator): academic profession of, 98, 99; children of, 100, 101; education of, 95, 97, 99, 104, 108, 135; financial decisions by, 102–3; marriage of, 98–102, 110; middle-class pursuits of, 103; mobility attainments of, 95, 98, 104; motherhood of, 100; parents of, 95, 96; travel by, 103
Netherlands, immigrant women in, 5–6

Palestine, Moroccan immigrants to, 22
patriarchy: division of labor in, 66, 83, 126, 136; Jewish, 20; Middle Eastern, 147
politics: ethnic, 105–6, 116; Israeli women in, 100–101; mobility through, 14
Portes, Alejandro, 96, 146
professionalization, mobility through, 17

Ransford, Edward, 130
Reay, Diane, 52, 139
residence, as site of mobility, 14, 57, 73, 91–92, 112–13, 132, 138
Ruddick, Sara, 58
Rumbaut, Rubén, 96

Ruth (life history narrator), 141; children of, 58, 59; education of, 52–53, 124; ethnic feminine identity of, 64–65; financial decisions by, 57; independence of, 56; marriage of, 54–57, 126; military service of, 53; mobility attainments of, 51, 54, 64, 80; motherhood of, 58–59, 127; occupations of, 51, 64; parents of, 51–52, 124; professional skills of, 53; residential mobility of, 57; siblings of, 52; structural-material constraints on, 64; supporting of family, 124

Safilios-Rotschild, Constantina, 112
Sapsford, Roger, 18
Sara (life history narrator): children of, 72, 74, 78–79, 80; education of, 68–69, 70–71, 72; ethnic femininity of, 67, 78, 79, 80; marriage of, 71–72, 78, 130, 131; mobility attainments of, 71, 73–74, 80; occupation of, 69, 71–72, 73–74, 75, 78, 80; parents of, 68, 128; residential mobility of, 73; salary of, 131
Schely-Newman, Esther, 164n104
second-generation women: hegemonic, 6; mobility of, 2–3, 149; self-worth of, 3; social integration of, 3–4; subordinate, 6, 105; youthful, 7. *See also* immigrant women
second-generation women, Israeli: hegemonic, 13; status attainments of, 14
second-generation women, Moroccan, 23–26; academic professionals, 98–99, 107, 112, 113, 115–18, 133–38, 142; agency of, 1, 121, 146–49; autonomy of, 44–45, 83, 128; class attainments of, 25, 26–29; class awareness among, 7, 122; clerical workers, 67, 69–70, 75, 128–32; differences among, 121–22; divorced, 80, 81–94; dual identity among, 145; educational achievements of, 5, 7, 24–25, 27–29, 31–32, 38–39, 46–47, 80, 96–97, 123–24, 129, 130; employment of, 5, 9–12, 27, 31–32, 35, 38–39, 48, 49, 51, 64, 69, 71–75, 78, 80, 129–30; expectations for children, 112; family formation patterns of, 29–33; femininity of, 4, 40, 138–46; financial decisions by, 45–46, 57, 86–89, 102–3, 126; generations of, 9; goals of, 122, 145; housewives, 41, 82; identification with Israeli society, 145–46, 148; as innovators, 149; kindergarten assistants, 9, 23, 35, 38–40, 47, 53, 57, 64, 125, 152, 153; in labor market, 28–29, 40; lack of confidence, 62, 63; life history narratives of, 9–12; marriage age of, 41, 71–72, 78, 125, 130; middle-class mobility of, 1–2, 3, 5, 6–7, 13, 23–26, 27, 28, 106, 119, 150; midlife, 6–7, 8; military service of, 53, 82; motherhood among, 42–44, 58–59, 74–75; motivations for mobility, 12; obstacles facing, 1, 39, 64, 123–24; parents' aspirations for, 36–37, 96–97, 144; paths to mobility, 12; representations of, 33; residential mobility among, 57, 73, 91–92, 112–13, 132, 138; salaries of, 73, 86, 118, 131, 135–36, 140; self-confidence of, 106, 114, 133; self-empowerment of, 128; semiprofessional, 26, 35–49, 51, 123–28, 135, 152, 153; in social hierarchy, 6, 12, 41–42, 122–23; subordinate position of, 119, 123, 138, 140–41, 144–45, 150; working-class origins among, 3, 5, 36, 37, 43, 49, 63, 69–70, 81, 93, 99, 122, 133. *See also* immigrant women, Moroccan; Jewish Moroccan women
Semyonov, Moshe, 32, 61; on home ownership, 86
Sennett, Richard, 49

Sharni, Shoshana, 32
Sharon (life history narrator): accomplishments of, 93; autonomy of, 83; car of, 87; children of, 83, 89–93; dissociation from Moroccan culture, 83; divorce of, 82–84, 85–86, 89; education of, 82, 90, 93–94; ethnic gender norms of, 83; financial planning by, 86–89; marriage of, 82, 83–84; middle-class identity of, 86; military service of, 82; mobility attainments of, 87–89, 94; motherhood of, 89–93; occupation of, 81; ownership of home, 86–88; parents of, 81–82, 84, 128; residential mobility of, 91–92; salary of, 86, 131; support networks of, 89
Shas Party (Israel), 15–16, 116, 171n5
Sidel, Ruth, 93; *Unsung Heroines,* 89
Skeggs, Beverley, 6
Smith, Bonnie, 87
Smooha, Sammy, 15
societies, Western: clerical workers in, 69–70; multicultural, 150; subordinate women in, 149–50; women's mobility in, 2
society, Israeli: class structure of, 16–17, 33, 48, 61, 92; cultural pluralism in, 16, 105, 115, 145; divisive tendencies in, 106; educational values of, 131; familistic, 85, 99; gender construction in, 57; intraclass differences in, 121; knowledge of languages in, 95, 96; marital status in, 42; mobility in, 4, 38; Moroccan ethnicity in, 144–45; professionalization in, 38, 122; second-generation women's identification with, 145–46, 148; shared traits within, 150; stratification of, 14–16, 17, 48, 119, 122–23; working-class, 36
spousal relationships. *See* marriage
status markers, Israeli, 14, 103
Steedman, Carolyn Kay, 6, 128
subordination: agency in, 148, 150; in colonial studies, 157n23; of second-generation Moroccan women, 119, 123, 138, 140–41, 144–45, 150
Swidler, Ann, 148

teachers, Israeli, 97–98; in administrative positions, 117; gender discrimination against, 117; in high middle class, 133–38; interpersonal relations among, 116. *See also* academic professionals; kindergarten assistants
tourism, as status marker, 103
Tsolidis, Georgina, 5

Wasserfall, Rahel, 32
Waters, Mary, 117
wealth, intergenerational transmission of, 14
work: in gender construction, 21; importance for Moroccan immigrants, 82; in social mobility, 51–52
working class, Moroccan immigrants in, 21, 36, 81–82, 122, 123, 128
working-class women, 2, 3; Ashkenazi, 26, 27; bodily markers of, 127; motherhood among, 128; upward mobility of, 3, 5; vocational education for, 52

Yaish, Meir, 15, 151

Zionist movement: in Morocco, 22–23, 95; and social mobility, 95, 96

www.ingramcontent.com/pod-product-compliance
Lightning Source LLC
LaVergne TN
LVHW010355080826

844660LV00016B/972/J
*9780814338810*